Other Book

Section Roads

"An ambitious, evocative small-town tale located somewhere between *Peyton Place* and *The last Picture Show.*"

—Kirkus Reviews

The Conman: A Baseball Odyssey

"Mike Murphey's writing style is simple, neat, and elegant, and the detailed narration takes readers into the world of baseball, and the ugly side that exists under all the glamour."

—Reader Views

Taking Time . . . a Tale of Physics, Lust and Greed

"Mike Murphey's novel is a masterpiece, from the gorgeous writing to the sophisticated characters, it deliver's entertainment at its finest."

—The Book Commentary

Wasting Time . . . Physics, Lust and Greed Series Book 2

". . . a quirky, enjoyable novel with some interesting speculations on the consequences and possibilities of time travel, lightened by a playful sense of humor."

—Indie Reader

Killing Time . . . Physics Lust and Greed Series Book 3

"Satire and subterfuge are paired flawlessly in this wildly entertaining and unexpectedly heartwarming piece of futuristic fiction."

—Indies Today

See more of Mike's books:
https://www.mikemurpheybooks.com

Get a free short story "Old Man Baseball" at:
https://www.mikemurpheybooks.com/freebies

We Never Knew Just What It Was...

The Story of the Chad Mitchell Trio

by

Mike Murphey

with

Mike Kobluk

and

Chad Mitchell

FROM THE TINY ACORN...
GROWS THE MIGHTY OAK

We Never Knew Just What It Was . . . The Story of the Chad Mitchell Trio
Copyright © 2021 Mike Murphey Books, LLC. All rights reserved.

Printed in the United States of America.

For information, address Acorn Publishing, LLC, 3943 Irvine Blvd. Ste. 218, Irvine, CA 92602
www.acornpublishingllc.com

Cover Design by ebooklaunch.com
Edited by Laura Taylor
Interior Design and Digital Formatting by Debra Cranfield Kennedy

Cover photos by Lori Ulm Gordon and Bob Mitchell

**Almost all the songs mentioned in this book are available through www.youtube.com.
Just search YouTube by song name, and you can sing along as you read.**

Anti-Piracy Warning: The unauthorized reproduction or distribution of a copyrighted work is illegal.
Criminal copyright infringement, including infringement without monetary gain, is investigated by
the FBI and is punishable by up to five years in federal prison and a fine of $250,000.

All rights reserved. No part of this book may be used or reproduced in any manner whatsoever,
including internet usage, without written permission from the author.

ISBN—978-1-952112-66-9 (hardcover)
ISBN—978-1-952112-65-2 (paperback)

This Book is dedicated to

the happy memory of

John Prine

— Foreword —

t was September of 1960. I was sitting in the Gaslight one early evening when John Stauber came in. John was a classical guitarist who accompanied Leon Bibb and he frequently dropped in to do a guest set at the Gaslight. To me, he said, "you should go up to Columbia Artists tomorrow; they're having auditions for the Chad Mitchell Trio. One of their guys is going back to school."

Now, I wonder what my life would have been like if I hadn't taken John's advice.

I was there the next day and found a long line of aspirants. Eventually I was admitted to the audition room. For some inexplicable reason, I did not have a guitar and had to borrow Jim McGuinn's instrument. (Jim, then eighteen years old, went on to become Roger McGuinn, founder of The Byrds.) I don't remember what I sang first, but then someone asked if I could sing *Jamaica Farewell*. Luckily, I could. Then, to my amazement, the word went out to send the rest of the auditioners home. I was in, provisionally. It was explained to me that we would rehearse for a week and then see how it was going. But for now, I was a member of The Chad Mitchell Trio.

I was gobsmacked.

We began rehearsals on a Monday at the home of Milt Okun, their musical director and record producer. Milt lived on West 10th St. in Greenwich Village and had impressive credentials, having been the conductor for Harry Belafonte. He stood about six feet two and had the slightly bemused expression of a philosophy professor. He also told great and funny stories. Above all, he knew what he wanted, and we got down to it.

One of the songs was a traditional southern folk song involving trains (what else?). Its chorus went:

Roll in my sweet baby's arms,
Roll in my sweet baby's arms.
Gonna lay 'round that shack,
Till the mail train comes back,
Gonna roll in my sweet baby's arms.

Well, maybe you needed to hear it with the banjo backing.

There was also some choreography involved, which hardly came naturally to me but which I figured I would eventually get the hang of. The singing, too, was of a full-voiced style that I wasn't used to. But I was having fun and thought all in all it was going well.

It wasn't.

I liked the guys. Chad Mitchell was medium height with a round, handsome face, blond hair and a stunningly beautiful voice. Mike Kobluk was a Canadian by birth, taller than Chad with a quieter voice and perfect intonation; he had a warmth about him that was very winning. He had (and has) a wicked sense of humor. We got on very well together and during one rehearsal break I sang the only good song I had: *The Marvelous Toy*. They liked it and so did Milt.

On Friday, though, the hammer fell. Milt took me into another room and broke it to me gently: the experiment was not a success. My voice did not blend well with the boys' voices, and I was not experienced enough to make that happen, so, sadly, I was out. I was crushed. But wait! There was good news, too. Everyone loved *The Marvelous Toy* and wanted to record it. Not only that; Milt had recently started his own publishing company and wanted to sign me to be his first writer. I was thrilled. I ultimately spent fifty years associated with Milt as my publisher.

The boys and I said our goodbyes. They went on to discover and sign Joe Frazier, a tremendous success in my view. Joe was a large-voiced singer with a big, extroverted personality who completed the trio beautifully. This was a trio of *singers;* they could compete with anyone vocally and sang with enormous vitality. I was blessed with many Trio covers of my songs and *Toy* became a hit for them in 1963.

In recent years we have done many shows together and I'm usually included in their encores. I like to think that I fill out the Chad Mitchell Quartet very nicely, indeed.

—Tom Paxton

— Introduction —

This book is my first attempt at non-fiction. The specific genre is "creative non-fiction." I have used creative license to flesh out some of the conversations related here because, with the passage of years and passing of principle characters, we cannot know exactly what was said at certain moments.

My hope, though, is that this is an accurate portrayal of the lives of Mike Kobluk, Chad Mitchell and Joe Frazier. For me, this has been a labor of love. Like many people you will read about here, as a teenager growing up in a small, conservative community, my opinions, values and outlook on the world were profoundly shaped by the songs of first the Chad Mitchell Trio, and then the Mitchell Trio.

Chad has not always been comfortable with that sentiment. But I think he's come to terms with it and can finally accept the compliment.

Like so many others, I learned to play the guitar, formed folk trios and performed so I could sing their songs. I took most of the values they inspired into adulthood, and I think those values have served me well. Along the way, I became a lifetime devotee to the folk music genre. I finally saw The Chad Mitchell Trio perform live in the 2007 Spokane concert that provides the framework for this book.

I chose that framework, because this is a story of missed opportunities, management mistakes, personal struggle, and sometimes bitter conflict. But forty-five years into it, I revisit this concert on Alan Jacobson's extraordinary three-DVD set "Then and Now," and I see three men performing almost flawlessly. Having a blast. Genuinely enjoying this experience and each other.

As fans we want the people we admire, whether athletes or actors or performers, to be the people we hope they are. The three-year association this book has created leaves me with the sense that Mike and Chad are those people. I genuinely thank them for having provided the opportunity to immerse myself in the music of my youth, and to tell what I think is an extraordinary story.

We Never Knew Just What It Was...

———— ❧ ————

The story of the Chad Mitchell Trio

— CHAPTER ONE —

"A trio is the worst combination you can have.
When there's three of you,
it always ends up being two against one."

—Chad Mitchell

OCTOBER 2007
Spokane, Washington

The last time The Chad Mitchell Trio performed before their hometown crowd—summer of 1964—a reviewer for a local newspaper called them "depressing." While allowing they were "fine sounding and fine-looking young men," Ed Costello bemoaned their choice of material. Making fun of Nazis and the John Birch Society, he said, were examples of something new being called a "social and political conscience," which, he intimated, had no place in popular entertainment.

Forty-three years later, Chad stood in the dark, off-stage wings at Spokane's Opera House and smiled at Tom Paxton's lyrics. Tom, who had written so much of their material, served as opening act this evening for The Trio's long-belated return to Spokane.

As Tom took his bows, a towering screen at center stage came to life with clips of a Chad Mitchell Trio appearance on the Ed Sullivan Show in 1963. While the Opera House sound system detailed every nuance of exquisite harmony from those twenty-year-old voices, Mike Kobluk stepped to Chad's side, resting a hand on his shoulder.

"Damn, we were good," Chad said, gesturing to the screen. "Can we still do this? Are we making a mistake?"

Mike laughed. "I guess we'll find out."

Chad glanced to Mike and could only imagine what emotions were shuttered behind his calm stoicism—what this performance must mean. When Mike turned The Mitchell Trio over to John Denver in 1968, he found his way back to Spokane and became entertainment director for Expo '74, the city's version of a World's Fair. He parlayed that gig into a three-decade run as Spokane's Manager of Entertainment Facilities.

Now, finally, Mike would perform here.

Mike seldom shared his feelings, but Chad wanted to know.

"This crowd is mostly here for you, Mike," he said. "You ran this building. They all remember that."

"They're here for The Trio," Mike said.

"You're the one who came back. You're this town's real anchor to who we were. Come on. Haven't you thought about performing here?"

Granted, this wasn't Carnegie Hall, where they'd sung on four different occasions. Still . . .

Chad and Mike exchanged a long glance—even after all these years, in many ways they remained strangers.

Of course, Mike had thought of performing here. A few days ago, Mike—who retired in 2003 after twenty-eight years of managing this building—told Chad that the people he worked with here knew few details of what he'd done before he'd finished his degree at Gonzaga and gone to work for the city.

"A few weeks ago," Mike said, "I visited the Opera House to see the promotional posters for our concert being installed and a janitor, who I'd known for years, approached me."

"That's you in that picture," the janitor said, pointing to a poster.

"Yes, it is."

"But why? What are you doing in a concert advertisement?"

"Those other guys are Chad Mitchell and Joe Frazier. We used to sing together. We're doing a concert."

The janitor regarded Mike quizzically for a few moments. "Yeah. But really. Why are *you* in that picture?"

Chad smiled as he glimpsed row after row filling with people, the crowd extending into the balcony. Among them were other curious people who came to see why their old boss or friend or neighbor *was* in this picture.

Chad thought of all the artists Mike had ushered to this stage. From Van Cliburn to Isaac Stern to Ella Fitzgerald. Harry Belafonte. Peter, Paul and Mary. Folk to rock to classical to opera. Hal Holbrook doing Mark Twain Tonight. Broadway shows. Every significant performer in America for almost three decades.

Chad prodded him again. "Really, how can this be just another show for you?"

Mike shook his head and took a breath. "Back when I was booking this building for Expo '74, when the Opera House was brand new, Bing Crosby came to see what the Expo development was doing to his hometown. He wasn't performing, but he wanted a tour. So, I showed him around. We walked to the stage in this empty building. Bing stood right over there." Mike pointed to place just beyond the curtain.

"And he crooned this *too-raloo-raloora* thing in that Crosby voice that rang through the auditorium, then turned to me and said, 'Boy, the acoustics in this place are great. Is this where Hope will perform?'

"I told him no. I said Bob Hope was scheduled to play the Coliseum, because we had more seating available there. Bing said, 'Good. This place is way too classy for Hope.'"

Chad smiled at the story.

"So, yes," Mike said. "I've thought about singing with The Trio on this stage more than once."

Chad flirted with the performing arts for twenty years following The Trio's demise. Not Mike. He became a husband, father, administrator. He greeted folk acts he knew from the old days as they came through Spokane. Catching up. Whatever happened to whoever?

During those two decades his three children grew up with a vague notion that Dad had done something once. Enjoyed some sort of celebrity in their pre-history. They saw a wall of 3,500 record albums their parents clung to while the world progressed from eight-track to cassettes to CD's to digital downloads. Mostly, though, he was just Dad. The responsible, steady one.

At that thought, emotion flooded Chad, a remorse he could not afford to take on stage with him. Mike did not know how much Chad still struggled with guilt over the anger with which he'd confronted their conflict more than forty years ago.

Ever the professional, Chad set those feelings aside.

Joe Frazier joined them.

"Okay, fellows," Mike said. "Let's go."

On a huge screen above the stage, Mike, who was raised in a rock-solid immigrant family in Trail, British Columbia, stood tallest of the three. Mike and Joe, both handsome and solidly built, had dark hair. While Mike had chiseled facial features, Joe radiated a more subtle hardness, drawn by childhood in a Pennsylvania coal town.

A year older than his compatriots, born in 1936, a young Chad Mitchell seen on the big screen still had to produce ID at liquor counters. Smaller and slight of build, with blondest of blond hair and an almost cherubic visage, he would have fit seamlessly on the set of *Leave It to Beaver*.

Back in 1960, he offered reassurance to mothers across America who might be otherwise concerned about their daughters getting mixed up with all this coffee house, beatnik, folk music stuff. The product of a single-parent home, raised by his mother in a blue-collar Spokane neighborhood, he might have looked like a choir boy. His childhood, though, was much more complex than that.

Then, as always, audience eyes and ears found Chad first.

All three were gifted choral singers. Joe offered a classically trained baritone voice with both range and power to slip down to bass or sneak up toward tenor. Milt Okun, The Trio's musical director, mentor and guardian, found Mike's voice most difficult to pin down. While as harmonically adept as his partners, Mike added a unique, lower-register smoky tone to their vocal blends. Milt described it as "this lovely low, rich, informal, untrained sound."

Just as his appearance stood in contrast to Mike and Joe, so did Chad's vocal instrument. He could rein in a powerful tenor to meld seamlessly with the others—always on pitch—but Milt's direction frequently sent it soaring above Mike and Joe's harmonies during a song's final stanza with a commanding, almost operatic, descant melody that no other folkies could begin to approach.

The Trio's genuine vocal distinctiveness, though, was their ability to blend. While Milt spent hours using studio tricks to achieve the right vocal mix for Peter, Paul and Mary, that was never the case with Joe, Mike and Chad.

"They were so good, their harmonies so intricate. And they measured their own voices against each other," Milt recalled wistfully during an interview related to an earlier reunion performance. "They almost mixed themselves." When a recording session occasionally failed to produce a good separation of the three individual tracks, Milt said, "I could take the initial mono track, and it would be as good as if I'd mixed it."

Arts and performance reviewer Jim Kershner of the *Spokane Spokesman-Review* sat front and center awaiting The Trio's appearance. He felt uneasy with this assignment. Unlike *Spokesman-Review* critic Ed Costello 43 years earlier, Kershner wasn't concerned about The Trio's social and political commentary. He wondered if they could still sing.

Most Spokane journalists knew the story of this Gonzaga University-born group and its iconic place in community history. So, if the guys were performing again, someone had to cover it.

Kershner could have asked another reporter to critique the concert. But he feared this review would require tact to soften criticism of legendary performers forty years beyond their prime. He winced when the giant video presentation transitioned from the Sullivan show to clips of the guys singing on the *Dinah Shore Show* in 1962. Every ear in the house tonight would be able to discern the difference if they failed to measure up.

Waiting for The Trio on-stage were two guitarists and an acoustic bassist. Bass player Eugene Jablonski came from the Spokane symphony. Lead guitarist Bob Hefferan had toured with The Mitchell Trio during its John Denver years. Paul Prestopino had been around for almost the full life of The Trio. His resume included seventeen years accompanying Peter, Paul and Mary. During the 60's Paul dressed in button-down fashion—like The Trio—with sport coat, tie, carefully combed but thinning hair, and a groomed goatee. Somewhere along the way, he'd relaxed. As he grew portly and bald, he compensated with a long beard. Wisps of hair below a bare crown fell over his collar. And overalls. He preferred pastels. Tonight, the overalls were a screaming yellow, a long-sleeved shirt beneath them bright orange.

When Mike, Chad and Joe trotted onstage to enthusiastic applause, Kershner again thought the video presentation a mistake. Joe Frazier had grown heavy and jowly. Mike, too, had added pounds, but wore his weight better than Joe. Chad remained trim. With a scruff of beard, though, he no longer appeared the fresh-faced, wide-eyed little brother. While Mike and Joe still had full heads of hair, grey tending toward white, the reddish-blond locks that bolstered the innocent appeal of Chad's youth were rapidly retreating. The comedic gleam in his eyes now resided behind glasses.

Coats and ties were consigned to the past. Chad wore jeans and an unbuttoned leather vest. Joe's shirt draped over his stomach. Mike came closest to the old uniform, dark slacks and a grey long-sleeved dress shirt.

Because the three vocalists did not play instruments, they had developed a stage presence unique to the folk music era. Many of their numbers involved subtle choreography relying on comedic timing that lent a theatrical flavor to their concerts.

The three stood silent on the Opera House stage, sheepish, allowing applause to taper off. Still, they stood, glancing to each other, quiet, awkward. The audience filled this space with its own nervous laughter.

Mike finally spoke. "Shouldn't we say something here?"

Chad, at center-stage, looked left and right, feigning confusion. "I thought we'd decided we *weren't* going to say something here."

"Well," said Joe, "somebody has to say *something*."

"We just saw a clip from forty-five years ago," Mike agreed. "I think we should probably *say* something."

"Forty-five years?" Joe scoffed. "That's nothing. I go back a lot further than that."

"As do I," Mike said. "In fact, *I was born about ten thousand years ago . . .*"

To enthusiastic applause, guitars and bass rang in. Mike picked up the melody to Woody Guthrie's *Great Historical Bum*, one of The Chad Mitchell Trio's comedic staples.

Mike and Joe traded verses, claiming responsibility for Biblical feats and historic battle victories as they squeezed the smaller Chad aside each time he tried to push his way to the microphone. As the braggadocio became more extreme, Chad stood to first one side, then the other, protesting just loud enough to be heard that it was he who had performed these epic exploits.

Finally, he broke through and that imposing tenor filled the house. A simple melody line became an intricate three-part weave of harmony and lyrics. In the final chorus, Chad's trademark obligato soared and The Trio became a choir.

Kershner relaxed to enjoy the show.

— CHAPTER TWO —

"... and it went zip when it moved,
bop when it stopped,
and whirr when it stood still.
I never knew just what it was,
and I guess I never will."

The Marvelous Toy
—Tom Paxton

F ate? Destiny? Providence? Or maybe just the music.

Something over the past fifty years keeps shoving Chad Mitchell and Mike Kobluk onto the same stage. It's not that they don't like each other. Although, there have been times...

See, the music was all they shared to begin with. They were acquaintances, not pals. Each knew little of the others' life story. They *did* know, though, that when they sang, the music was better than good. When they joined voices, people applauded. Agents jockeyed to represent them. Record companies offered contracts. Night clubs and television producers called.

Eventually, their political satire and commitment to social change doomed their commercial success. Not their talent. Vocally, they were better than anyone on the folk scene.

Anyone.

Initially, the music demanded everything. They were so busy finding material, building harmonies, rushing from performance to performance, they didn't have time to notice how different they were. But the bliss of that ignorance couldn't last forever.

As familiarity set in, they found they agreed on music and politics. But not so much anything else. Little things festered and became bigger things.

As Tom Paxton considered the vast differences between Mike and

Chad, he noted, "So often it happens that the one thing people have in common is musical talent. But if they have that one thing, they'd be fools not to use it."

When this marvelous toy finally broke in the summer of 1965, neither Chad nor Mike mourned the parting.

Mike's subsequent path has been deliberate and linear.

Chad strayed far outside the lines.

They didn't speak for twenty years.

Then, a call about a reunion performance. *I will if he will.* They stepped right back into rehearsal as if nothing had changed. Their conflicts had never intruded here. The process of practice, creative experimentation, finding harmonies, had always been sacred.

Milt Okun, their music director from the old days, cringed at the idea of their performing again. They couldn't possibly be that good after twenty years, could they?

They were.

The simple reunion spawned a broader interest among a generation from college campuses whose lives The Trio's songs had influenced two decades earlier. More opportunities appeared. Mike and Chad kept their day jobs—and their distance—but once again, they shared the music.

Today, they live only two blocks apart, another unplanned coincidence. When Chad decided to return to Spokane in the early nineties, he and his wife Chris found a house among all the others in a city of 200,000. A few days after they moved in, Chad left his driveway, drove up the avenue, and saw Mike standing in a front yard.

He stopped. "What are you doing here?"

"I live here."

"When did you move in?"

"Nineteen Sixty-Nine."

Despite this proximity, they typically see each other four or five times a year.

In their eighties, they don't perform any more. They don't feel they can do the music justice. And, once again, they thought their separation complete.

Then a guy contacted Mike and said he wanted to write a book. "Shouldn't we involve Chad as well?" Mike asked. "He lives just down the street."

So, three days a week, we talk. Once with both Chad and Mike present. And then each, separately. They spent more time together during the summer of 2018 than they had since 1965. They still see the world—especially those first few years—from distinctly different perspectives. But they agree to disagree without animosity.

If old acquaintances are lucky—especially when they've shared so many highs and lows—they can find ways to set aside those things that divided them, and cherish the moments of joy their combined talents created for both themselves, and countless others.

— CHAPTER THREE —

"They threw a friend from out a boat
And sad to say he did not float
He wore a concrete overcoat
In the town of Brook-lie-ann . . ."

The Ballad of Murder Incorporated
—Ernie Sheldon and Richard Powell

Given the benefit of the doubt, folk music's brightest era might be exaggerated to ten years. Carefully nurtured through the late forties and fifties by Woody Guthrie, Pete Seeger, The Almanac Singers and The Weavers, broad folk music popularity burst to life in 1958 with The Kingston Trio's entirely unexpected hit, *Tom Dooley*. Folk music's commercial success, though, was fading fast when Chad left The Trio in 1965.

The public's abandonment of folk began with the Beatles' 1964 appearance on The Ed Sullivan Show. This burgeoning rock scene, though, didn't render folk music irrelevant overnight.

Frank Fried, The Trio's manager—and, in Mike Kobluk's mind, the author of The Trio's demise—pretty much nailed it when he urged Chad to hang in there a while longer.

"You're walking away too soon," Frank told Chad. "I think The Trio has one or two more years of relevance."

Indeed, by 1967 folk music had evolved to folk-rock, the difference between the two largely being an abandonment of folk music's plea for social justice.

John Sebastian and The Lovin' Spoonful; The Byrds (fronted by The Chad Mitchell Trio's former accompanist Roger McGuinn); Judy Collins; John Denver; Crosby, Stills & Nash; Neil Young and so many others had their roots in the folk movement. All were deserting a sinking ship. The Mamas and Papas' *Creeque Alley,* a musical history of the early folk-rock movement, notes that . . . *John and Mitchy were gettin' kind of itchy just to leave the folk music behind . . .*

Bob Dylan, folk's poet laureate, signaled the coming demise when he went electric at the 1965 Newport Folk Festival.

One folk group that managed to maintain popular relevance was Peter, Paul and Mary, who, like The Mitchell Trio, couldn't get along and went their separate ways in 1970. Their final collaboration—*Album 1700*—bore little resemblance to their hits of a decade earlier.

Those few years—1958 through 1968—produced amazing music with a remarkable brand of social conscience. And none were better or more profound than The Chad Mitchell Trio.

Ironically, folk purists embraced neither this era nor The Trio.

The Kingstons adapted *Tom Dooley* from a North Carolina folk song based on the 1866 murder of a woman named Laura Foster. Tom Dula, the alleged culprit, was hanged for his crime. The Kingston's version came out of nowhere and reached number one on 1958's Billboard chart, sending every record company in America searching for anyone who could sing a folk song.

This song on which *Tom Dooley* was based is included in a sub-genre defined by folk purists as *Appalachian Sweetheart Murder Ballads.* Apparently, a lot of Appalachian sweethearts manage to really piss off their significant others.

The Kingston's sin was in altering the song—making it more palatable to a commercial audience's ears. To purists, this transgression and those that would follow were unforgivable.

These purists defined folk music as a body of work that had been handed down orally from generation to generation without taint of commercialism. These songs needed to be homespun and unsophisticated. To be entirely legitimate, they had to be performed by those who experienced the events sung about, or who represented a direct lineage to those who had.

The purists had hiked through hills armed with recording devices, seeking any folk who played a guitar, a dulcimer, a washboard or jug, and sang songs born of local antiquity.

Often, these renditions, though authentic, were hardly palpable for commercial appetites.

For the popular folk movement, adaptations were a godsend.

At some point in the distant past a horse race took place in Kildare, Ireland, featuring an underdog nag named Stewball. The favorite was a grey mare named Griselda. Stewball's upset of Griselda—and the subsequent payoff for those who bet the longer odds—resulted in several variations of songs celebrating this event.

The better-known version, sung by Peter, Paul and Mary, features a plodding tempo.

The Chad Mitchell Trio also recorded that version with lyrical variations on their *Reflecting* album in late 1963. *The Slightly Irreverent Mitchell Trio* album, recorded a year later, included *Stewball and Griselda*, which Chad adapted by combining two different musical versions of the race:

"Come all you men of sportin' blood and listen to my story, Tis' of the noble Stewball, a gallant racing pony . . ."

And:

"Bet on Stewball my boys and you might win, you might win . . ."

This up-tempo version better captures the excitement of a village sporting event so significant, it spawned an enduring legend.

Chad was reminded firsthand the importance of adaptations late in The Trio's revived career when performing a song called *Tell Old Bill* at a benefit concert to raise funds for Father Joe Frazier's Episcopal diocese.

Chad had adapted the traditional song years before to make it more palatable to modern audiences. Rather than singing his rewritten line

"...*tell old Bill when he gets home to leave those downtown women alone...*" Chad sang the traditional line "... *tell old Bill when he gets home to leave them damn white women alone...*" Joe's bishop, who was in attendance, told Joe in no uncertain terms the song was unsuitable for a diocese audience.

Another advantage in adapting songs of uncertain authorship is that the adaptor owns this new version. To this day, both Chad and Mike get an occasional royalty check, sometimes amounting to as little as one cent, for their adaptations.

An adapter must be sure, though, the material is in the public domain before they go adapting. Chad discovered this when he added music to an A.A. Milne poem called *Disobedience*. The Trio performed it as *James James Morrison Morrison* on their *Live at the Bitter End* album, and the Disney Corporation, which owns Milne's copyrights, came calling for payment.

In any case, the purists discounted all these adaptations as a corruption of folk music.

Thus arose a debate as to what is legitimate folk music, and who can rightfully call themselves folk?

If anyone could claim to be a folk, certainly Pete Seeger should qualify. This patriarch of the folk movement hails back to Woody Guthrie and the Depression Era, *The Almanac Singers* and *The Weavers,* who shepherded folk music through the post-Depression '40s and the Joe McCarthy '50s.

Seeger told the New York Times in 1995, "There are as many kinds of folk songs as there are folks."

Seeger said in the current climate of multiculturalism, a distinction between folk and non-folk music grows more obscure. He argued that every musical style has an association with some cultural or socio-economic group. What music, he wondered, could be a more direct, outspoken expression of cultural sentiment than Rap?

Back in the sixties, neither purists nor proponents of commercial folk music would likely have gone that far. But comedian and writer Wally Cox— later famed for occupying the upper left-hand corner on the television game show *Hollywood Squares*—did tackle this question: what is *folk music* and who are *folk?*—on an intended comedy album recorded in RCA's New York studios in 1961.

Cox hired The Belafonte Singers and The Chad Mitchell Trio to sing for his project, during which Cox poses as an academic addressing these weighty questions. At one point he suggests that folk music legitimately could have urban, as well as rural hill country roots.

Chad narrated an introduction: *In my search for material among the rich and complex traditions of the city in which I dwell—Brooklyn—I came across, in a candy store, an old man of forty-five singing a song which had been sung by his father before him. I asked him to give me the name and copyright. He said it didn't have a name, rightly, but he called it* The Ballad of Murder Incorporated.

Composer Richard Powell and lyricist Ernie Lieberman wrote *The Ballad of Murder Incorporated*, and The Trio sang it for Cox's project. Lieberman, performing under the name Ernie Sheldon, was a member of the Gateway Singers and later the Limeliters. He is best known for writing lyrics to Glenn Yarbrough's biggest hit, *Baby the Rain Must Fall*.

A group called The Womenfolk included the only recorded and released version of *Murder Incorporated* on their *Womenfolk at the Hungry i* album in 1965.

Cox's venture never got out of the studio.

Over the past thirty years, Mike has made it his mission to recover master recordings, film and video tape of The Mitchell Trio's television, stage and recording performances. Among these treasures is the only known copy of Cox's comedy LP.

So, virtually no one has heard The Chad Mitchell Trio sing *The Ballad of Murder Incorporated*. Until now.

PART ONE

1958–1965

— CHAPTER FOUR —

ather Reinhard Beaver described himself as a "real priest as opposed to the Jesuits," who ran Gonzaga University and spent their time administrating or teaching or contemplating. He looked after baptisms, confirmations, burials and marriages. As assistant pastor at St. Augustine's in Spokane, routine tasks fell to him while more senior clerics got to pick and choose their assignments.

Many years later, Beaver would be implicated in the sexual abuse scandal that haunts the Catholic Church. But in these early years of their relationship, neither Chad nor Mike had any inkling their benefactor was plagued by those particular demons.

Short, balding and built along the lines of the Pillsbury Doughboy, had Father Beaver not chosen the priesthood, promotion would have been his forte. He spoke with a used-car-salesman's smile in his voice, ebullient with enthusiasm for his causes. Beginning in 1958, the priest's focus had been a group of three singing Gonzaga students.

Father Beaver saw himself as the Sol Hurock of the priesthood. Hurock, a Jewish impresario, promoted such talents as Van Cliburn, Isadora Duncan, Andres Segovia, Arthur Rubinstein and Isaac Stern. Father Beaver adopted The Trio as his cause the first time he heard them.

Chad Mitchell, Mike Kobluk and Mike Pugh were members of the Gonzaga Men's Glee Club, a forty-man choral group in which they were, at best, nodding acquaintances.

Chad had been raised in Spokane by his single mother and was accepted to Stanford University. At Lewis and Clark High School, Chad was the golden boy, one of those kids who did everything well. Class president, Boy's State representative, three-point-nine GPA. He played football and ran track. The acme of his high school athletic career came when he won the Washington State championship running the 880 his senior year.

Chad also sang. He recruited three friends and formed the Lewis and Clark Sophomore Quartet, which by and by became the Senior Quartet.

They even had a short-lived local television gig.

When he departed for college, Chad thought of folk music as "hoohaw western kind of stuff." His Stanford roommate, though, altered that perception.

"The first time I heard Harry Belafonte was when my roommate played Harry's *Mark Twain* album. I became fascinated with his music."

His roommate also initiated Chad's interest in musical satire when he played a Tom Lehrer album. Lehrer, a mathematician by vocation, wrote brilliant satire and accompanied himself on piano as he sang songs like *The Vatican Rag*.

Chad was further intrigued at a gathering for incoming Stanford freshmen as he gravitated to a young man who sat among an admiring audience playing a banjo. Chad liked the sound. He thought his tenor would blend nicely with this guy's baritone.

"Gee, who's that?" Chad asked the person next to him. "You think he might be interested in forming a singing group?"

"That's Dave, and no. He's an upper classman. He wouldn't want to sing with a freshman."

A couple of years later, Dave Guard would form The Kingston Trio.

Planning to study aeronautical engineering, Chad attended Stanford on a Navy ROTC scholarship. On Christmas break he saw a movie called *Not as a Stranger,* which inspired him to become a doctor. He shifted his major to pre-med, not realizing NROTC scholarships weren't available to pre-med students. So, he transferred to the University of Washington for his sophomore year.

At UW, he heard a couple of guys harmonizing at his frat house and joined in.

"Hey, you're pretty good," one of the guys told him.

"So are you," Chad said. "When I come back after the break, we should form a folk group. I think our voices work well together."

They agreed.

After the break though, Chad stayed home and enrolled at Gonzaga. The guys at UW remained intrigued by Chad's proposal. They found two other singers and, in the next couple of years, became The Brothers Four.

So—an unwitting veteran of two flirtations with folk music history—

Chad accepted a partial scholarship in exchange for singing in the Gonzaga Men's Glee Club. The basketball team got nowhere near as much notice as the men's glee club on the 1958 version of Gonzaga's campus.

Mike's introduction to the glee club occurred when it performed at his Trail, British Columbia high school during one of the club's Northwest tours.

The son of Ukrainian and Polish immigrants who were devout Catholics, Mike had a rich family and school life. He sang in his school choir and played violin in the orchestra. He sang High Mass as a member of his church's Gregorian choir each Sunday.

Like Chad, Mike was an accomplished athlete. A member of Trail's juvenile hockey team, he was voted most valuable player each of his final two seasons. Trail made it to the British Columbia championship game, winning the B.C. Trophy the second year. In that game, Mike scored two goals and assisted on a third as Trail defeated Kamloops 6–3.

Mike's Catholicism has not always provided a smooth path. As chairman of his high school's graduating class, he headed a committee responsible for planning graduation activities, including the graduation banquet which was to be held on a Friday. The committee voted for a main course of Baron of Beef, a delectability most Trail families could not otherwise afford.

Nearly forty percent of the graduating class, though, was Catholic and forbidden to eat meat on Friday. Mike appealed to his parish priest for dispensation. Father Martin said he would have to contact the bishop. The bishop denied the request and directed the Catholic students to substitute fish for the beef.

When Mike reported this edict to the committee, the Catholic members were disheartened until Mike said, "I'm going to eat beef on Friday and enjoy it, then seek forgiveness in confession on Saturday."

All but four of the Catholic students had the beef and lined up at the confessional the next day.

Being Catholic, though, fit right in with Mike's ambition to attend Gonzaga.

"When I heard the glee club," Mike said, "I was amazed. I'd never heard a group so good, so intense. And they sang with such heart. I decided on the spot I wanted to go to Gonzaga and sing with that group."

Director Lyle Moore had presided over the glee club for thirty years. "Nothing was ever good enough for Lyle Moore," Mike said. "He was a taskmaster and a perfectionist."

Both Mike and Chad credit Moore with development of their vocal and choral skills.

"He emphasized listening to other singers," Mike said, "blending your voice with theirs rather than trying to make your voice dominant."

When Moore heard The Trio in concert several years later, Mike and Chad invited him backstage, anxious to hear his critique. Moore looked at Chad and said, "Too much tenor."

In addition to the full choir, Mike sang with the club's men's quartet. As a scholarship student, Chad was expected to develop solo material and be available when called upon during a glee club performance. Chad recruited another club member who played guitar and, for his solo presentations, did his best to imitate Belafonte's calypso sound.

Chad and Mike were thrust together when Moore told them they would represent the glee club during Campus Days at Gonzaga. Each university club sponsored an information booth in a county fair atmosphere to recruit new members.

"What should we sing?" Mike asked at their first meeting.

"I know some Belafonte tunes," Chad said.

Mike voted for The Kingston Trio. "How about *Tom Dooley*?"

To duplicate the stylings of the Kingstons, they required a voice to fill between Chad's tenor and Mike's bass range, so they drafted a baritone.

Because they entertained a wandering audience, the three pretty much had their fill of *Tom Dooley* that weekend. The priest, though, couldn't get enough.

"How would you like to sing at the Job's Daughters meeting on Saturday?" Father Beaver offered. "They'd probably pay a few bucks for the entertainment."

"Sure," echoed Mike and Chad.

The baritone, a law student who didn't have the time to devote to rehearsal and performance, begged off and Mike Kobluk recruited Mike Pugh as a replacement.

Throughout his high school years—he graduated in 1955—Chad Mitchell had been pushed to the front. Best singer, best grades, prettiest girlfriend. The winning personality. Whatever group he joined chose him to lead. He accepted these roles with humility and outward enthusiasm.

"I was always the golden boy in high school," Chad said, "but I led a double life."

Chad's mom worked hard. His father contributed nothing—either financially or emotionally—to the family.

Every summer Chad held various manual labor jobs to help pay for college. Among those jobs, he worked on the night shift at the Armour Meat packing plant where his crew loaded animal carcasses and boxes on trucks. He was a rock crusher monitor at a gravel company where he stood all day ensuring the crusher's jaws didn't get jammed. And he was a maintenance helper at Sacred Heart Hospital where his job was to organize a basement area containing jars filled with organs and body parts. He still remembers with a shudder the day he examined one of the jars and found an eyeball looking back at him.

His mom had managed to provide him with a car, a 1940 Chevy coupe. But he couldn't afford gas, "We didn't have any extra money," Chad said, "so I improvised."

Sometimes, late at night, he roamed the neighborhood with a siphon hose and gas can.

On one other occasion he and another car collided in a minor accident. The Chevy's elaborate metal grill was damaged. He couldn't afford insurance, so again, he improvised.

During the fifties Spokane's auto dealers were all located along Third Avenue downtown. Chad found another 1940 Chevy with an identical grill on one of the lots. He observed for a couple of days, learning that first thing each morning, car lot employees put keys in each car so customers who wanted to take a test drive wouldn't have to wait. Chad chose a moment when no one appeared to be looking and lifted the Chevy's keys. He went to a nearby hardware store, had duplicates made, then slipped the original keys back into the car.

Late that night, he snuck back, and drove the car to Spokane's Comstock Park. Today, the park is surrounded by Spokane's South Hill neighborhood. Then, it bordered an unpopulated wooded area full of dirt roads and trails. He removed the Chevy's grill and hid it among some brush, then returned the Chevy to the car lot.

He planned to drive his car to the wooded area the next day and swap the new grill for his damaged one. As he approached, though, he saw a police car cruising one of the dirt roads.

Looking closer, Chad saw a couple of cops on motorcycles along the trails. If indeed they were looking for the stolen grill, Chad couldn't afford to let them spot his car sporting an identical damaged grill.

He parked among dozens of cars at Comstock Park and fled to a crowd watching a tennis tournament. Still not sure whether the cops had seen him, he took off his shirt and sat among tennis fans for two hours. Finally, he risked the drive home.

He waited for the cover of darkness a couple of nights later to install the stolen grill on his own car.

Still the golden boy. No one the wiser.

———~———

True to his word, Father Beaver booked the unnamed trio with the Spokane chapter of Job's Daughters on a regular basis, even landing them a performance at a state Job's Daughters Convention. He arranged a week-long booking at the Early Bird's Club at the Davenport Hotel as well as a date at the Fairchild Air Force Base Officers' Club. On a good night, the singers and Dennis Collins, their guitarist, would split fifty dollars among them.

During the 1959 spring semester, Chad abandoned Gonzaga in favor of the University of Washington's pre-med program. He didn't leave The Trio, though. He found himself driving across the Cascades and through the Palouse wheat country on weekends to perform at the priest's various bookings, now as far-flung as Wenatchee or Walla Walla.

Following that spring semester, Father Beaver announced his grand plan.

"I'm driving to New York to attend a training program for Army chaplains," he told them. "The Army is paying my travel fees and giving me a room on base for the summer. Why don't you guys come with me? We'll find a record company and get you guys a recording contract."

Chad and Mike Pugh were at loose ends. Mike Kobluk's options were to paint his sister's house, work at Trail's lead/zinc smelter, or bag Elephant Brand Fertilizer. A trip to New York looked good to him.

They had no designs on making a career of folk singing. They didn't believe for a moment they'd really make records. But a free trip to a place they'd never seen? Count us in. Each fully expected to be back at Gonzaga when fall semester began.

Dennis Collins obtained a leave of absence from his job at his neighborhood Rosauers Grocery Store.

— CHAPTER FIVE—

"And I can't help but wonder where I'm bound . . ."

—Tom Paxton

July 1959

The priest lied.

A fairly innocuous lie as lies go, but a lie, nonetheless.

"Can you do that? Without getting in trouble with, you know, God?" Chad asked.

A smile stole across the priest's face and he said, "Well, we don't know for certain it's *not* the truth, now do we? And they'll feed us supper."

Considering the three Gonzaga University students and their guitarist had only about a hundred and fifty dollars among them, supper was a big deal, regardless of how they came by it.

Father Beaver had called ahead to arrange a booking their first night on the road in Butte, Montana. They played a set at Raymond's Bar in exchange for dinner and a place to stay. Funding for the rest of their journey, though, was a craps shoot.

The folks at Raymond's wondered what to call the group.

"Boys, we need to come up with a name," Father Beaver advised as they rolled through western Montana. "Something catchy, like The Kingston Trio."

"That one's already taken," Mike said.

"How about, the Palouse Trio?" Father Beaver suggested.

The singers exchanged indifferent shrugs.

The priest had no inkling his next suggestion would ultimately doom this vocal collaboration he worked so hard to encourage.

"Okay, then, how about The Chad Mitchell Trio?"

When the priest suggested The Chad Mitchell Trio, Father Beaver was only following a pattern set by a host of others over Chad's early life. His voice, his personality, his all-American glow, once again shoved him to the front.

"Why not name it after all of us?" Chad suggested. "Kobluk, Mitchell and Pugh?"

"That won't work," Mike Pugh said. "It'll sound like we smell bad."

"The Kobluk Trio?" Mike Kobluk said. "They'll think we're Russian subversives."

"Okay," the priest said. "The Chad Mitchell Trio it is."

As a theologian, the priest certainly understood the curse of original sin—that one misstep that ultimately unravels even the most earnest of endeavors. In his choice of the group's name, the priest had introduced a serpent into this vocal Garden of Eden.

Once they reached AM radio range of Miles City, Montana, the priest hunted up a weak signal from a local station. Chad and Mike listened in hopes of hearing *Tom Dooley*. The Kingston Trio offering had sold six million copies the summer of 1958. Now, a year later, *Tom Dooley* hung on at number forty, but the charts didn't hint at an impending folk music explosion. Bobby Darin's *Dream Lover* rested at number one as the priest's Ford pulled into Miles City. The closest thing to a folk song on the chart was the gimmicky *Battle of New Orleans* at number three. *Ragtime Cowboy Joe*—charting at number fourteen—might be considered a little folky, were it not performed by Alvin and the Chipmunks.

The priest continued to fiddle with the radio dial. His interest lay in snippets of local news bleeding through the static. *". . . the new Miles City Country Club will hold its first-ever annual meeting tonight at . . ."* A blare of fuzzy noise wiped out the rest.

"That's it, boys," the priest said. "That's where you'll perform."

They got directions at a gas station and headed north of town where the priest pulled to the roadside as a golf course came into view. He rummaged through his luggage to find a black cassock and clerical collar.

He parked at a sprawling ranch-style building situated among the green grass and fledgling trees of a new golf course and a sign that said, "Annual Meeting and Dinner, 7:00 P.M."

The boys stretched their legs and were cautioned to wait there. Mike and Chad wandered onto the lawn next to a doorway covered only by a screen in deference to summer afternoon heat.

Chad heard the priest's opening pitch before the cleric followed his quarry through a second inner door.

"Can I help you, Father?"

"How do you do? I'm taking a folk-singing trio from Gonzaga University to New York so they can perform on The Ed Sullivan Show . . ."

———— ∾ ————

". . . and I'm sure you folks would enjoy some entertainment this evening when you finish conducting your business," the priest continued as a man in a white shirt and bolo tie pulled a door closed behind them, then pointed to a seat opposite a cluttered desk.

"Well, that's a nice offer, Father," he said, "but I'm afraid we don't have the budget for that sort of thing."

"Oh, my good man," the priest waved his hands before his face as if to clear the air of misconception, "I'm not asking for money. The boys need to run through their songs and playing for an audience is good experience. They're quite accomplished. After all, this is Ed Sullivan we're talking about."

The man seemed fixated on the clerical collar. "Well, I guess we might—"

"Excellent! I'll tell the boys." The priest rose and reached for the door before turning again. "I don't suppose you might be able to include them at dinner?"

"Do they know *Tom Dooley*?" the man asked.

The priest smiled. "I'm sure they do."

"Okay, I expect we'll have enough food."

When the priest returned, Mike Pugh and Dennis Collins had joined

Chad and Mike leaning against the car.

"Ed Sullivan?" Chad asked.

"Why not?" the priest said.

The country club's lack of a sound system presented no problem. Mike, Chad and Mike sang with power and fullness, easily filling the medium-sized banquet room. They performed a half-dozen traditional songs, along with *Tom Dooley*, to their audience's delight. Their reception was so enthusiastic the crowd passed a hat, producing about thirty dollars to add to The Trio's bank.

"I manage a hotel in Glendive, about seventy miles up the road," a middle-aged woman told Chad as she shook his hand. "I'll call ahead and hold a couple of rooms if you boys want to stay there tonight. No charge. I really enjoyed your music."

Their third night out, the aspiring troubadours sang at a Minneapolis nunnery in exchange for lodging. The sparse setting and severe glances from senior nuns kept the guys from wandering the halls and cured any thoughts they might have entertained concerning the priesthood.

Once again, though, they'd managed to keep their meager bank intact.

Having grown up in Trail, British Columbia, Mike Kobluk regarded Spokane as a big city. Their drive through Chicago disabused him of that notion.

"Is New York like this?" he asked as he craned his neck to see the peaks in this canyon of towering buildings.

"Yes," the priest said, "only more so."

In Chicago, they stayed with a friend of the priest and the next day were back on the road. With the day fading fast, they arrived in downtown Toledo where Father Beaver stopped at a phone booth. As the boys crowded close, he thumbed through the Yellow Pages nightclub listings.

"This one," he said, pointing to a half-page ad for The Roundtable.

They stopped at a gas station so the priest could change.

"You want the black stuff and the collar?" Chad asked as he tugged the priest's suitcase to the top of the pile.

"No," the priest said after a moment of thought, "I think my Army chaplain's uniform is the one to go with in Toledo."

Although dusk approached as they drove into the nightclub parking lot, the blacktop expanse was empty except for the cars of early-arriving employees.

"I'll be back," the priest told them.

———❧———

Chad and the Mikes sat with windows rolled down to temper the humidity of a Toledo parking lot and waited for Father Beaver to reappear.

"He's taking a long time," Mike said. "What do you think that means?"

"You know how much he likes to talk," Chad said. "He's probably just found someone willing to listen."

A half hour passed before Father Beaver emerged through shadows of the Roundtable's entryway. Drooped shoulders and absence of a characteristic bounce in his stride told the story.

"Guys," he said, his voice empty, "I'm sorry. I don't know what to say. I ... I couldn't ..."

"Did you tell him about Ed Sullivan?" Mike asked.

"I did. But he said it didn't make any difference. He asked to see union cards. He said he only books through the union."

"Don't feel bad, Father," Chad said. "This is the first time anyone's turned you down. We'll find something else."

"Not here," Father Beaver said. "I'm afraid every place we go will have the same rules."

"Then we'll just keep going," Mike said. "We don't have to stay here tonight. We can drive straight through to New York."

"I suppose that's the thing to do," Father Beaver said. "Push on. I feel so strongly you boys have a destiny ..."

He had his hand on the ignition switch when The Roundtable's front door burst open, and a tall, bearded man with reading glasses perched low on his nose sprinted toward them.

"Father! Father! Wait!"

The man skidded to a stop, placed one hand on the driver's side window frame to balance himself and wiped a heavy dew of sweat from his forehead with the other.

"Thank goodness . . . I . . . caught you," he said, gasping for breath. "I need . . . I need your group tonight."

"I thought the union—"

"Never mind that," he panted. "I have an emergency. I just found out the lead singer for the group we hired fell off a barstool and is comatose, or something. I need an act."

Father Beaver turned and winked at his four charges. "God looks out for His own, boys," he said. "God looks out for His own."

He stepped half out of the car door with an extended hand.

"You do understand," he told the nightclub owner, "that our price just went up?"

"He loved your performance," Father Beaver told them. Mike couldn't help noticing, though, a missing hint of triumph in the priest's voice. "So much he wants to book you for two more weeks."

Silence gripped a tiny off-stage dressing room where Dennis re-strung his guitar and Chad dabbed at his face with a cold washcloth. Mike still felt an adrenalin glow from their performance. They'd played two twenty-five-minute sets, stretching their repertoire to its max. They earned $100, dinner, and a place to stay for the night.

"He offered $1,300 a week," Father Beaver finally said.

Chad's eyes lit up. "You've got to be kidding."

"That's what he said. Two hour-long shows a night. He'll take care of your union cards . . ."

The priest's voice trailed into silence.

"But you can't wait for us," Mike said. "You have to be in New York."

The priest offered a confirming nod.

"Thirteen hundred dollars," Chad said. "We could take a train."

Mike knew, though, any train they took would be headed west instead of east. The priest provided the confidence propping them up. Made all things seem possible. Without him, New York would fade into next year, then into forever.

"That's thirteen hundred divided four ways," Mike said, adapting the practical realism that would define his role with The Trio. "We'd have to rent a place, buy food, not to mention travel costs. We came on this trip to go to New York. Let's go to New York."

Father Beaver smiled. Mike Pugh shrugged.

Chad took a last longing look at a corner sink, the little makeup table, clothing racks, the cracked mirror. "Yeah. Let's go to New York."

The boys had been in New York two days when the Toledo gig began to look pretty good.

They rolled into Manhattan early afternoon, having driven all night. The sheer, colossal fact of New York City, though, trumped their exhaustion. Father Beaver booked a room at the Schuyler Hotel located on 46th Street between Fifth and Sixth Avenues. Four blocks from 42nd and Broadway, a block further to Times Square.

The Trio and their guitarist left the priest at the hotel as they braved the streets and, gaping and stretching like rubes, went to see the sights.

A sense of intimidation left them uncertain about what lay ahead. At the same time, though, amid the honking and clatter and shouting, Chad felt the thrum of the place, like the dangerous buzzing wind makes when it whistles across a taut strand of wire.

They made their way to Times Square and walked from the gargantuan Admiral Television and Appliances sign, below the neon Canadian Club tower at the north end, past a looming half-block long testimony to Kleenex, to a Coca Cola and Planters Peanuts colossus at the south end.

Along the way, elegant old theaters advertised the latest Hollywood offerings, while smaller movie houses spawned an adult film industry featuring peep shows and seedy remnants of burlesque. They returned to the hotel, feeling a little soiled, but excited for the adventure ahead.

The priest escorted them to a few clubs in Greenwich Village the next day. They couldn't find anyone willing to listen at the Village Barn but were directed to mid-town and a place called The Upstairs Downstairs, managed by the flamboyant Julius Monk. Monk listened to The Trio sing, then joined them at a table in the dark and empty lounge.

He placed a hand on Chad's thigh, smiled and said, "My, but you boys are certainly a healthy lot."

Chad had just learned the first of many lessons about the difference of life in Spokane and life in the big city.

A week of auditions produced no takers. Each day represented a drain on their meager resources. The priest's despair multiplied as he realized his clerical collar didn't hold as much sway in New York as it did in Billings, Montana. If he said anything about Ed Sullivan, most of these guys would pick up a phone and call Ed. The Trio needed a real agent, or they would end up hitchhiking back to Spokane.

Father Beaver checked himself and his wards out of the Schuyler and drove to Fort Slocum, located on David's Island at the western end of Long Island Sound where he would be quartered during the six weeks of his army chaplain training. He'd assumed The Trio and their guitarist could stay with him. They couldn't. Base officials granted them a single night, at fifty cents apiece, but no longer.

The priest's ebullient nature faded. "I've brought you boys all the way here, and I have no idea what to do. We can't afford for you to stay, and I've no way of getting you home."

He took them back to the Schuyler, negotiated a deal with someone at the front desk, and left them with the promise that, "I'll figure something out."

"So, where do we find an agent?" Mike wondered.

The priest snapped his fingers. "I have a cousin, a piano player. He lives somewhere in the city. I think he plays clubs. He must know an agent."

Beaver reached his cousin by phone. "A woman named Bertha Case helps him with his bookings. He called her for us, and we have an appointment."

Bertha, in her early fifties, had made her mark as a literary agent. She'd been raised in Paris, where she eventually worked for the U.S. Embassy. She moved to New York and began working in the office of the Audrey Wood Agency. Next, she headed the literary department of the A.S. Lyons Agency in Hollywood before returning to New York to oversee the television department of the M.C.A. Agency. She opened her own office to handle the works of Lotte Lenya, and the Kurt Weill and Bertolt Brecht estates. In 1958, she met an aspiring singer named Nina Simone. So taken with Miss Simone's haunting voice and piano virtuosity, she branched into talent management.

Bertha welcomed the priest and his charges to her Manhattan office, listened to three songs and said, "You boys have extraordinary gifts. I will be happy to represent you. We need to get you an audition at one of the respectable clubs."

"We've auditioned at several clubs and made no progress," the priest told her.

She smiled. "We'll choose someplace where they know me."

"How long will it take?" Mike asked. "To get an audition?"

"I'll start working on it today," Bertha said. She'd apparently noticed some anxiety in Mike's tone, because she asked, "Why? Is there a problem?"

"We're broke," Mike said. "Flat out of money. We can afford maybe one more night in our hotel. After that, we'll be on the street."

"You're staying at the Schuyler?" Bertha picked up her phone and gave someone instructions to arrange another couple of weeks at the hotel.

"We'll sign a contract," Bertha told them. "I'll advance the money you need. It won't be extravagant. You'll be on an allowance. You'll pay me back through your bookings."

"We'll have bookings?" Chad asked.

Bertha smiled. "Oh, yes. You'll have bookings."

The priest bid his charges good luck. The army chaplain's program had begun in earnest, and he would be confined to Fort Slocum for six weeks. He shook hands with each young man, and then told them, "I'm counting on you. You know, the whole Ed Sullivan thing? It's only a lie if it doesn't come true. My mortal soul is in your hands."

So, it came to pass that, during their second week in New York City, The Chad Mitchell Trio auditioned at The Blue Angel, among the most sophisticated of New York nightclubs booking major acts.

Bertha knew the management.

Seven p.m. might as well have been early morning at the Blue Angel. Self-respecting New York City nightclubbers didn't hit the streets much before 10 p.m. Bertha led the guys into an empty lounge.

As his eyes adjusted to the shadows, Chad poked Mike and pointed to a poster. "Look. Harry Belafonte performs here."

They were directed to an empty stage. Dennis tuned his guitar.

"What sort of microphone setup do you need," asked a voice from the darkness.

The only time The Trio had sung into a microphone was the Toledo gig where they fought with feedback as a sound man tried to adjust to the unanticipated power of their voices.

"I think we'll be fine without it," Chad said.

The club manager offered a questioning look to Bertha.

She smiled and nodded.

Three songs later, the manager waved them off stage.

"You guys are good," he said. "Better than good. But I can't book an act that does someone else's material. Not in New York. Everybody knows who sings *Tom Dooley*. Bertha, go find your guys their own material and then come back."

As they trooped onto the sidewalk, slumped shoulders betrayed their discouragement.

"What's wrong?" Bertha asked.

"Same old thing," Chad said.

Bertha laughed. "You didn't hear what he said, did you? He said to come back."

"Where do we find our own material?" Mike asked.

Bertha rolled her eyes. "Don't worry, boys. I know a guy."

— CHAPTER SIX—

Spokane Opera House
October 2007

"Well, here we are in Spokane, just a few, short, forty-five years later," Chad told their audience as Mike and Joe deferred to him for introductions. "You know we'd really like to thank our promoters, Jack Lucas and Kevin Twohig, for being so persistent in convincing the folks at the home to let us out and be with you this evening.

"As has been the case for people who haven't seen us in some time, there's been some confusion as to exactly what the identity is of the people up here. Let me try and ease that for you. My name is Chad Mitchell, and I am, indeed, happy to be here."

The audience, particularly those knowledgeable of Chad's history, laughed and applauded. Mike laughed too as he and Chad exchanged a meaningful glance.

Chad continued. "After The Trio, among other endeavors I was a cabaret performer, a realtor, and director of entertainment for The Delta Queen Steamboat Company. To my right I have Mr. Mike Kobluk . . ." Mike garnered applause and cheers. ". . . and for those of you who might not know, for thirty years Mike was the Spokane City Entertainment Facilities Director, which included the Convention Center, the Arena and, of course, the Opera House. Well, he spent thirty years booking people onto this stage, and has finally earned his way to be here tonight."

Chad paused to let applause ring.

"And to my left is Father Joe Frazier—"

"Far left," Joe corrected.

"Far left, yes. Farther left than you might think."

Joe crossed himself and bowed.

"After The Trio," Chad said, "Joe attended Yale Divinity School, where he got his license to—"

"Ordained," Joe said. "The word is ordained."

"—where he got his license to be *ordained* as an Episcopal priest, and now he is the brand-new vicar at Big Bear Lake, California. So, you see, none of us really ever left show business."

New York City
August 1959

Bertha took The Trio on a tour of recording companies. Columbia Records liked them but had just signed Lou Gottlieb's Limeliters, featuring Glenn Yarbrough. RCA loved The Trio, but had just signed The Brothers Four, including the two singers whom Chad had encouraged to form a folk group back at the University of Washington. Uncertain where the whole folk thing was headed, neither company wanted to dilute its promotional efforts by adding a second folk act.

Columbia, however, sent them to ColPix, which shared Columbia Pictures offices at 711 Fifth Avenue. This offshoot handled music for Columbia Pictures and had moved into record production. After the guys sang, Bertha huddled with a couple of company honchos in a corner.

"Do they already have a folk group?" Chad asked after the brief conference.

Bertha smiled. "They do now."

Two weeks into their New York City adventure, The Chad Mitchell Trio had a recording contract.

Now, Bertha explained, they needed a booking agent. General Artists Corporation, the country's largest booking agency, signed them immediately.

ColPix assigned Hecky Krasnow as The Trio's Artist and Repertoire representative, a lucky break because Krasnow had a deep interest in folk music. He recognized immediately that The Trio needed a musical director to help develop material.

"I was thinking Milt Okun," Bertha told Krasnow when the topic came up.

"That's the guy," Krasnow agreed.

"But isn't he going on tour with Belafonte?" Bertha asked.

"Nope. Harry got pissed off about something. He's not taking Milt to Europe."

———— ❧ ————

Milt Okun couldn't hide his amazement. He listened to the three young men sing in Bertha's office and at first said nothing. Mike, Chad and Mike waited in silence.

"And you said your choral training is from...?"

"The Gonzaga Men's Glee Club," Chad said.

"Gonzaga University," Mike added. "Spokane... Washington. The state..."

Milt turned to Bertha. "And ColPix signed them?"

"Yes." She smiled. "You're surprised?"

"I am surprised," Milt said. "Not that ColPix signed them. But at how chorally adept..." His voice trailed off as he studied the song list Bertha handed him. "These are almost all Kingston Trio songs," he said. "But your harmonies are different."

"We work out our own harmonies," Mike said.

"These are very good. Better than the Kingston's arrangements. But you need your own material."

"So we've heard," Chad said.

"Sing something not on this list," Okun said, "something not Kingston."

They sang the *Ballad of Sigmund Freud*, a song written by Larry Glasser and Bob March in the early fifties and recorded by The Gateway Singers. *Sigmund* always got a laugh at The Trio's beer money performances around Spokane.

Ahhh, Milt thought, *these boys have a sense of humor and a grasp of comedic timing.*

A tall, soft-spoken academic with round face and black-rimmed glasses, Milt Okun had been a high school music teacher when he went to work for Harry Belafonte as a sometime member of the Belafonte Singers, a pianist, musical arranger, and conductor. Working for the mercurial Belafonte, though, could be an exercise in frustration. Milt had committed some sin and had been excluded from Belafonte's current tour.

When Bertha Case called and asked Milt to work with her newly discovered folk trio, he was intrigued. An aficionado of opera and symphony, his love of folk music had been ingrained through personal experience.

Milt's parents were Jewish cousins who, like Mike Kobluk's parents, emigrated from Russia. These left-wing political activists settled in Brooklyn and eventually purchased the Schroon Crest, an Adirondacks resort, where each summer they sponsored folk music festivals. During the previous two decades a rich vein of music had been spawned by Depression era hardship. Folk music celebrated the little guy and protested a hardscrabble life that follies of the wealthy had handed him.

During his teenage years, Milt sat at the feet of performers like The Weavers—Pete Seeger, Ronnie Gilbert, Lee Hays and Fred Hellerman. Some years at festival time, a hobo named Woody Guthrie would show up to perform.

Conservative America turned mean and paranoid following World War II. Joseph McCarthy reigned, and Milt watched as these childhood heroes were hauled before Congress to answer for music and lifestyles leaning sharply left, flirting with fringes of the American Communist Party.

When the U.S. House Unamerican Activities Committee decided certain opinions should be punished, folk music was indicted right along with movies, books and the arts in general. People who would not swear loyalty oaths to the United States of McCarthy were blacklisted, denied their ability to make a living according to their talents. The arts no longer spoke out or poked fun. Popular music shifted to tales of adolescent angst and teenage girls mutilated in automobile accidents.

Milt looked forward to a day when popular music could once again *say something*. And when it did, he believed folk music would provide the platform.

Beyond saying something, though, the music had to be good. Too much of what Milt heard in the current folk revival was not. The songs themselves were okay. Many of the singers, though, had only a nodding acquaintance with melody and didn't grasp harmony at all. They strummed their instruments and sang their songs almost in agony.

So, when he heard these young men—all with limited formal training—who seemed to have an intuitive grasp of harmony, humor and stage presence, he realized how much he wanted to direct them.

Milt, his wife Rosemary and their daughter Jenny occupied a tiny apartment on Twelfth Street above the Cherry Lane Theater in Greenwich Village. This apartment became The Trio's rehearsal venue, the scene of many post-rehearsal meals and some legendary Monopoly games. Milt's sole moral failing, Chad believes to this day, is that he cheated at Monopoly.

Although scores of clients would come later, including Peter, Paul and Mary, the Brothers Four, the Limeliters, John Denver, and Placido Domingo, Milt remembered The Chad Mitchell Trio as his first and favorite.

For Chad and Mike, even during the tumultuous times that lay ahead, these rehearsals—the most intensely creative aspect of their performing careers—were what they enjoyed most. Milt termed what they were fashioning as "head arrangements." They wrote nothing down. They didn't need to. The Trio members remembered what they rehearsed.

Milt presented a song. The Trio experimented with melody and harmonies, straightforward at first, but as the full extent of their musical aptitude became apparent, Milt suggested and nudged them toward greater complexity.

As they prepared to record their first album, Milt, The Trio and their guitarist met each day for several hours. Rosemary and Jenny sought to keep a certain distance to let The Trio work, but the apartment was small, and they couldn't help being caught up in the process.

Milt found the boys "extremely flexible, anxious to learn, and really quite gifted."

"Okay, fellows," Milt could suggest, "let's take these two lines and build to a crescendo, then hit the final chord fortissimo and hold it. And Chad, we need a nice high obligato through the final verse. Mike and Mike, adjust the blend. Give Chad his space, and it will sound heavenly."

And there the music would be, seamless, ready for stage or studio.

⁓

The Trio carried off the vocal aspect of their first album superbly. The songs themselves, though, were hardly top forty material.

ColPix saw The Chad Mitchell Trio as Kingston Trio clones—a little smart-alecky, a broad sort of presentation that mocked some of the traditional songs they performed. Everyone sought to emulate success.

Always careful about budgeting an unknown group, ColPix had Milt joined with Rose Warwick and Irene Olson to write lyrics and attach them to the melodies of traditional Jewish songs long since consigned to the public domain. The Trio sang words like *Hey, Nanine, get your tambourine* to a traditional folk melody.

And, of course, the record company wanted a hanging song. By now, *Tom Dooley* had been perched on the gallows for years. So, they found *The Gallows Song*, based on a traditional Scottish ballad about the impending hanging of a fellow named MacPherson. Unlike Tom Dooley, MacPherson's crime is not detailed, but MacPherson is clearly not pleased with his circumstances.

The harmonies they contrived made *The Gallows Tree* The Trio's favorite on *The Chad Mitchell Trio Arrives* album. Faced with the choice, however, of leaving either MacPherson or their listeners dangling, they closed *Gallows* by adding a single clarifying line: *And he was hung.*

The Trio recorded their debut album during August. Following its completion, ColPix gave Hecky Krasnow a different assignment, replacing him with Stu Phillips, a man The Trio regarded as slimy. Phillips arranged for them to record a dubious single.

"*The Guns of Navarone?*" Chad asked.

"It's a movie. A Columbia Pictures movie. And this is a theme song."

"Why would we do a movie theme song?" Mike asked.

"It's a job. You need exposure."

They ran through the song. Chad agreed when Mike said, "This is awful."

They thought the song even worse when, at a recording session, thundering cannon sound effects punctuated the rhythm as they sang of *Six Men*.

"Don't worry about it," said a studio technician. "Nobody will ever hear it. The guy directing the movie is writing his own song."

———

The Trio received no advance on that first album, so while they had a record contract, they remained without funds. Bertha's allowance kept a roof over their head, but they often ran short at week's end.

"What do you want for dinner?" Chad asked the other three.

"You still have money?" Mike asked.

"No. But I have a raincoat."

"What's that have to do with it?"

"The raincoat has lots of inside pockets."

"You'll get yourself arrested," Mike said. "What will Bertha think when she has to bail you out?"

"I don't plan on being caught."

He wasn't. Chad managed to return from the deli next to the hotel with a whole chicken.

Chad never planned on getting caught.

———

The Trio and their guitarist eventually escaped The Schuyler Hotel. They found an apartment on East 93rd Street, and they sub-let it for two hundred dollars a month from a couple locked into a lease who had moved to Chicago. They rehearsed relentlessly. Their sessions with Milt added songs almost daily. In the meantime, ColPix released a single from the first album—*Walking on the Green Grass*—that enjoyed some radio airtime. Bertha found a ten-day August booking in Pittsburg.

Armed now with their own material, Bertha returned them to The Blue Angel where they were booked for two weeks in November. Their national television debut occurred during that two-week run when they appeared on *The Pat Boone Show*. The Angel extended their appearance three more weeks, and Arthur Godfrey booked them for a week's worth of appearances on his daily radio program. They'd leave The Angel between 1:00 and 2:00 a.m., crash at their apartment for a couple hours, then get to mid-town to tape the Godfrey show by 9:00.

Their summer lark to New York had stretched into December. They began their trip intending to be back at Gonzaga when Fall classes resumed. Parents wondered just what their sons had gotten themselves into. Chad's mother thought singing was a nice enough hobby, but her plan called for Chad to attend medical school.

"My mother didn't like Father Beaver at all," Chad said. "She saw him as the man who took me from a promising medical career. She blamed him for everything."

Mike's adventure became legitimized in the eyes of his parents when they heard their son singing on the radio. They listened to Arthur Godfrey religiously. And Mike's new job came with an unanticipated bonus. They didn't have to help pay for another semester at Gonzaga.

—CHAPTER SEVEN—

January 1960

The Trio returned to The Blue Angel in January for another two-week date. They shared billing with Miriam Makeba, a South African singer and protégé of Harry Belafonte.

Five years older than Mike, Mike and Chad, she enjoyed not only an outstanding performance career, but also became active in civil rights movements and humanitarian causes in both the United States and her native country.

Belafonte, present to hear Miriam's performance that night, listened to The Trio's opening set and sought them out backstage.

"You fellows are wonderful," he said. "I understand you're working with Milt Okun?"

Not sure if Belafonte had yet forgiven whatever Milt's sin had been, Chad acknowledged the association.

"That's great," Belafonte said. "Milt knows what he's doing. I had a thought listening to you. You should work something up with Miriam as a transition between acts."

The Trio welcomed this collaboration. They didn't realize that a musical partnership between Miriam and The Trio fit other aspects of Belafonte's agenda.

The Gateway Singers, based in San Francisco, had made significant commercial inroads during the 1950's. They were Dave Guard's inspiration for The Kingston Trio, and Chad drew on the Gateways' material in The Trio's early years. The Gateways consisted of three white male singers and Elmerlee Thomas, a young black woman. Like Chad, Elmerlee had a powerful, commanding voice that gave the Gateways their unique vocal identity.

Not long before Belafonte matched Miriam with The Trio, the Gateways had been booked on *Ed Sullivan*. Their appearance was canceled at the last minute when CBS refused to allow the performance of a racially mixed group.

Chad and Mike were still naïve enough not to realize that, even in New York, white and black performers didn't share the same stage.

For the rest of the Blue Angel booking, though, as The Trio closed their set and Miriam came on, they offered a joint rendition of *Mbube,* the traditional South African version of *Wimoweh*, which later evolved into *The Lion Sleeps Tonight.*

Belafonte loved the result. He told Bertha he'd like to include The Trio in a concert performance scheduled for May that would be recorded for Harry's next album. The Trio joined Belafonte, the Belafonte Singers, Miriam and Odetta for *Harry Belafonte Returns to Carnegie Hall.*

Meanwhile, they did another week at The Blue Angel, sharing billing with Dorothy Loudon, singer and actress, who later won the Tony Award for Best Lead Actress in a Musical for her performance in *Annie.* Loudon and The Trio followed with a week at Chicago's Palmer House.

After their set the first evening in Chicago, Frank Fried, a short, overweight man holding a smoldering cigarette introduced himself to Chad.

"In many ways," Chad said, "Frank was a repulsive character." He chewed with his mouth open. His mind wandered during conversations. He gnawed on bits of paper. He was seldom without a cigarette smoldering in one hand or the other, never mindful of where a growing lump of ash might fall. During their long association, Chad lost track of how many shirts and pants he'd thrown away because Frank's ashes had burned holes in them.

Years later, a woman to whom Frank had proposed marriage came to Chad, seeking an honest assessment. "Chad," she said, wearing an earnest, almost fearful expression, "Is Frank a good man?"

"Yes," Chad answered without hesitation. Then added, "As long as he doesn't set you on fire."

That night in Chicago, Chad might have politely steered himself away from this unsavory-looking character had he not followed, "I'm Frank Fried . . ." with ". . . and I manage the Gateway Singers."

Despite his first impression, Chad found Frank to be knowledgeable and engaging. A former union organizer and unapologetic lefty, he espoused liberal causes, backing them not only with sentiment, but cash as well. He was plugged into Chicago's folk scene and on both coasts. An original partner in Frank's company, Triangle Productions, had been Al Grossman, who would manage the careers of both Bob Dylan and Peter, Paul and Mary.

Chad and Frank talked late into the evening.

———⤸———

The Trio's booking agent could have easily filled the rest of the summer, but everything had to be put on hold to honor Chad's military commitment.

"No, I can't get out of it," Chad explained. "They say I have to go back for basic training."

To circumvent his draft board, Chad had signed on with the Washington Air National Guard during his stint at the University of Washington. As a pre-med student, the guard assigned him to dispensary duty. The air guard required Chad to be present one weekend a month. They didn't specify where. So that first summer, Chad tracked down the closest Air Force National Guard unit and showed up in uniform. Although the unit supervisor wasn't expecting him, he put Chad to work administering inoculations.

If The Trio happened to be on the road when Chad's weekend obligation rolled around, he found the nearest Air Force base or Air Guard unit and presented himself for duty.

The Trio had just completed its appearance at Carnegie Hall when the Washington Air National Guard contacted Chad and asked him why he hadn't been meeting his weekend obligations. Chad explained he had faithfully complied with his commitment. An unhappy officer told Chad he must report for six weeks of basic training. If he tried to get creative again, he would be drafted and would fight the Cold War in less comfortable circumstances than a state-side Guard unit.

"What can we do?" Mike asked. "We've got bookings."

"I don't see that I have a choice," Chad said. "We'll get Bertha to rearrange things. You guys can take the summer off."

Bertha salvaged what bookings she could, pushing dates to September.

Chad bought a banjo, and went to Lackland Air Force Base in San

Antonio, not suspecting that one day, San Antonio would represent quite a speed bump along his life's path. That episode, however, lay many years in his future. The only thing he got in trouble for this time was his banjo.

"Why did you bring a banjo?" demanded his drill sergeant.

"I thought I might learn to play in my spare time, Drill Sergeant!"

"Have you had any spare time?"

"No, Drill Sergeant!"

"Didn't you know a banjo amounts to contraband?" the drill sergeant hollered.

"Not until I arrived, Drill Sergeant," Chad hollered back. "That's why I hid it behind the ceiling tiles!"

"What are you, some kind of fucking folk singer?"

"Yes, Drill Sergeant!"

Mike Kobluk spent the summer in Trail, enjoying time with his high school sweetheart.

The Trio planned to meet in New York in early September. Bertha's initial booking took place a couple of weeks later. They figured they'd have plenty of time to polish their song list and add a few new numbers.

On August eighteenth, Chad and Mike each received a letter postmarked three days earlier.

> I have decided to remain at Gonzaga and continue my education. I resign my partnership in the Trio. Please consider this my two-weeks notice.
>
> Sincerely,
>
> Mike Pugh

"A letter!" Mike lamented to Chad over the phone. "He could at least have called. His *two-weeks* notice is now down to ten days."

"So, there go any September dates," Chad said. "I talked with Dennis, and he's willing to come back, but until we get another singer and some bookings, we don't have anything to offer him."

"Milt has said all along that we need a stronger musician backing us," Mike said. "So, when we find a replacement singer, we need another guitar player lined up. Where do you find guitar players?"

Chad thought for a moment. "Do you remember the guy who talked to us when we did that week at the Palmer House in Chicago, just before Carnegie Hall?"

"The short guy?" Mike asked. "The one who said he managed the Gateway Singers?"

"Yeah, Frank Fried. He claimed to be really connected to the music scene in Chicago. Milt wants a backup musician, who can play both guitar and banjo. I'll call Frank and see if he can put us in touch with someone."

"Okay," Mike said. "I'll contact Milt and start looking for a singer."

———— ✵ ————

"Yeah, I know someone who would be exactly what you're looking for," Frank told Chad. "He's a kid. Eighteen years old. Plays guitar and banjo like a virtuoso."

"Eighteen?"

"Yeah, but he's good. I hooked him up with the Limeliters when they were playing Chicago a couple of months ago. He did fine. His name's Jim McGuinn. He's a graduate of the Old Town School of Folk Music here."

Frank said he'd talk to McGuinn and put him in touch. "By the way," he added, "are you guys happy with your current management?"

"We're with Bertha Case and General Artists," Chad said. "Why do ask?"

"You can't do better than General Artists, but I don't know about Bertha. She's not as . . . connected . . . with the folk scene as you might need her to be. Look, I've got to tell you how impressed I am with you guys, Chad. You, especially. That voice of yours."

"Thanks, Frank. I—"

"How's everything else with The Trio?"

"Besides looking for a backup musician, we're also looking for a singer.

Mike Pugh decided not to come back and left us hanging."

"Bertha helping you find a singer?" Fried asked.

"She asked Milt Okun to do that. Milt put an advertisement in one of the trades. We'll be auditioning people as soon as we can."

～

Milt called Lou Gottlieb of the Limeliters to get his take on Jim McGuinn. Gottlieb confirmed Frank's assessment. Mike and Chad both talked with Jim by phone and hired him, sight unseen, sound unheard.

The Trio's business structure assigned each trio member an equal one-third partnership. Their guitarist, Dennis Collins, had been an employee. Chad and Mike decided to retain the same structure. The new singer would become a partner. The guitarist would not have a partnership share.

Chad met Jim at Idlewild Airport. He found a scrubbed and polished young man, who somehow did not seem to fit the constraints of his youth. Which made sense, Chad thought. Frank had filled him in. The young man's musical acumen had propelled him past his high school peers into an older crowd. He'd been accepted into Chicago's Old School of Folk Music, an advanced academy that specialized in all aspects of the folk genre.

While Chad was constantly taken for someone younger than his twenty-four years, people expressed surprise to learn Jim was still in his teens. He wore a tie and jacket for their first meeting, hair carefully in place with that *little-dab'll-do-ya* look. The slender young man had pleasant, hawkish facial features. Soft-spoken, he exhibited a quiet sort of tension, or distance, that Chad attributed to lack of familiarity.

On their ride into the city, Chad sought to put him at ease by detailing The Trio's brief history. Jim nodded and commented appropriately, but the distance remained.

Chad thought a part of Jim's reticence might be nervousness born of pressure to impress his new employers. That theory fell by the wayside when Jim joined The Trio and Milt at Columbia Artists on Fifty-Seventh Street where the vocal auditions were taking place. Milt asked Jim to play. He unpacked both guitar and banjo. With either instrument in his hand, Jim

McGuinn played with supreme confidence, and for good reason. He could handle anything Milt asked of him.

Milt's advertisement attracted would-be folk singers like trout rising to a mayfly hatch.

Over the course of a couple of weeks, Milt, Mike and Chad listened to almost a hundred aspirants.

"I don't know," Milt said. "I'm just not hearing the right voice."

"You don't think Tom will work out?" Mike asked. "He's very good."

"No question," Milt said. "More than his voice, though, I'm impressed with his songs. Clearly, he's someone who can provide great material. The problem is that while his voice is pleasant, it's too much in Chad's range, but without the power. We're looking for a blend."

Tom Paxton had mustered out of the army a few weeks earlier. An aspiring songwriter and folk artist, he'd been doing open mic appearances at the Gaslight in Greenwich Village when he heard about The Chad Mitchell Trio auditions. He knew of The Trio and hoped he wasn't too late.

He stood behind dozens of others, many of them holding sheet music, humming quietly to themselves, warming their vocal cords. When the audition room door swung open from time to time, he heard a piano.

Was he supposed to bring music for the pianist? Should he have brought a guitar?

When his turn came, Milt introduced himself and said, "What would you like to do for us today?"

"Well, I didn't know what to expect," Tom said. "I suppose I could do one of my own songs, but I don't have anything for the piano player, and I didn't bring a guitar."

"You can use mine," said Jim.

Tom heaved a sigh of relief. "Do you want me to sing anything specific?"

Milt requested *Jamaica Farewell*. Tom performed Harry Belafonte's hit from memory.

Milt, Mike and Chad huddled.

"Are you available to work with us for a week or so to see how it goes?" Milt asked.

A week later, Milt borrowed an office at Columbia Artists where auditions were ongoing and beckoned Tom to follow. Tom felt his stomach sink. As the rehearsals progressed, he knew Milt's ear hadn't been satisfied.

"Tom, I'm sorry," Milt said, "but the blend just isn't there. We are appreciative of the time and effort you've put in. I think you have a real future in this business."

Tom tucked his disappointment into his chest and offered his hand. "Thank you for the opportunity. I've learned a lot here."

He felt particularly disheartened because he'd hit it off so well with Mike and Chad. These were people he wanted to know better. His plan had been to be a solo performer, but he liked the camaraderie of a group. He liked the creativity of Milt's rehearsal process. He liked the liberal slant and satirical nature of their material.

"The golden side of that experience," Tom said, "is that during a break, I sang a song I'd just written—*The Marvelous Toy*. They loved it."

"Don't be too discouraged," Milt said. "We're recording a live album at the Bitter End early next year. I'd like to include *Come Along Home*."

On the evening The Trio recorded *Live at the Bitter End,* Tom was playing a set at a club in the Village. As soon as he finished, he raced to the Bitter End and arrived just in time to hear The Chad Mitchell Trio perform the first Tom Paxton song ever to be recorded.

"And that song you sang for us yesterday, about the toy?" Milt said. "I love that one. I'd like to publish it."

Milt explained he was starting his own publishing company to be called Cherry Lane Music. "I'd like to see anything else you've written," Milt said. "You do have others, don't you?"

"Yes," Tom said. "I have others."

Tom Paxton became the first writer to sign with Cherry Lane Music, a company that would become a giant in the industry. Tom's songs over the years included *The Last Thing on My Mind, Ramblin' Boy, Bottle of Wine, Can't Help but Wonder Where I'm Bound* and countless others. His songs have been recorded by Pete Seeger, Bob Dylan, The Weavers, Judy Collins,

Joan Baez, Doc Watson, Harry Belafonte, Peter, Paul and Mary, The Seekers, Marianne Faithfull, The Kingston Trio, John Denver, Dolly Parton and Porter Wagoner, Johnny Cash, Willie Nelson, Flatt & Scruggs, The Move, The Fireballs and many others.

"That became the biggest break I ever had," Tom said. "I remained associated with Milt and The Trio for fifty years, which is kind of an amazing figure."

<hr>

The vocalist search continued. With each passing day, The Trio fell further in debt to Bertha as she continued to finance them while they weren't working. Milt and guitarist Jim McGuinn had to be paid. September bookings fell by the wayside. October and November were in jeopardy.

Jim remained quiet and reserved, but musically fit everything Milt wanted in an accompanist. Jim mentioned that people he'd worked with in Chicago had gone to Boston to immerse themselves in an emerging folk scene there. Milt dispatched Jim and Chad to Boston while he and Mike continued auditions in New York.

On the plane ride, Jim asked Chad if they'd consider a female singer for their third voice. Chad hadn't thought about it, but said, "I suppose so. It would depend on the voice."

"There's a woman performing around Boston who people I know are impressed with," Jim said. "We should listen to her."

They went to Club 47 where they heard several acts, none of which offered the answer they sought.

"Okay, this is her," Jim said late into the evening.

A woman carrying an oversized guitar walked onstage wearing a grim expression of purpose. Her thread-bare sweater hung on a thin, almost fragile frame. Jet black hair draped her shoulders. She might have been, Chad thought, a Jewish refugee pictured in a film clip at the end of World War II.

A cat followed her on stage and wound its way through her ankles as she sang. Something very traditional and—eventually when she got through all the verses—a little boring, in the vein of folk purists. The song, though, hardly mattered. Chad found her voice exquisite.

"Wow," Chad said. "I should talk to her."

At the entrance leading backstage, an attendant pointed to a man standing at the bar. "That's Manny Greenhill, Joan's manager."

"I'm Chad Mitchell, with The Chad Mitchell Trio." He shook Manny's hand. "I don't know if you've heard of us."

"Sure. You do stuff with Belafonte. I heard the Carnegie Hall album."

"The Trio is looking for a singer," Chad said. "If Joan is interested, I think we could certainly make that work."

Manny chuckled. "I'm sorry, but Miss Baez is a solo act. Nice meeting you, though."

Chad emerged from the restroom when he saw Manny and Joan in conference at a table a few feet away. He thought of introducing himself and complimenting her performance but didn't want to interrupt. He waited for a break in the conversation and overheard Manny say to Joan, "By the way, did you know Chad Mitchell was in the audience tonight."

"Chad Mitchell?"

"You know, The Chad Mitchell Trio?"

Joan laughed. "Are those the idiots who sang *Wimoweh* with Miriam Makeba?"

Chad decided not to intrude.

———✺———

Milt wanted more than just the right voice. He wanted the right ideology. He wanted each member of The Trio to believe in a social and political direction in which he'd gently been steering the group. By now, he'd begun working with The Brothers Four. He'd mentioned some of his frustrations with his new clients to Mike.

"Milt says he's rehearsing a group that sings four-part unison," Mike told Chad.

The Brothers could do *safe* songs like *The San Francisco Bay Blues*, or *The Green Leaves of Summer* or *Five Hundred Miles*. The Trio did that type of song beautifully as well, but Milt had other ambitions for them. He wanted someone to return folk music to its Depression-era status as the political and social conscience of America.

Finally, in November, they found Joe Frazier.

The same age as Mike, Joe had been involved in New York City's music scene for several years. His wife, Charlotte, aspired to a stage career and appeared in a Broadway chorus as a dancer and singer. Joe had sung and danced in choruses and proved theatrically adept.

"This is an impressive résumé," Milt said, "but are you into folk music?"

Joe's response was to sing *If I Had a Hammer* and *Banks are Made of Marble,* both Pete Seeger contributions to The Almanac Singers.

He brought a strong baritone with a broad range. He could easily sing the parts Mike Pugh handled and added versatility to jump to tenor or sink to bass when needed. Milt loved how the three voices blended. He loved Joe's politics as well.

The son of a Pennsylvania coal miner, Joe had been raised on unions, and he knew first-hand a working man's hardships. A member of the W.E.B. Society, he'd flirted with the American Communist Party in 1955. "They were the only people around who saw things the way I did," Joe explained.

Additionally, Joe had a sense of humor, willingly played the roles Milt suggested, and grabbed a chance to be regularly employed.

The Chad Mitchell Trio had found its third partner.

— CHAPTER EIGHT —

Spokane Opera House
2007

Comfortable there would be no embarrassment to mitigate, critic Jim Kershner settled into his seat to make notes.

Mike sang lead in Ian Tyson's *Four Strong Winds* as Chad and Joe built soft harmonies behind him. The remnants of Mike's Canadian accent lent a subtle authenticity to the piece.

When The Trio banded together in 1959, World War II remained fresh in historical memory. War had always been a theme of traditional music, and neither the folk revival nor The Trio ignored that aspect of history.

The Trio, however, sang of war's price rather than its glory.

Following *The Banks of Sicily,* a traditional song about a Scottish regiment occupying Sicily during World War II, Joe handled the next introduction.

"Some of the unsung heroes of that war were on those ships that went on the run to Murmansk on the North Sea and carried supplies," Joe told his audience. "And all the way over they faced the danger of U-boat attack, and many didn't make it. Woody Guthrie wrote a song about one of those ships, *The Good Ruben James.*"

The song, perfectly suited to The Trio's mounting harmonies, closed with its poignant final verse:

"Many years have passed, but still, I wonder why
The worst of men must fight, and the best of men must die."

—∾—

Las Vegas, Nevada
December 1960

"She hung her false hair on the wall on a peg
Then she proceeded to take off her leg
Her trembling husband got quite a surprise
When she asked him to come and take out her glass eye."

The Unfortunate Man
—Traditional, Adaptation by Jimmy Driftwood

When he met Bob Crosby, Chad beheld a sad man.

Bob's older brother Bing, when he wasn't hamming it up with Bob Hope, played serious movie roles and perfected a sort of hang-dog world-weary look.

Bob had that look about him most of the time.

Milt and Bertha explored safe circumstances for The Trio and guitarist Jim McGuinn to get up to speed following Joe Frazier's addition, and earn some money as well. They settled on Las Vegas where Bob Crosby and the Bobcats sought a singing act to augment their month-long appearance at the Riviera Hotel.

The Trio had only managed to get a handful of songs performance ready, but that was adequate for three quick sets an evening. During the day, they would have plenty of time together in an apartment provided by the Riviera to rehearse their full repertoire with Joe and Jim.

Bob Crosby's sadness, Chad learned, manifested itself on several accounts. By this stage of his career, he'd long-since tired of being the other Crosby. "It got so bad," he admitted to Chad, Mike and Joe one evening when he was in his cups, "that whenever someone asked me what my occupation was, I'd automatically answer 'Bing Crosby's brother.'"

By December of 1960, the Bobcats had long gone the way of big bands and other dinosaurs, but Crosby gathered who he could for Vegas reunion gigs. Partly to make a buck and perform again, but more probably, The Trio guessed, Bob was in arrears to the casinos, and was working off his debt.

Why Crosby wanted a folk singing act to augment a Dixieland group that also paid homage to big bands and torch singers was a mystery to the guys until they met Bob.

"I've got a soft place in my heart," he said, "for kids from Spokane."

The Crosby clan grew up in Spokane, and, according to their Catholic upbringing, attended Gonzaga Prep and Gonzaga University. During Chad and Mike's time there, Bing starred as Gonzaga's most famous alumnus. He'd made generous donations to the school.

Following his death, his widow commissioned a statue of Bing which stands in front of the Crosby Student Center depicting Bing in his familiar hat—a golf bag and clubs at his feet—and a pipe. The pipe is used only for special events because people keep stealing it. After the third or fourth theft, the statue was modified so the pipe can be unscrewed for safekeeping, then reattached when the occasion demands.

At their first meeting, Bob outlined the show. The Trio would be placed somewhere toward the end. As a finale, Bob would call them back to the stage and ask, "Don't you boys have an encore . . . ?"

Chad and Mike exchanged a cautious glance. They didn't have an encore. They had four songs.

". . . and then you'll say yes, and you'll ask me to perform it with you."

The glance became incredulous.

"We'll do a song and dance to *Three Little Fishes*."

Nobody spoke.

"You know?" Crosby said, and sang "*Tree little fishies in de itty bitty poo, tree little fishies in de itty-bitty poo . . .*"

Crosby added a few soft shoe steps to his rendition.

Oh, my God, thought Chad. *What are we doing here?*

They were folk singers. They didn't do songs about fishies. Plus, Chad and Mike knew nothing about dancing.

Crosby offered a couple more steps, then finished with the traditional soft-shoe flourish, a little bow with right hand extended in a palm-up gesture inviting applause.

An awkward silence only became more awkward, Bob frozen in his pose, Chad and Mike beyond comment.

"Um . . . Mr. Crosby," Joe said. "I . . . I don't dance."

Chad and Mike exchanged a look of surprise. Joe was the only one among them who *could* dance. He'd spent the past couple of years auditioning for parts in dancing and singing choruses for Broadway shows.

"It's not difficult, son," Crosby said. "We can teach you a few steps."

"No, you don't understand. I *don't* dance. I was frightened . . . by dancers . . . when I was young, and . . . well, I have flashbacks . . ."

"Oh." Crosby frowned. "Okay. I'll figure something else out. You guys just sing."

Chad understood at that moment they'd chosen the right guy in Joe Frazier.

The Bobcats consisted of a five-piece Dixieland combo fronted by Crosby, who did not play an instrument. Saxophone and clarinet player Matty Matlock represented the other original Bobcat. Back in the day, Matty arranged most of the group's repertoire. Bob and Matty dated back to 1935 and, by 1961, generally despised each other.

Bob had plucked what big band veterans he could find to fill out the group, with mixed results. These were old pros—old being the operative word—who could still produce a hot sound when things went right. They had their quirks, though.

The Trio's introduction to this cast occurred at the first show as they watched from the wings with Rudy, the Bobcats' roadie.

House lights dimmed. Curtains swept open. A drumroll clattered from the darkness. Bob bounded onstage under the halo of a single spotlight, holding his director's baton. He bowed deeply, then whipped the baton to a quick downbeat. The Bobcats were off and running.

The first tune went well enough, but Chad thought the audience seemed a little . . . disengaged? The room was only about half full and he asked the stagehand about it.

"This is the lounge," Rudy explained. "You get two kinds of customers here—the ones drinking to celebrate their wins and the ones drinking to forget their losses. Mostly, lounge acts are just background noise."

So, Chad supposed, much of the audience probably didn't notice when, with the next downbeat, the pianist launched into a different song than everyone else. Bob glared, the remainder of the band persevered, and after a few bars, the piano player joined them.

"Wow, what happened there?" Mike asked.

"The piano player, Sol," Rudy said. "He drinks."

"He shows up for performances drunk?" Chad asked.

"Yeah, well, at least he shows up. He used to do heroin, but Bob laid down the law. Said if he came late anymore, he'd fire him."

"So, showing up drunk is better?" Mike asked.

"He played great on heroin," Rudy said. "Booze?" He wiggled his hand back and forth in an *I-don't-know* gesture. "But he gets here on time."

As the second number ended, Bob again made his best attempt at charming the lounge crowd. A slurred voice wafted through from the bar: "Play *Big Noise from Winnetka.*"

Bob ignored the request. The demand came a little louder at the next break. "Play *Big Noise from Winnetka*!" Bob's charm seemed a little more strained.

"What's with *Big Noise from Winnetka*?" Mike asked.

"That was the Bobcats big hit," Rudy said.

"So, are they saving it for the finish or something?" Chad asked.

"Nah, they don't play it. See, there's this big drum and bass solo." Rudy gestured to Joey, playing standup bass. "The bass player goes over by the drummer who hits the base strings with his sticks while the bass guy does the fingerings."

"So, why—?"

"Benny, the drummer, has cataracts and he don't see so good no more. Sometimes he misses the strings and beats hell out of Joey's bass. Joey gets pissed off."

The voice from the bar took a different tack. "Play *Shummertime!*"

Bob's shoulders raised and lowered with a sigh as he turned from the audience and cast a searching glance toward Matty Matlock. Chad saw the clarinet player respond with a subtle middle finger salute.

"I take it they don't play *Summertime* either?"

"No. *Summertime* was the Bobcats' theme song in their heyday. Matty's sick to death of *Summertime.*"

Instead, the next number was a rollicking Dixieland tune that included a vocal by Bob and a short but emphatic drum solo. This being the first night of the engagement, the adrenaline rush got the better of Benny the drummer, and he ended his solo with a trick he employed to great effect in the thirties. He banged out a final measure and tossed his sticks into the air. Thirty years ago, he could catch the sticks and keep pounding. Given his cataracts, though, on this night Benny didn't have a prayer as the sticks clattered to the floor. Heroically, Benny pumped away on the bass drum pedal and the other musicians soldiered along, as, without missing a note, Bob crooned into his handheld microphone, snaking the cord deftly through the band in search of Benny's sticks. He retrieved them with a graceful little half bow and slipped them into Benny's hands.

"You guys ready?" Rudy asked. "You're up next."

Their performance consisted of *Vayiven,* a driving Jewish folk song with difficult, precise harmonies sung in Hebrew; Chad's calypso take on *I Do Adore Her;* and the comic *Ballad of Sigmund Freud.* They quickly realized the Riviera lounge crowd was neither sober enough nor attentive enough to keep up with the *Freud* lyrics.

As it turned out, though, *Sigmund* received a standing ovation. Not so much the song as the aftermath. *Sigmund's* choreography called for The Trio to close with a jump, arms extended, and transition to a bow. Joe, betrayed by his theatrical training, added a flourish to his leap that backed him right into the drums.

If falling into a drum set is funny, getting out of the drum set is funnier. Buried among cymbals and snares and drum stands, Joe clanged and crashed his way toward freedom for two or three minutes.

"You know what happens now, don't you?" Chad asked Joe as The Trio took one more bow.

"What?"

"Bob will want you to fall into the drums every night."

While many emerging folk stars treated performance like a somber, almost religious ritual, The Chad Mitchell Trio had always enjoyed making audiences laugh. Milt encouraged songs like *Sigmund Freud.* They had a new comedic piece ready for performance and planned for its debut in Las Vegas. *Unfortunate Man* tells the story of a lawyer who marries a widow for her beauty and money, only to discover on their wedding night she has several hidden flaws, including a glass eye and a wooden leg.

This would be the obvious replacement for Sigmund Freud.

"Thanks, guys." Bob returned as laughter at Joe's percussion accident subsided. "Well, that's a hard act to follow. But, believe me, we've got the lady who can do it."

Stage lights blinked off. Dark silence ensued as Mike, Chad and Joe returned to the wings. The audience's dumbfounded and gaping expression of disbelief reminded Chad of the scene in *The Producers* when the chorus performs *Springtime for Hitler.*

The audience had gone silent with the darkness. Finally, the Bobcats had the audience's attention.

As the gloom lingered, though, coughs, whispers and a general resumption of conversation spoiled the intended effect.

"What's going on?" Mike asked.

"Bob's waiting for a drum cue," Rudy said. "I guess they haven't quite got the traps set put back together."

From somewhere mid-stage came a heavy thump, followed by a disembodied, "I'm all right. I'm all right."

"Sol again," Rudy explained. "Sometimes he goes to sleep and falls off the piano bench if it's dark too long."

Finally, a drum roll.

"And here she is," Bob's voice drifted through the hall, "Our Red-Hot Mama, Miss Toni . . . Lee . . . Scott!"

Benny's drums took up a boom-ba-da-boom rhythm befitting a red-hot mama's seductive gate. A spotlight glared revealing a beautiful, sequined lady wearing a low-cut evening dress, her platinum curls piled high. Her walk toward center stage was, indeed, seductive on the first boom and the ba da, but she punctuated the latter boom with a lurch. This pattern repeated itself on her brief journey to Sol and his piano.

"Oh, God," Chad whispered to Rudy. "Is she all right?"

"Yeah. She had an accident a few years ago. Fell out of a streetcar or something and severed her leg. She sings great, though."

Once arrived, the red-hot mama leaned seductively against the piano and, true to Rudy's word, displayed a beautiful, melancholy alto voice as she sang *Someone to Watch Over Me*. After a three-song set, the darkened stage covered her withdrawal.

Over dinner that night, Joe said, "I guess *Unfortunate Man* is out, huh?"

The Trio and their banjo/guitar accompanist endured their month's engagement.

Mike felt bad for Crosby, a sorrowful man who'd harbored lofty ambitions only to find himself lost in the shadow of a famous sibling.

He saw Bob one afternoon standing at a craps table. Mike's instinct was to hurry past, hoping Bob hadn't seen him. But avoidance wasn't in Mike's nature. Instead, he greeted Bob and watched him throw the dice, giving back his week's wages. Finally, Bob stacked his remaining chips for the croupier and tugged at Mike's sleeve.

"Let's get a drink."

"You guys are good," Bob said as Mike sipped at his beer and Bob drank bourbon. "I don't know much about this folk stuff. But I do know you guys can sing. Your harmonies are really tight."

"Thanks, Bob," Mike said. "We've enjoyed listening to the band. You guys can really—"

Bob offered a dismissive wave. "No, we can't. Not anymore. I know it's a train wreck up there sometimes. But the guys need work. I need work."

Bob studied his highball glass.

"I was where you guys are. Once. In the thirties. The Dorseys put together a band. A good one. I mean a real good one. They hired me as one of the singers."

He sighed.

"Probably because of Bing. But I thought I was on my way. Then, the third night out, Tommy Dorsey comes over to me and says, 'Look, this is the best band in the world and, I'm sorry, but you ain't even the best Crosby.'"

The guys became acquainted with Toni Lee Scott beyond her red-hot momma persona and found they liked her. She was only a few years older. She'd lost her leg in a motorcycle accident at nineteen, and despite a handicap that certainly limited her ambition to be a singer in the mold of Doris Day or Peggy Lee, persevered and found a place in show business.

Late in their Riviera engagement, she offered to make dinner for the guys. She came to their apartment, and they enjoyed conversation as she worked. Partway through the meal preparation, she sat on a kitchen chair and said, "I'm sorry, but this thing is just so damned uncomfortable. Would you guys mind?"

She hiked up her skirt, took off her leg and propped it in the corner. Deftly, she hopped through the rest of the evening. While dining, she rested her stump next to Chad's salad.

Mike and Chad avoided looking at each other.

". . . then she proceeded to takeoff her leg.
He's a very unfortunate, very unfortunate,
very unfortunate man . . ."

— CHAPTER NINE —

*"But you can't chop your poppa up in Massachusetts
And then get dressed and go out for a walk
. . . you can't chop your poppa up in Massachusetts,
Massachusetts is a far cry from New York . . ."*

The Ballad of Lizzie Bordon
—Michael Brown

JANUARY 1961

"So, how's Jim McGuinn working out?"

Frank Fried and Chad huddled at a table at Chicago's Edgewater Polynesian Village where The Trio performed for a week. Frank had caught the evening show and invited Chad to join him for a drink.

"He's a great musician," Chad said. "Good singer, too."

"Yeah, having him do his own set during your act is a nice touch," Frank said.

"I wish he'd just relax, though," Chad said. "We lived together for a month in Vegas, and he's still pretty reserved."

"Your new guy, Frazier," Frank said, "fits really well. He's a better singer, got better stage presence than the other guy. Did Bertha find him?"

Chad shook his head. "No. We auditioned people for ten weeks before we hired Joe."

"Well, I've got something for you," Frank said. "A Chicago television producer and I have come up with a concept for a half-hour TV pilot we call *Folk Song*. My company, Triangle Productions, will produce it. We want The Chad Mitchell Trio to be the show's house band." He paused briefly. "And we want you to be the host."

"Me?" Chad said. "Why me?"

"I love The Trio," Frank said, "but you've got something the other guys don't. You've got that something that draws the eye, and the ear. You're the spark plug."

Chad shook his head. "The Trio is three equal partners."

"Maybe so, but whether you like it or not, your voice and your charisma put you out front in audience perceptions," Frank said. "If this pilot goes anywhere, the result will be great for all of you. There's real income potential for you guys if a network picks it up. Your record sales would go way up."

Frank conceived of a show recorded before a live audience, featuring different folk music acts each week. The pilot, he said, would include Josh White, The Clancy Brothers, and a newcomer named Judy Collins.

Frank asked Chad to take the proposal to Bertha, Mike, Joe and Milt.

Everyone expressed delighted enthusiasm until Chad got to the part about him being the show's host.

"Everything stopped all of a sudden," Chad said. "For the first time, I'd placed the thought in Mike's mind that he and Joe were being cast as backup singers. After that moment, nothing was the same."

Bertha asked Chad to stay behind as the others left.

"Whether you understand it or not," Bertha said, "Fried sees you, not The Trio, as the star of this show. I've got both a financial and emotional investment in the three of you. I deserve to know if you're planning to leave."

"Leave The Trio?" Chad couldn't disguise his shock. "Of course not. We're just getting started."

———— ✐ ————

Frank shot the pilot on a shoestring at The Village Gate in New York. His partners were producer Jim McGinn, not to be confused with guitarist Jim McGuinn, and director William Friedkin.

Mike, Joe, Bertha and Milt all realized what an opportunity the pilot offered and reluctantly agreed to Chad's role as host. Mindful of their discomfort, Chad exhibited a self-conscious approach that irritated Friedkin. He saw the dynamic, charismatic character Frank Fried had described when The Trio sang. Alone on stage, though, Chad became subdued and kept improvising on Friedkin's script.

Friedkin's words rang hollow to Chad.

"I can't do it this way," he said. "I'd rather say it my own—"

"Doesn't matter what you'd rather," Friedkin told him. "Just follow the damn script."

With cameras rolling, though, Chad did it his way and Frank's $6,000 shoestring budget didn't allow for multiple takes. A typical pilot was budgeted at $60,000 or $70,000.

Friedkin didn't control his fury. "You're a real sonofabitch, you know that?" he told Chad following the taping.

Friedkin went on to become one of Hollywood's prominent film directors. His projects included *The French Connection*, *The Exorcist* and *To Live and Die in LA*.

McGinn stayed up all night editing the tape. The next day, he took it to Mike Dann, vice president of New York programming for CBS. Despite Friedkin's dissatisfaction with Chad's performance, Dann loved it. He said if Frank could come up with a half sponsorship, CBS would air the pilot.

An industry insider had warned Frank that pitching a show to sponsors in April would be a mistake. April represented the end of the selling season and potential sponsors had already committed their budgets. If Frank shopped the pilot and nobody bit, the project would be old news by the next selling season.

Mike Dann's enthusiasm, though, spurred Frank to go ahead. He rented the Gate of Horn in Chicago and screened the pilot for ad agency executives, suggesting *Folk Song* would be a perfect candidate for the following summer when regular programming went on hiatus. Advertising honcho J. Walter Thompson liked *Folk Song* so much, he didn't want to wait for summer. He wanted to air the pilot in January and screened it for executives of Schlitz Beer. The Schlitz people loved it as well. As legal papers were being drawn up, though, Thompson lost the Schlitz account to the Leo Burnett Agency.

Frank relayed the bad news to Chad.

"So?" Chad asked. "Don't the Schlitz guys still love it?"

"There's no way," Frank predicted, "Leo Burnett will go ahead with a project recommended by the ad agency he just replaced."

Indeed, when Frank screened the pilot for Burnett's team, the new agency said Schlitz's money would be better spent on something else.

———— ✎ ————

Like many behind-the-scenes managers and promotors during the sixty's folk movement, Frank Fried was an avowed and unrepentant leftist. After serving in the Navy at the end of World War II, he joined the Socialist Workers Party, hiring on as a welder in a Chicago steel plant where he became an activist in union causes.

One evening in 1956, he wandered into The Gate of Horn, a Chicago nightclub catering to people of liberal persuasion. He went to hear Austrian folk singer, Martha Schlamme. Her material championed progressive artists whose lives were being dismantled by McCarthyism and the blacklist.

Following her set, Schlamme introduced Frank to her manager, Albert Grossman. Frank convinced them that Schlamme should perform a benefit concert for the Eugene Debs Forum, a speakers' program that had the support of Chicago radical groups.

Grossman subsequently hired Frank to assist in his management company. He dispatched Frank to the West Coast to handle booking agreements there. One evening Frank went to San Francisco's Hungry i where he heard the Gateway Singers, the most dynamic folk group he'd ever experienced. They were managed by legendary Hollywood agent, Abner Greschler, who hadn't been able to move their career much beyond San Francisco. Within a few months, Frank had convinced the Gateways to become his clients instead.

Frank first heard The Chad Mitchell Trio at The Blue Angel during a visit to New York in January of 1960. This was the Mike Pugh version of the group. Two songs Frank heard The Trio perform were Gateway numbers: *Puttin' on the Style* and *The Ballad of Sigmund Freud*. As good as the Gateways were, Frank thought The Trio's harmonies were better.

Frank didn't introduce himself until he met Chad at Chicago's Palmer House later that spring.

Chad and Frank met again during The Trio's January 1961 booking at Chicago's Edgewater Polynesian Village. In addition to the *Folk Song* television show, Frank told Chad of his plans to promote a folk concert series for Orchestra Hall, home of the Chicago Symphony. He invited The Trio to participate on an October date. This subscription concert series—a concept new to folk or pop music—became a success, launching Fried on a storied promotional career that later included acts as varied as Frank Sinatra, Pete Seeger, Frank Zappa, Led Zeppelin and The Beatles.

———— ❧ ————

Frank did not mount an overt campaign to supplant Bertha Case as The Trio's agent and business manager. He did, though, make it clear he would be willing to provide those services should the guys want to make a change.

Frank saw Bertha as a well-intentioned dowager, who had neither the connections nor energy to guide The Trio's career. He did not think, for example, they should be embarking, in March of 1962, on a three-month tour of South America.

"You've got an album coming out," he told Chad. "You won't be in any position to promote it. Other folk groups will be raising their profiles with U.S. audiences while you're gone."

Indeed, The Trio had no shortage of U.S. bookings. They followed the January Edgewater appearance with a thirty-nine-show, nine-week tour of college campuses through the East and Midwest. During April they opened for a newcomer named Bob Newhart on a two-week tour that included their second appearance at Carnegie Hall.

They'd agreed to an alliance with Belafonte, who moved them from ColPix to Kapp Records, a company with which Belafonte was associated. Kapp assigned Bob Bollard as The Trio's artist and repertoire guy, and they began to assemble material for their second album. Bollard arranged to record the album during a live performance at Brooklyn College.

Their set grew to include traditional folk pieces: *Mighty Day*, *The Whistling Gypsy*, and *Whup Jamboree*. With Milt, they created their first and most enduring anti-war statement, *Johnnie*—in which Chad and Milt melded the triumphant *When Johnny Comes Marching Home* and a tragic Irish ballad, *Johnnie I Hardly Knew Ye,* from which the American version was derived.

For their campus audiences, they added more humor, *Away, Away with Rum by Gum; Super Skier; Hang on the Bell, Nellie;* and, a song they initially resisted, *The Ballad of Lizzie Bordon.* Bollard chose *Lizzie* for them from an old Broadway musical revue called *New Faces of 1952.*

"Since when do we do show tunes?" Mike asked.

"It's a funny song," Bollard said. "You can work up something theatric."

Neither Milt nor The Trio cared for Bollard, particularly when he fouled up the Brooklyn College date. In Bollard's effort to attract a crowd that would sound good on a live album, his promotion of the Brooklyn College concert implied that Harry Belafonte would perform in some fashion.

The scheme produced a sell-out, but Belafonte had no plans to be there.

As The Trio prepared to go on stage, a chant started. "We want Harry!" Clearly, the crowd would not be happy when they learned the truth. A panicked Bollard phoned Belafonte and begged him to drive across town to make an appearance. Belafonte reluctantly agreed to come save the day.

Bollard assured the crowd Harry would be there soon.

"In the meantime, please welcome The Chad Mitchell Trio."

The audience offered tepid applause for a group they knew little about, and from whom they expected even less.

A few bars, though, into *Mighty Day*—a hard-driving account of a hurricane that devastated Galveston at the turn of the century—the audience had come aboard.

The students laughed at *Away, Away with Rum by Gum,* and Bob Gibson's *Super Skier.* Harry showed up in the middle of *Whup Jamboree,* heard the cheering laughter, and seemed confused as to why he'd been summoned. He joined The Trio on stage to rabid applause, apologized for not being able to sing this evening, thanked the students for coming, and turned the show back to The Trio.

To Bollard's credit, *Lizzie Borden* brought down the house.

Chad offered its introduction. "One very exciting area of folk idiom and folk music to us has always been … the hatchet murders in Massachusetts. And I think that this quaint bit of suburban living can best be explained through our poet laureate, Joe Frazier."

Joe stepped to center stage and recited in somber tone:

"Elizabeth Borden took an axe
And gave her mother forty whacks.
And when the job was nicely done,
She gave her father forty-one."

Chad sang the first verse:

"Yesterday in old Fall River, Mr. Andrew Borden died
And they got his daughter Lizzie on a charge of homicide.
Some folks say she didn't do it, and others say of course she did
But they all agree Miss Lizzie B. was a problem kind of kid …"

The album recorded that night wasn't released until late in 1961, but soon after the Brooklyn College concert, Kapp released a single with *Lizzie Borden* on the A side and *Super Skier* on the B. Lizzie reached number forty-four on radio charts that year.

Ironically, while Lizzie became one of The Trio's most successful singles, it took them one more step along a path that would stifle their commercial success.

SPOKANE OPERA HOUSE
OCTOBER 2007

Among the songs on the *Mighty Day on Campus* album is an innocuous tune called *Tail Toddle*. The song's rapid tempo renders the Scottish dialect unintelligible. Its lilting charm and clever harmonies—punctuated by an abrupt halt—made it a concert favorite of Trio audiences for years to come.

The audience also liked Chad's, Mike's and Joe's knowing expressions—as if they were sharing an inside joke.

On the Opera House stage, Chad revealed the secret. By way of introduction, he said, "Speaking of dirty Scotch folk songs . . ."

"What?" said Father Joe, feigning shock.

". . . here's one about a bonnie lass named Tammy."

The Trio sang. The audience produced charmed laughter, and Chad offered his explanation. "That song is an example of what is called Scottish mouth music . . ."

"Mouth music," emphasized Joe.

Chad offered Joe a quizzical look and in his best Irish brogue said, ". . . Thank you very much for that clarity, Father," then returned his focus to the audience. "Mouth music is formed by alliterative consonants that really make up the gist of the, the, fabric of the . . ."

He paused. "It's very strange that I just said that. But it's true. Now what you don't know is this song escaped the censors for forty-five years. And tonight, you are going to have the real translation. Because this was just a cute little Scottish ditty all these years.

"Okay, let's start with the chorus: *Tail toddle, tail toddle, Tammy gars me tail toddle.*

"I don't want to be too explicit about the phrase tail toddle. But if you use your imagination, I'm sure most of us have had our tails toddled or been involved in a variety of forms of tail toddling.

"All right, *Tammy made my tail toddle, but an' ben with diddle doddle.*

"But and ben is *in the kitchen and in the living room with diddle doddle.* Well, if you understood tail toddle, I think diddle doddle is self-evident."

Chad paused for laughter, then, "So, let's go to the verses.

"*When I'm dead, I'm out of date. When I'm sick, I'm full of trouble. When I'm well, I step about, and Tammy makes my tail toddle.*

"Second verse takes place at a bridal shower.

"*Jessie Mack, she gave a plate, Helen Wallace gave a bottle. Quote the bride, it's a little too late for to mend a broken doddle.*

"We can assume the bride did not wear white.

"Third verse: *My good wife went over to Fife, for to buy a bucket of coal. Long before she came back, Tammy had made my tail toddle.*

"And then once again we see, the world-wide over, all men are despicable beasts. So, with new understanding and insight, we'd like to offer this song one more time for your prurient pleasure."

1961

As *Lizzie Borden* continued to gain air play and *Mighty Day on Campus* showed strong sales, Milt Okun made a difficult suggestion. Milt's relationship with The Trio had grown beyond the music. He'd taken a direct hand in shaping their political and social values. He'd come to feel an almost paternal responsibility for these young men, and he wanted badly to see them succeed at every level.

He'd observed Mike's consternation—born of Frank Fried's failed television pilot—that in some minds he and Joe were relegated to Chad's backup singers.

Milt knew many performers. He knew all about ego. He realized Chad might one day be tempted to go his own way, where he'd find himself fighting for recognition as only one among hundreds of talented solo acts. Chad's ability to combine his voice and personality with Mike Kobluk and Joe Frazier is what produced something entirely genuine and utterly unique.

Look what they'd achieved vocally in only a couple of years! Milt wanted to see where the evolution of their combined talents could take them. For that to occur, though, no single member could be bigger than The Trio.

"Fellows," he said following a rehearsal in his tiny apartment above the Cherry Lane Theater, "I'm bringing up something that may be hard to discuss, but I think it's important to your future."

Mike, Chad and Joe waited in silence.

"It's the group's name," Milt said. "And please, Chad, don't think this in any way suggests that I underestimate or don't appreciate your role. But I think it's a mistake to have The Trio named for any one member."

"Why?" asked Mike.

Chad appeared puzzled but said nothing.

"What, for example," Milt said, "happens if Chad gets hit by a bus? The Trio would be as dead as he was. But that's an extreme example. You have other considerations."

Milt talked about expectations of booking agents, promotors, and the general public, who all made assumptions based on the name. At least some of The Kingston Trio's success could be attributed to individual anonymity inherent in their name. Neither Dave Guard nor Bob Shane bore any more responsibility for the group's image or fan and media relationships than the other.

Mike and Joe asked questions. Chad said little.

"Will you at least think about it?" Milt asked.

On an impulse he has regretted ever since, Mike disagreed. "I understand what you're saying, Milt. But things are working fine. We've released two albums. We've been on television. We've done tours. If we change the name now, we'd be starting over."

"Yes, there would be disadvantages to overcome," Milt conceded.

"I think," Mike said, "the name should stay the same."

Joe, who tried to steer himself away from controversy when it came to internal workings of The Trio, agreed.

Chad shrugged his consent.

In truth, he would have been relieved at a change. When The Trio arrived in a new city, entertainment reporters and disc jockeys assumed he was spokesman. Mike would be far more comfortable in that role. While Chad enjoyed being on stage and took pride in the quality of their work, when a show ended, he sought escape without really understanding why. Mike and Joe enjoyed mingling with the crowd or attending afterparties where fans expressed their praise, where college students thanked them for raising their social and political awareness, for influencing their opinions, changing their lives.

Chad felt dishonest when confronted with such adulation.

"I didn't feel," he said, "that we were influencing anyone. I thought we were simply reflecting what was happening in American society. I didn't understand until far later that we *had* been an influence."

More important to Chad and Mike both was the craftsmanship of their work. In performance, the complexity and uniqueness of their harmonies often slipped past audiences caught up in the humor or emotion of a piece.

Several years after he'd left The Trio, Chad lived at One Christopher Street in New York where musicians often performed in a triangular courtyard just outside his building. One day he saw a small crowd listening to Phil Ochs.

Chad smiled at memories of Phil's *Draft Dodger Rag* and slipped into the crowd to hear better. A young man touched him on the elbow. "Pardon me, but aren't you Chad Mitchell?"

Surprised anyone would recognize him, Chad shook the man's hand.

"I'm a student at Julliard," the young man said, "and in our choral arranging classes, we study your music. We listen to your albums."

Wow, Chad thought, nodding his appreciation, *somebody actually* did *get it.*

"Oh, where are your legs that used to run,
when first you left to carry a gun?
Indeed, your dancin' days are done.
Oh, Johnnie, I hardly knew ya."

Johnnie
—Adapted by Milt Okun and Chad Michell

The rest of 1961 became a crush of activity. They played the Carter Baron Amphitheater in Washington, D.C. with Odetta and The Belafonte Singers.

Following their tour with new comedic sensation Bob Newhart, The

Trio performed on *The Bell Telephone Hour*, the most prestigious of television venues available to popular musicians. During the blocking for their segment, they sang *Johnnie* with its lament on the tragedy of war.

The Bell Telephone Hour's director listened in rapt attention as Chad sang his haunting solos backed by Mike and Joe's harmonies while *Johnnie* transitioned back and forth between triumph and tragedy.

"Wow," the director said as the last notes of the song died. "Just, wow. I don't think I've ever heard such a powerful and beautiful statement on war. Will you do it again? I'd like to assemble the whole crew, so they can hear it, too."

"Won't they hear it on the show?" Mike asked.

The director smiled and shook his head. "Sorry, boys. There's no way that song can be performed on network television."

It never was.

A three-week tour with Miriam Makeba took them to both New York's Town Hall, and Orchestra Hall in Chicago, the latter a performance booked as part of Frank Fried's subscription series. They played ten days at the Elizabeth Hotel in Montreal, ending 1961 with a booking at La Concha in Puerto Rico. The *Mighty Day on Campus* album had its release late that year, once again raising *Lizzie Borden* in the public consciousness.

Early in 1962, Michael Brown—thrilled that his composition of *Lizzie* had finally emerged from the shadows of the 50's and was attracting notice on radio—approached Milt with another song. Milt jumped on the opportunity. *Lizzie* had humor going for it but making fun of axe murderers didn't really push anyone's envelope. *The John Birch Society* would thrust The Trio into a whole new realm of political satire and fix Mike, Joe and Chad firmly on the path Milt Okun wanted for them.

"Oh, we're meetin' at the courthouse at eight o'clock tonight.
You just come in the door and take the first turn to the right.
Be careful when you get there, we'd hate to be bereft,
But we're taking down the names of everybody turning left.
Oh, we're the John Birch Society, the John Birch Society
Here to save our country from a COMMUNISTIC PLOT.

Join the John Birch Society, help us fill the ranks.
To get this movement started we need lots of tools and cranks."

John Birch would be the cornerstone of their third album, A*t the Bitter End*, recorded live in March. Suddenly, The Trio no longer grasped for material. Songs flowed to them as an entire sub-genre of writers living lonely lives of topical satirists and commentators realized that someone, finally, had the daring to perform their music.

The Bitter End album included several more songs that would become staples of Trio concerts for fifty years: *The Great Historical Bum*; *Unfortunate Man*; Chad's adaption of A.A. Milne's whimsical *James James Morrison Morrison;* Tom Paxton's *Come Along Home*; and a song that remains the anthem of peace movements, Ed McCurdy's *Last Night I Had the Strangest Dream.*

— CHAPTER TEN —

MARCH 1962

"... We'll teach you how to spot 'em in the cities or the sticks,
For even Jasper Junction is just full of Bolsheviks
The CIA's subversive and so's the FCC.
There's no one left but thee and we and we're not sure of thee ..."

The John Birch Society
—Michael Brown

"Suppose *The John Birch Society* takes off when Kapp releases it as a single and you're somewhere in the middle of South America with no way to promote it?" Frank asked Chad. The bond between Frank Fried and Chad had become closer. Frank had loaned Chad the use of his apartment during The Trio's Chicago engagement the previous October, and he continued to make Chad aware of his availability should The Trio seek new management.

Bertha Case had arranged a three-month tour of Central and South America under the auspices of President Kennedy's cultural exchange initiative. They were not, however, traveling as emissaries of the United States government. The American National Theater Academy sponsored the tour. The Trio would journey from Brazil to Mexico, playing in eleven countries over fourteen weeks spreading American good will. This wasn't an *entertain the troops* sort of endeavor. They targeted small towns and backwaters where South and Central Americans could see an example of young Americans and popular American culture. Clearly, though, the State Department wanted to supervise. When Mike, Joe, Chad and Jim landed in Rio de Janeiro, they were met by embassy officials who warned them to avoid drugs, women, beaches, and bars.

"Good luck with that," Joe said as the embassy guys walked away. Joe and Jim McGuinn were clearly intrigued by the possibilities.

Chad, though, bristled at the embassy's attempt to impose its authority.

The Trio had decided to censor themselves in terms of political and satirical material in their growing repertoire. Not to toe any line of official policy, but because people in rural Brazilian or Chilean villages—even through interpretation—wouldn't have any idea what the songs were about. Still, their material almost immediately got them into trouble.

They had been told by American National Theater Academy officials that the only circumstance in which they would perform at an American Embassy was if at least fifty percent of their audience consisted of citizens of the country they were visiting. When they were summoned to perform at the U.S. Embassy in Rio that first week, their audience certainly appeared to be mostly American. An embassy representative who greeted them as they arrived thanked them for coming, introduced them to dignitaries, and showed them where they'd be singing.

"And by the way," he said, "I was in Chicago last week, and I heard your new song."

Mike and Chad exchanged glances. "What song is that?" Chad asked.

"The one about the Birchers," he said. "It's really funny. Would you do it for us tonight?"

"Um . . . sure?" Chad said.

As the official walked away, Mike said, "Kapp must have released the single."

"Yeah," Chad said. "I thought that wouldn't happen for a few more weeks."

"Do you think we should sing it tonight?" Mike said.

"Well," Chad shrugged, "he asked."

———— ∾ ————

They placed *John Birch* toward the end of the program where it drew laughter—only some of it nervous—and applause. Following their performance, a different embassy official, scowling all the way, hustled The Trio to an empty room.

Chad suspected that these Kennedy Administration cold warriors might take exception to a song satirizing the most vehement anti-communist group in America. He braced for the tirade to come.

Instead, the man demanded, "What do you think you're doing singing that Russian song?"

The Trio performed several foreign language songs. Mike, whose parents had emigrated to Canada from what is now Russia, had an interest in Russian music. When he found a song he liked, he asked his parents to teach it to him phonetically so The Trio could learn proper pronunciations. *Moscow Nights,* a song about a group of friends spending a happy evening in the historic Russian capital, appears on the *Bitter End* album.

"Russian song?" asked Chad. "You mean *Moscow Nights*?"

"I don't know what the damn thing's name is," the man said. "I don't speak Russian."

"What's wrong with it?" Mike asked.

"Don't you understand what's happening in the world?" he said. "We're here fighting the spreading influence of communism! And you think you're going out to all the villages and sing an anti-American song?"

"It's not an anti-American song," Mike said. "It's a song about friends having dinner in Moscow."

"It's Russian!" the official said.

Chad, whose fuse was shorter than either Mike's or Joe's, responded accordingly. "Wait a minute. You can't dictate what we sing or don't sing. We're not here representing the State Department."

"Oh yeah? We'll see about that. You sing that song again, and this tour will be canceled before it even gets started." The man stomped away.

No one said a word about *The John Birch Society.*

They continued to perform *Moscow Nights* during that first week. Summoned back to the embassy they were informed the State Department would send a representative to evaluate "that Russian song" and determine the viability of The Chad Mitchell Trio tour.

A few days later, State Department representative Joe Salyers arrived from Washington, D.C. Salyers had helped arrange the tour and had met The Trio during that process.

He caught up with them in São Paulo.

"So, you've already managed to get yourselves in trouble," Salyers said, greeting the guys with a smile.

"Look," Mike said, "the song is innocuous. There's nothing political about it. It's about the beauty of Moscow on a winter evening and a gathering of friends."

"Jim," said Chad, "get your guitar. We'll do it now. Mike can translate as we go along."

Salyers dismissed Mike's defensive mood with a waving motion, like erasing a blackboard. "I speak a little Russian. I won't have any trouble following. And I'll wait until tonight."

"You're letting us sing it tonight?" Mike said. "Aren't you afraid we'll incite village dwellers to join the rebels?"

Salyers smiled again. "This evening will be soon enough. If I spot any rebels, I'll ask them to leave."

Salyers toured with The Trio for two weeks as they played cities, towns and villages throughout western Brazil. He helped them find locals who spoke enough English to at least tell their audience what each song was about.

"Well, guys," he said before catching his plane, "I've thoroughly enjoyed myself."

"So, what's the verdict on *Moscow Nights*?" Mike asked. They'd performed it at every stop along the way.

"Love the song. Keep doing it with your State Department's blessing."

He shook hands all the way around. As he turned to go, he stopped and added, "One more thing. As a favor to me? Don't do the *John Birch* song."

Puzzled, because the only time they'd done it was at the request of an embassy official, Mike asked, "You mean you've heard it?"

"Oh, yeah," Salyers said. "I flew here from Chicago. There's some disc jockey there who plays it like every hour or so. The tune's causing some controversy, I'll tell you."

"You're kidding," Chad said. "Um . . . don't worry. We understand that some embassy people might not like—"

"That's got nothing to do with it," Salyers said. "Your set is great as it is. That song will just confuse everyone. The locals never heard of John Birch."

———

The John Birch Society was blowing up the Chicago market. Chad placed a call to Frank, who confirmed Salyers' account. "Yeah, a radio personality named Dan Sorkin is pushing the song like crazy," Frank said. "He gives it lots of airplay, and it's getting a big reaction. Made headlines in the Tribune. Liberals like it. Conservatives hate it. Moderates are undecided. But they all listen to it. You guys need to be here so you can capitalize on this. Every newspaper and radio station in the city would interview you."

Chicago music critic Len Chaimowitz called Birch headquarters in Massachusetts for reaction. A secretary told him while she supposed the song was "not very complimentary, we have no comment."

"The record, which was released late last week on the Kapp label," Chaimowitz wrote, "has been aired on WNEW and WNBC and has been banned from WCBS, WABC and WOR. A WCBS spokesman declared the decision to ban the record had nothing to do with political considerations, though program director Gene King said it was done on legal advice. 'We have no set policy about such stuff,' King declared, 'but in this case we thought it was too controversial and not entertaining.'"

"Controversial or not, 'Billboard,' a record industry trade publication, yesterday chose *The John Birch Society* as its 'spotlight hit' of the week.

"The Mitchell Trio recorded *The John Birch Society* single March 22 before an audience in a Greenwich Village coffee shop, a spokesman said. The Trio left for a State Department-sponsored tour in South America the next day and hasn't been heard from since."

A second Chicago music critic, Gabriel Favoino, wrote, "KAPP Records, at first reluctant to record the song, had relented and put it on the back side of a single release. But a spirited song with such timely lyrics cannot be hidden for long. Nonetheless, the attempt was seriously made.

"First, the Columbia Broadcasting System banned the record from its network radio stations. The American Broadcasting Company did the same, but in a swift about-face, rescinded the ban. Every single radio station in the Los Angeles area kept the song off the air. (California is a Birch stronghold.)

"One Chicago AM station also nixed the tune, but WCFL disc jockey Dan Sorkin was so delighted with the record, he ritually played it at least twice a day—with reverence."

Favoino added his own editorial note: "The Lunacy typified by the Birchers can best be attacked with richly deserved laughter—a weapon The Chad Mitchell Trio knows how to use—because it also implies a certain security and sanity for the rest of us. But when out of sheer fear broadcasters don't want to offend the lunatic fringe—on the left or the right—then we have questions to ask."

———

"Frank's prediction is coming true," Chad told Mike and Joe as they learned details of the *John Birch* controversy. "We're missing an opportunity to promote the single. Frank knows what he's doing. I think we need to consider a change."

"What kind of change?" Mike asked.

"Bertha just isn't connected to the folk music scene," Chad said. "Not the way Frank is. He promotes concerts. He put together the *Folk Song* pilot."

"Bertha has been good to us," Mike countered. "We wouldn't even have recorded *John Birch* without her interest and support. Just look at the prestigious bookings we've had. And we owe her money, for heaven's sake."

They both looked to Joe.

Milt had established a rule for The Trio, to which each member agreed. Each partner had an equal say in any debate. All three had to agree on material. If one member was uncomfortable with a song, they wouldn't do it. On business decisions, though, legal standards applied. The Trio was a three-member equal partnership and the majority ruled.

Throughout The Trio's life, Joe was reluctant to take a stand in disputes between Mike and Chad.

Joe shrugged. "I don't know, guys. I guess I agree with Mike. Sticking with Bertha, at least for now, seems like the right thing to do."

———⁓———

The tour's pace became more demanding as days passed. They played tiny villages. They played huge venues, including the performance center in Brasilia, the new capital being built in central Brazil. Brasilia's buildings and art and streets were beautiful. The only people there, though, were construction workers. Brasilia stood in the middle of nowhere, and the Brazilian Congress had thus far refused to relocate.

At another stop, the Venezuelan government ordered them to remain in their hotel. Tanks prowled the streets to put down the latest rebellion. They found the political climate in Peru tense as well.

Chad discovered wine in Argentina. Jim and Joe discovered marijuana in Recife, Brazil.

"We need to score some grass," Jim suggested. Joe agreed. The problem was how to do so without being thrown into a third-world jail. They finally decided to simply ask someone on the street.

"Um . . . Dónde . . . podemos comprar . . . marijuana?" Joe asked a man who looked like he might be hip, after consulting his English to Spanish dictionary.

The man seemed confused. Joe put his fingers to his lips in a simulation of smoking. The man grinned. Pointed at a bench and said, "Espera aquí voy a volver en . . . ah . . . half of an hour."

Joe consulted his dictionary. "I think he wants us to wait here." They sat.

"You know," Joe said to Jim as time dragged by, "this could be a set-up. If any cops come, just say the guy misunderstood us."

The man eventually returned with a companion who carried a large paper bag. Inside Joe and Jim found a marijuana plant, roots and all. The second man spoke broken English and conveyed a price. When Joe and Jim ponied up their pesos, the man shook his head. "American dollars, por favor."

State Department people had warned them they risked robbery if they carried U.S. currency. "We only have travelers checks," Joe said.

"American Express?" the man asked.

"Yes, um . . . si."

The man grinned and made an OK sign with his thumb and forefinger.

They continued touring by train, bus, van, plane and boat. In Brazil, Chad and Mike looked to their left and right outside the square windows as their DC-1 struggled for altitude through a mountain pass. They saw goats standing on steep hillsides staring into the plane at eye level.

A boat in Paraguay took them to an island inhabited by a village whose women were all topless. Mike had a new single lens reflex 35mm camera that had a complicated look to it. Chad had a tiny Minox, which used 8mm film.

As Mike clicked his first photo, a man stepped in front of a smiling woman posing for him and said, "Dollar, por favor?" Mike gave him a dollar. Another woman smiled. Mike raised his camera. Again, the man intervened. "Dollar."

Mike and Chad consulted. "At this rate," Mike said, "we'll go broke."

Chad thought for a moment. "I've got an idea." He thumbed through Joe's dictionary, then pointed the little Minox at another woman. When the man asked for a dollar, Chad waved his hand back and forth and said, "No, no camera. Medidor de luz necesario..." he pointed to Mike's camera, "... para la cámara."

The man offered a suspicious look, then waved for Chad and Mike to go ahead. So, they got their topless photos for half price as first Chad took his picture, passing the Minox off as a light meter, and Mike followed.

As they walked back to the boat, bare-breasted women waved and Chad heard the man on the dock say, "Bien, señoritas, los gringos se van. Puedes volver a ponerte las tapas."

He consulted his dictionary and laughed.

"What?" Mike asked.

"As near as I can tell, the guy said, *okay, girls, the gringos are leaving. You can put your shirts back on.*"

The tour wore on. As weeks passed, Jim McGuinn appeared to grow bored.

Which Chad understood. The Trio still rehearsed relentlessly. While Chad, Mike and Joe loved this creative process, Jim played the same chord patterns over and over while The Trio worked. When he'd occasionally express his boredom by breaking into an improvisational guitar run, Milt would offer a disapproving frown and shush him.

Jim played a three-song solo set during some shows on the South American tour to display both his instrumental and vocal talents, but his material wasn't part of this group process.

Following the marijuana episode, Joe and Jim hung out together more often. And more often, they were late for rehearsal or departure deadlines.

Their tardiness grated on Mike and Chad because of their history with Lyle Moore and the Gonzaga Glee Club. In Lyle Moore's world, five minutes early was too late. Few sins trumped wasted time, particularly if the waste was imposed upon those who were not late.

Tardy departures for destinations that might be a drive of several hours, particularly troubled Jerry Bell, the road manager traveling with The Trio.

"You've got to do something about this," Bell said to Chad. "It's getting worse."

In these instances, Chad felt one more burden of having his name on the marquee. Although he, Mike and Joe were equal partners, Bell assumed Chad was in charge.

"Look, Jerry," he said, "I'm not the boss. I can't tell Joe what to do. Seeing that those guys are on time is your job."

Chad still felt the weight of responsibility. While it might not be appropriate for him to reprimand Joe, he felt he could hold Jim accountable. The issue came to a head as they prepared to leave the town of Belem for a long car ride to their next stop. Chad waited in the hotel lobby for the others. Mike, as usual, arrived early.

"I'm heading to the van," he told Chad.

"I ordered a cheese sandwich," Chad said, pointing at a little cafeteria just off the hotel lobby. "Do you want one?"

"No, thanks. I'll meet you outside."

Chad waited. He glanced to the lobby where he saw Joe and Jim. On time for once.

He checked his watch. Five minutes to go. *How long*, he thought, *does it take to make a cheese sandwich?*

Five more minutes. He got the counter guys attention. "My sandwich?"

"Un momento, por favor."

"Listen, I'm late. I've got to—"

"So, what the hell, Chad?" He turned to find Jim. "Everyone's waiting for you."

"My sandwich—"

Days of boredom and frustration spilled over. Inches from Chad's face, Jim began yelling. Why was it okay for Chad to be late and not him? As the rant went on it grew louder, then louder still.

"Jim, stop," Chad said. "This is stupid. Just . . . stop!"

Jim didn't stop. Chad hit him—a sort of karate chop to the side of Jim's neck.

The blow shocked both Chad and Jim into silence. Chad spun on his heel and went to the van.

———

"He says you punched him in the face," Mike said.

Mike and Chad sat in back. Jim seethed in the front seat.

"I didn't punch him. More like a slap."

"You shouldn't have hit him."

"I know. I can't remember the last time I hit anyone. He was going on and on, and he wouldn't stop."

The tour continued. Jim and Chad avoided each other as best they could.

———

". . . McGuinn and McGuire, just a-gettin higher
In L.A., you know where that's at? . . ."

Creeque Alley
—John and Michelle Phillips

The Trio returned to the U.S. and went their separate ways for a three-week break. Their next date was a booking at Hollywood's Crescendo Club with Lenny Bruce. Jim flew directly to Los Angeles where he hung out at a folk club called The Troubadour and heard a group calling themselves The New Christy Minstrels. Randy Sparks, the Minstrels' founder and director, listened to Jim play his banjo and offered him a job.

While Jim had grown disenchanted with The Trio gig, he didn't want to be a backup musician for an even larger group and declined the offer. He did, though, start hanging out with a scratchy-voiced Minstrels singer named Barry McGuire with whom he shared an affinity for marijuana.

Jim returned to The Trio as they opened at the Crescendo. Bobby Darin caught one of their performances. Darin, who had become interested in shifting toward folk music, asked Jim to join him. Jim gave The Trio proper notice, affording them time to search for another musician.

Jim took up residence in a Laurel Canyon house which became a frequent stopover for McGuire and other members of the L.A. area folk scene, including John and Michelle Phillips, on their way to becoming The Mamas and the Papas.

Jim worked with Darin for a year and a half, then played as a studio musician in both New York and Los Angeles where he spearheaded folk music's evolution toward folk-rock. In 1964, he and Gene Clark formed The Byrds. Enamored of The Beatles, they equipped themselves with the same instrumentation the Fab Four used, including a Rickenbacker twelve-string guitar for McGuinn. When Columbia Records released the band's debut single—Bob Dylan's *Mr. Tambourine Man*—in April of 1965, The Byrds' electric twelve-string sound became the prototype for the folk-rock movement. The term folk-rock was coined by the music press to describe *Mr. Tambourine Man's* unique sound.

As Jim joined a parade of rock musicians experimenting with Eastern religions, an Indonesian guru told him he would "vibrate better with the universe" if his name began with R. From mid-1967 on, Jim performed as Roger McGuinn.

— CHAPTER ELEVEN —

July 1962

"The saddest thing about the history of the group, which I think was the most gifted of all the groups that appeared in the folk-pop period, is that they had much less commercial success than they deserved. Looking back, I imagine some of the blame falls on me as their producer. I think the real difficulty was that they were not managed well, nor were they handled well by their record companies."

—Milt Okun

The Trio returned stateside, having missed their window for *The John Birch Society*. The song managed to make its way into Billboard's Top One Hundred for a brief appearance at number ninety-nine for 1962, then became old news.

Worse, they found *John Birch* had branded them in the opinion of both radio and television as controversial.

"When we'd do interviews with DJ's as we arrived in a city for a concert," Mike said, "he'd show us the back of our album cover, and most songs had black lines through them, meaning *don't play this*. We weren't exactly black-listed, but we were certainly black-lined."

Thus, the listening public heard two different Mitchell Trios. Radio and television listeners heard and saw a straightforward clean-cut group singing safe, beautiful folk songs. The college concert audience saw a funny and outspoken performance offering biting satirical comments on the political and social scene.

Only once was *John Birch Society* performed in its entirety for an American television audience—on Hootenanny in 1963.

John Birch had another profound influence on The Trio's future. The missed promotional opportunity wrought by their South American tour helped persuade Joe to Chad's side of the management argument, and in July of 1962, The Trio hired Frank Fried as agent and business manager.

Bertha could not hide her hurt and disappointment when told of their decision.

"I have to say," she said, "I think you boys are making a mistake. But I won't stand in your way. I wish you best of luck."

The Trio owed Bertha about $25,000.

As Chad and Joe left her office, Mike stayed behind.

"I didn't want this, Bertha," he said. "We'd be back at Gonzaga if it wasn't for you. You took a chance on us, and I think this is a poor way to treat you."

"Don't ever forget, Mike," Bertha said, taking his hand, "this is business. And difficult decisions must sometimes be made."

"I'll make sure you're repaid every cent," Mike said.

"I know you will, Mike. I know you will."

———— ᴘ ————

Abandoned by an alcoholic father, Chad fought an inner turmoil much of his life. He was quick to rebel against authority. At the same time, he hungered for a father figure. During the first five years of The Trio's evolution, two men stepped forward to play that role.

Both Mike and Chad came to New York City in 1959 as blank slates, socially and politically. Milt Okun, their musical director, did much to mold not only their music, but the political and social conscience for which The Trio would become known. Frank Fried did not disguise his belief in Chad's talent and potential. He eventually made Chad a partner in Triangle Productions, The Trio's management company.

Tensions between Milt and Frank continued to escalate. Their fraught relationship only complicated Chad's dilemma.

Like Bertha, Milt Okun thought The Trio had made a mistake. Initially, Chad hoped Frank and Milt might get along. Both had strong leftist backgrounds, although Frank's roots were significantly more blue-collar than Milt's. Both saw folk music as a vehicle for social justice. These two men, who had become powerful influences, both felt music should say something.

Milt, a tall, understated, elegant man from a well-to-do background, and Frank, a short, overweight, coarse man who'd organized steelworkers, were doomed to clash.

Frank charged that Milt's subsequent work directing and producing The Trio, Peter, Paul and Mary, and The Brothers Four simultaneously represented a conflict of interest creating competition for The Trio's future bookings.

Milt believed Frank's focus on Chad as The Trio's most talented member became the catalyst that tore The Trio apart before they could realize the success they deserved.

———

Although they had missed an opportunity with *John Birch*, the *Folk Song* television pilot rose like Lazarus from the dead in the Fall of 1962. Despite Schlitz's rejection, Jim McGinn continued to show the half-hour pilot to anyone who would watch. Manny Kaplan, vice president of Sara Lee Bakeries, loved it.

"He wants us to do the pilot again?" Mike asked.

"Yes," Frank said. "But he wants an hour-long program this time. He says he'll air it as an hour-long special in Chicago and the Midwest, then option it to the networks. If one of them likes it, Sara Lee will sponsor a series."

In addition to The Trio, this version of *Folk Song* would feature Chicago's Second City comedy ensemble and The Weavers. Kaplan insisted on The Weavers.

The Trio's reception at Brooklyn College, where their *Mighty Day on Campus* album had been recorded, inspired Frank and McGinn to film the new pilot before a live outdoor audience at the University of Chicago.

Taping the program became an ordeal as October weather turned cold and windy and both audience and performers suffered through take after take. What really dampened The Trio's enthusiasm for the project, though, was Fred Hellerman's visit to their dressing room later that evening.

The Weavers had gone through several permutations since Pete Seeger left them in 1958. The current version consisted of Hellerman, Ronnie Gilbert, Lee Hays and Frank Hamilton.

"Fellows," Hellerman addressed Mike, Chad and Joe, "ABC has demanded that the members of the Weavers sign a loyalty oath, and we won't do it. We know you guys are counting on this pilot going somewhere, and we hope this doesn't mess everything up."

"A loyalty oath?" Chad asked in disbelief.

"That's not right," Mike said. "They didn't ask us to sign loyalty oaths."

"Yeah, well," Hellerman said, "you aren't The Weavers."

———∿———

By 1950, U.S. Sen. Joseph McCarthy had convinced many Americans that Communists and Communist sympathizers lurked behind every government agency, every union, every plea for peace, every demand for social justice and every liberal cause in America. Writers, actors, composers and singers of folk songs were McCarthyism's targets.

Unlike traditional oaths of allegiance to uphold the Constitution and the country's laws, the McCarthy-era loyalty oaths required people to disavow the Communist Party and other radical movements. They were oaths directed at beliefs rather than illegal actions, a fundamental violation of the First Amendment.

A publication named *Counterattack* issued a story called *Red Channels: The Report of Communist Influence in Radio and Television*. The report listed a hundred and fifty-one Reds in show business. They included Pete Seeger, Oscar Brand, Richard Dyer-Bennet, Tom Glazer, Burl Ives, Earl Robison and Josh White.

Seeger became a protégé of Woody Guthrie in 1940. Seeger, Lee Hays and Millard Lampell founded the Almanac Singers, a group that aligned itself with political ideologies of the American Communist Party. After returning from army service in World War II, Seeger founded People's Songs, Inc., a group that attracted a core audience of intellectuals interested in folk music and radical political philosophies. Seeger subsequently combined with Lee Hayes, Fred Hellerman and Ronnie Gilbert to form The Weavers.

With the '50s Red Scare in full swing, The Weavers became targets of FBI investigations and protests that made promoters reluctant to hire them. In 1950, the group had three huge hits: *Goodnight Irene, Midnight Special* and *On Top of Old Smokey*, three completely innocent and apolitical songs. The Weavers' scheme, a witness testified before the House Unamerican Activities Committee, was to attract "bobby soxers" through their concerts where "the Communist Party organizer took over and stood a good chance to recruit many of the young people." Five years later, the witness recanted his testimony, admitting he lied about The Weavers under pressure from McCarthyites.

When called to testify before the House Unamerican Activities Committee, those who fell under the scrutiny of McCarthyism were asked to name names of Communist sympathizers, and to sign loyalty oaths. Those who refused found they could no longer make a living as actors, writers, singers, directors or artists. Many of the people being accused made the blacklist by refusing to answer under protection of their Fifth Amendment right from self-incrimination. Not Seeger. He told the committee he would not testify, because they had no right to ask him these questions in the first place. "But I'll be glad," he said, "to sing you a song."

A jury convicted him of ten counts of contempt of Congress, which could have landed him in a federal prison for a decade. The convictions were eventually overturned.

In the meantime, The Weavers lost their recording contract with Decca in 1951. Unable to book most concert venues and banned from television and radio appearances, they disbanded. By 1962, though, banned artists and writers were beginning to emerge from the blacklist's long shadow.

When Hellerman told Mike, Chad and Joe of the loyalty oath request by ABC, they were appalled. They considered refusing to cooperate further in the production. Hellerman gave them dispensation to continue.

"There's no point in giving up your voice," he said, "simply because someone wants to silence ours."

The issue became moot.

A few months earlier, Sam Levinson had filled in as guest host for Jack

Paar on NBC's *Tonight Show*. Levinson, like Manny Kaplan, was a huge Weavers fan, and, like Kaplan, felt time had come to put the blacklist to rest and allow the Weavers to appear on national television. NBC disagreed. The Weavers were not permitted on *The Tonight Show*, and controversy regarding the group was renewed in the eyes of network television.

When the Weavers wouldn't sign ABC's loyalty oath, the second *Folk Song* pilot died a quiet death.

Chad is not sure the real story is quite so simple.

Also, in 1962, Dan Melnick, vice president of ABC TV, conceived of a remarkably similar show featuring folk music acts to be taped at college campuses before student audiences. ABC video-taped the pilot late in 1962 at Syracuse University. The network and sponsors liked the concept so well that production of *Hootenanny* began immediately.

"If you've got two similar ideas, and one of them is backed by a network vice president," Chad said, "what better way to get the other one to disappear than by demanding that The Weavers sign a loyalty oath?"

Hootenanny was an ABC hit for three seasons before folk music slipped by the wayside. Some folk acts, like The Kingston Trio, refused to appear on *Hootenanny* because the show would not invite Seeger or the Weavers to perform. Chad, Mike and Joe, however, taking Hellerman's advice to heart, appeared on *Hootenanny* eight times during that run.

During the fall of 1961, Milt was coerced by Albert Grossman into providing musical direction for another trio. Grossman, co-owner of Chicago's Gate of Horn, had recently begun spending time in New York, trying his hand at talent management. Grossman had several individual performers as clients, but—partially based on The Chad Mitchell Trio's success—saw vocal groups as folk music's future.

In his tours of New York folk clubs, Grossman rounded up a male solo performer, a female solo performer and a stand-up comic. He wanted Milt to help them develop material.

The three gathered at Milt's apartment on 12th Street in Greenwich

Village above the Cherry Lane Theater—just as Chad, Mike and Joe did—and attempted the few snippets of songs they'd been rehearsing.

Rosemary Okun listened from the kitchen.

When the group departed, she said to Milt, "Those poor people! They were out of tune. Their voices clash. Whatever are you going to do with them?"

"Nothing," Milt said. "They're terrible. I can't believe anybody will ever record them. I'll tell Albert he has to find someone else."

Milt passed the buck to Fred Hellerman, who listened to one rehearsal and told Milt, "What are you trying to do to me?"

Milt would have simply walked away from the project, except Grossman represented other singers with whom Milt wanted to work—Odetta and folk singer/songwriter Bob Gibson. So, Milt resigned himself to hours and hours of rehearsal with Peter Yarrow, Mary Travers and Noel Paul Stookey.

History shows that Peter, Noel and Mary were enormous talents. Grossman wouldn't have chosen them if he hadn't liked what he heard from them as solo performers. Peter and Noel were excellent guitarists. The three knew little about harmony or blend, though. Each wanted to sing lead. As they tried to learn harmonies, Milt sat next to each in turn and sang the part with them over and over.

Songs Mike, Chad and Joe would have mastered in an afternoon or two required three weeks of three-hour-a-day rehearsals for Peter, Paul and Mary to nail down. They worked with Milt for seven months to develop the nine songs that comprised their first album. Milt found the process of recording PP&M an ordeal as well, using studio tricks to raise segments of Mary's tracks so she wouldn't be singing flat.

"It never occurred to me," Milt said, "that they would be successful."

But the first album, released late in 1962, was an immediate smash. *Lemon Tree, If I Had a Hammer* and *500 Miles* all became hit singles. Warner Brothers executives called Milt, congratulated him on his work, and said they wanted PP&M's follow-up album ready for release by May of 1963. Milt told them a May release would be impossible. He said teaching them parts for enough songs to fill another album would require a delay to October.

One mistake the group did not make was in choosing a name. Grossman wanted to call them The Willows. They wanted to be less generic, but Peter, Noel and Mary didn't have the right alliteration. They heard *The Great Historical Bum* and fixed on the line: *Peter, Paul and Moses playing ring around the roses*. Noel's middle name is Paul.

Noel later explained in an account of the group's history on the Peter, Paul and Mary website, "Symbolically, if the group had been the Willows, I'm not sure that we would have felt a value to our individual identities in the same way that being called Peter, Paul and Mary has encouraged us."

Milt's original understanding with Grossman was that he would prepare PP&M for their first concert, then walk away. Once he'd coached them through the initial album, though, neither Grossman nor Warner Brothers wanted to mess with the formula. Milt continued as the group's musical director and producer through their break-up in 1970.

They produced a reunion album and went on tour in 1978, then reunited in 1981 and continued to record and tour until Mary's death in 2009. They earned millions over the course of their long career.

———— ❧ ————

Winter 1962

The kid from Minnesota couldn't sing a lick, but he wrote a damn good song.

When Milt heard the kid's audition tape, he almost winced at the nasal nails-on-blackboard voice lurching along with the balky rhythm of a car firing on only five cylinders. But Milt had the ear to hear past all that. He heard lyrics. He heard tune. He heard other voices.

And he heard gold in this song. Milt Okun knew The Chad Mitchell Trio could make a hit out of Bob Dylan's composition.

Milt had been working to augment The Trio's considerable vocal skills with a point of view that would take folk music beyond a collection of old ballads and archaic rhymes of uncertain parentage, to songs bearing relevance to the season of change unfolding all around them.

With the exception of the haunting anti-war statement made with *Johnnie* on their *Mighty Day on Campus* album, their political commentary had taken the form of satire. Milt wanted folk music to return to serious social commentary as well, and Bob Dylan's song fit that plan to a tee.

The boys were beginning to get it. Joe, who'd labored the longest to find a place in New York City's performing arts scene, knew all about union struggles, the working class and a liberal agenda. Chad and Mike, though, had essentially come under Milt's wing with blank political slates. They knew only that they wanted to sing and were good at it. So, as Milt instructed them musically, he also encouraged them to ponder issues previously beyond their consideration. He raised questions that demanded answers.

Now, two years into the collaboration, they understood Bob Dylan's song. They embraced its spirit. They wanted the song as much as Milt did.

They were preparing an album for release in January, still working with Harry Belafonte and Kapp records. When they proudly presented a demo tape of the new song to their producer at KAPP, Bob Bollard clearly did not share their enthusiasm, but conceded, "We'll put it on the album."

Milt, whose patience with Bollard had been waning for some time, spoke carefully. "You do understand," he said, "that Albert Grossman (Dylan's manager) has granted me exclusive first recording rights for this song. We can make a single that will finally get some radio airplay for The Chad Mitchell Trio. This song will be a hit."

"We're not investing in pressing a single of this song," Bollard said, knowing that radio stations at that time didn't play album cuts.

"Why not?" asked Mike, his voice reflecting his disbelief.

"The song's a dead end. We wouldn't make money, and neither would you."

"What do you mean, a dead end?" asked Joe.

"No song with the word *death* in it has ever been a hit, or even made top fifty on the charts," Bollard said. "The whole industry knows that."

Chad played the Tom Dooley card.

"Tom Dooley is all about death," Chad said. "The guy is in the process of being hung."

"Yes, but he's not dead yet, is he? We know that, because he's singing the song. He can't sing if he's dead. Your song, on the other hand, has death all over it. Hundreds of deaths. Hell, maybe even millions of deaths. Who knows?"

Milt's anger rose to the point he didn't trust himself to speak. He decided to go over Kapp's head and appeal to Harry. Belafonte didn't want to fight with Kapp over the song. He chose to let Bollard's decision stand.

"It's ironic," Milt said years later, "because Harry fought the establishment in so many ways in his own career. But when it came to a chance for The Trio to challenge conventional wisdom and have a hit, he was absolutely stubborn."

Chad and Mike sought out Belafonte and made their own appeal, to no avail.

"I'm sorry," Milt apologized to Mike, Chad and Joe. "I had no idea— I'll have to take the song to my other clients and hope the representative of their record label isn't quite so obtuse."

So, while Milt and The Trio had created a beautiful arrangement in only a couple of rehearsal sessions, Milt started on the long and deliberate process of working with Peter, Paul and Mary on a simpler arrangement that better suited their skills.

The Chad Mitchell Trio became the first group to record *Blowin' In the Wind*, one of thirteen songs on their third album entitled *The Chad Mitchell Trio in Action,* released early in 1963.

When Peter, Paul and Mary's single hit number seventeen on 1963's Billboard Top 100, Bob Bollard rushed to re-release *The Chad Mitchell Trio in Action* under the title *The Chad Mitchell Trio Blowin' In the Wind,* one more example of too little, too late.

The song became the cornerstone of Peter, Paul and Mary's storied career.

Belafonte and his music had provided a significant influence for The Trio. During his early college days, Chad's interest in folk music had been driven by Belafonte's records. Belafonte had championed The Trio's cause and had provided them their first significant exposure by including them on the *Harry Belafonte Returns to Carnegie Hall* album. He'd teamed them with Miriam Makeba. He'd guided them away from ColPix to Kapp Records.

In the intervening time, though, they'd witnessed his moods and mercurial temper.

During an afterparty at a concert promoter's home one evening, Chad walked into a kitchen to find Harry and the promotor's son involved in a political discussion. The scene was civil enough until Chad heard the phrase "you people" pass the younger man's lips.

"You people?" shouted Belafonte. "You people!" He drew back his fist and had to be restrained from pummeling the man.

Like many artists, Belafonte came to be haunted by his trademark song. He first recorded *Matilda* in 1953. The silly calypso classic tells a story of a man robbed by a woman with whom he had a relationship. He ended his concerts for many years with the song, dividing the audience to sing the chorus line over and over: *Ma-til-da, Ma-til-da, Ma-til-da she take me money and run-a Venezuela.*

"Did you hear about the time in the Philippines," Miriam told Chad, "when a promotor got mad at Harry because he didn't do a full two-hour show?"

"What happened?"

"I don't know why we were there in the first place," Miriam said. "Harry hated Fernando Marcos. But somehow this promoter booked us in the Philippines. He came up to Harry after the first show and told him his contract required two hours. The guy timed it. Harry had only done an hour and fifty-seven minutes.

"So, for the rest of the booking, Harry would finish with *Matilda*, like he always did, but he'd start about ten minutes early, and to fill the remaining time, he'd sing over and over, '*time-killah, time-killah- time-killah, she took me money and ran a-Venezuela.*'"

The Chad Mitchell Trio's association with Belafonte, Bollard and Kapp Records ended when they blew *Blowin' in the Wind*. Frank Fried moved The Trio to Mercury Records. The Mercury years were the finest musically for The Trio, and the most chaotic in the relationship between Mike and Chad.

— CHAPTER TWELVE —

You might think a couple of young singers with a few record albums on their résumés, who were wildly popular on college campuses, would have no shortage of sordid details concerning those first five years. But you'd be wrong.

Joe Frazier was married during that time to Charlotte, who performed in chorus lines of Broadway productions. Mike and Chad knew few details of the relationship, only that by the time Chad left in 1965, the marriage had become strained. They didn't know until later of Joe's struggles with sexual identity. Joe masked all that with the gregarious nature of a social butterfly.

Mike left for New York City in 1959, believing his high school sweetheart from Trail, B.C. was the one. They maintained a long-distance relationship, and Mike's adherence to commitments are strong. Two years younger than Mike, she attended college in Vancouver, B.C. Mike returned to Trail for Christmas of 1961. When he stepped off the bus after arriving in his hometown, he saw her getting off a different bus.

With a grin on his face as he rushed to greet her. "What a happy surprise."

She shrugged from his embrace and gestured to a man standing behind her. "Mike, I'd like you to meet my fiancé."

During the months before The Trio embarked on their South American tour, Rosemary Okun tried to set Mike up with some young women she knew, but nothing sparked. Socially, Mike was The Trio's conservative. When not rehearsing or performing, he tended to keep to himself, or share company with the Okuns.

Midway through the South America tour, Mike, Chad and Joe performed at the American Embassy in Mexico City.

Clare Foran, from Corpus Christi, attended the University of Texas in Austin, but spent her junior year at Mexico City College where she lived with two girlfriends. Before sending her to Mexico, her father told her the American Embassy hosted programs each Tuesday evening to which American citizens were invited.

"I want you to go eat all the food and drink all the tequila and beer you want," he told her. "My tax dollars are paying for that."

So, Clare and her friends usually appeared at the embassy on Tuesday nights and were in the audience as The Chad Mitchell Trio performed. Following the show, someone announced an after party to which everyone was invited and gave an address in one of this city's historic districts.

Clare and her friends found their way to a beautiful, sprawling hacienda—dating back a few centuries—where the Brazilian soccer team was staying. The Brazilians had defeated Mexico that day. A raucous party ensued, and beer became scarce. Clare volunteered to search for cervezas. She found herself lost in a maze of hallways when she entered a small kitchen, opened the refrigerator, and returned to the hallway with beer in hand. A tall man walked toward her.

"Is this where the bar is?" he asked.

Clare handed him a beer. "Aren't you one of the guys who sang at the embassy tonight?" she asked.

Mike introduced himself. They talked as they returned to the party. She asked where they were staying. Mike gave her the address. "But we're leaving tomorrow," he said. "We have a concert in Tampico. We'll be back in a couple of days."

Two days later, Clare called the hotel. "Estoy buscando un americano alto que se aloja en este hotel. Sólo sé que su primer nombre es Mike—Miguel."

The hotel clerk asked, "Se llama Clare?"

She smiled. "Si, senor."

The clerk laughed. "He is at the American Embassy looking for you."

"When he gets back," Clare said, "tell him I'll pick him up here for dinner tonight."

On their way to dinner, Mike asked the cab driver if he knew the words to a song he'd heard along the tour. "I believe the name is Malaguena Sal Arosa?"

"Oh, si, si, senor," the cab driver said. "This is a beautiful love song. I can sing it for you if you'd like."

He pulled to the curb, then turned to face his passengers. "To sing this song properly, though," he said, "I must be in the back seat with the beautiful lady. You can sit in the front."

Mike laughed and shook his head. "I don't think so."

The driver sang for them anyway.

By the time Clare graduated from the University of Texas in 1963, Mike and Chad had both relocated from New York to Chicago. Clare found a job in The Windy City. She and Mike became engaged that summer and married on Dec. 30, 1963. Their daughter, Lydia, was born in March of 1966.

Chad also felt spurned by his high school girlfriend. Befitting his elevated status at Spokane's Lewis & Clark High School, she was hot and popular. This being Chad and the 1950's, they shared a rather chaste, although devoted, relationship. The trouble began in their senior year when she ran for Spokane Lilac Queen and won.

Spokane's Lilac Parade and celebration, held each spring, honors the relationship between Spokane and Fairchild Air Force Base. Each city high school chooses a Lilac Princess and from among those, the Lilac Queen is selected. She appears at many events leading up to the June parade. The Lilac Queen handles all these duties in the company of a young Air Force officer chosen by the base commander.

"Chad, what's wrong?" his girlfriend asked after he'd been stewing for days.

"I don't like you hanging around with that Air Force guy," he told her.

"I don't have any choice," she said. "It's a part of my job."

"Well, you certainly appear to be enthusiastic about that part of your job," Chad complained.

Everything came to a head during the regional Tri-City track meet in Spokane that determined who would advance to the state meet. Chad won the regional 880-yard event. His Lilac Princess girlfriend and her Air Force partner presented medals to each of the winners.

Chad boycotted the medal ceremony, although by the time he won the state 880 title a couple of weeks later, they were on speaking terms again.

Their paths crossed again when she attended a Chad Mitchell Trio performance a few years later. By that time, though, he had moved on.

Chad's sexual initiation occurred during The Trio's two-week engagement at The Blue Angel when Harry Belafonte teamed The Trio with Miriam Makeba. After closing the show one evening, Chad returned to his dressing room to find a small envelope bearing his name in a flowing script. He couldn't quite believe the message inside.

"Chad, I find you quite attractive. We should get together before we go our separate ways. Miriam"

Chad held the note to his chest and checked over his shoulder to discern whether Mike or Joe might have seen its contents. In his fantasies, he might have imagined the life of a performer to be liberally populated with women anxious to share his bed. But so far, given a hectic cycle of performance, travel and rehearsal, he didn't know how anyone could sit still long enough to arrange a seduction.

Miriam was certainly no star-struck fan. She came from a part of the world in which sexual activity proceeded at an earlier pace than in Spokane, Washington. And now this beautiful and exotic woman wanted him?

Thoroughly intimidated, he thought to himself, *Crap. She probably couldn't even imagine I've never been with a woman. Should I tell her? No, no, that would be a mistake. Maybe I'll just pretend I never got her note?*

Having decided on the latter strategy, he couldn't account for finding himself in Miriam's hotel room following the next night's show. As for being the same smooth performer in bed as on the stage, things couldn't have gone much worse.

"Well," Miriam said as they rested a few frantic minutes later, "that was . . . fast."

"Yeah, um . . . you're just so, so . . . I couldn't help . . . um . . . you know?"

"Yes. I think I do. But right now, I'm tired, and I have to get some sleep."

Awakened to sex, Chad vowed to himself that next time he'd prove to Miriam he wasn't some neophyte who couldn't please a woman. But for the remainder of the Blue Angel run, Chad found she was either tired or had a headache following each show.

When The Trio toured with Miriam late in 1961, Chad was again disappointed.

"Once having 'dipped,' so to speak," Chad recalled, "I was anxious to repeat, but when we did other concert tours with Miriam, there was always an excuse. I'm sure from her point of view, she thought, 'Why bother?'"

—✦—

Neither Chad nor Mike knew anything about Joe's high school sweetheart. They knew when he joined The Trio that he was married, but his wife wasn't much of a factor in the life of The Trio.

Joe's gregarious nature made him the socialite of the group. While Chad escaped post-performance mingling and parties as soon as he could, Mike happily stayed to chat and sign autographs. Joe seemed to love the adulation and association with fans. As years went by, though, Mike and Chad both saw Joe's social interests evolving toward the male members of their fan base.

The subject came up in casual conversation. Joe laughed and told Chad, "Well, you do know I seem to have an affinity for the boys."

No announcements were made. Joe never had a heart-to-heart discussion with his colleagues, but both Mike and Chad gradually came to understand that their versatile baritone was probably gay.

Which didn't matter to them.

Ironically, though, Chad seemed to be the one who kept getting mistaken for that sexual persuasion.

Chad's thigh was the one that got squeezed by Julius Monks at the Upstairs-Downstairs during their first week in New York. On a plane ride following a performance, Anthony Perkins made a subtle pass, as did Roddy McDowell a few years later.

Joe had no gay affectations, but neither did Chad. Perhaps his boyish, blond naiveté encouraged assumptions.

One evening in New York following a *Hootenanny* performance, Chad and Tommy Smothers stopped at P.J. O'Rourke's for a drink. They'd met when The Trio appeared on the same bill with the Smothers Brothers at a Denver venue in 1962.

And here they were, not just one fresh-faced blond young man, but two seated together, laughing and enjoying themselves.

Finally, their bartender could tolerate the scene no longer.

"You gentlemen will have to leave," he told them.

Chad looked at the man with puzzlement. "I beg your pardon?"

"You gentlemen need to leave," he repeated. "We don't serve your kind in this establishment."

"Our kind?"

Tommy nudged Chad with an elbow, stood and affected a lisp. "Come, Chadbourne," he said. "We don't have to put up with this."

They held hands as they walked out, then stood on the sidewalk looking through a window, thumbs in their ears, fingers wiggling, while they stuck out their tongues at the bartender.

— CHAPTER THIRTEEN —

October 2007
Spokane Opera House

"Well, I think we should introduce our orchestra this evening," Mike announced. "Our lead guitarist is a man who played with us during the three-year John Denver incarnation of The Mitchell Trio, Mr. Bob Hefferan of Scottsdale Arizona. And this man is Paul Prestopino, who plays anything with a string on it. Paul was with us for almost all the ten years of The Trio's life."

Paul smiled through his beard and nodded to the audience as Mike continued, "This is the more mature Paul Prestopino as opposed to the one you might remember."

Paul played a half dozen bars of introduction to the next number as The Trio turned to him with quizzical expressions.

"Oh, wrong song," he said. "Sorry."

"The *very* mature Paul Prestopino," Chad said.

This time, the guitarist's choice proved correct, and Joe sang the first verse of Tom Paxton's *The Last Thing on My Mind*.

———

SUMMER 1962

Jim McGuinn's resignation again left The Trio searching for musicians.

Chad can't recall who told him about a guitar player who lived way out in the sticks. Chad drove into the depths of a California canyon where he found a ramshackle house and Jacob Ander. The house might have been shabby, but Jacob's guitar playing wasn't. Chad offered him a job on the spot. Jacob, however, didn't play banjo. Jim McGuinn had played both.

At the time, Paul Prestopino worked as a lab tech for the University of Wisconsin's physics department. As his avocation, he played guitar, banjo and mandolin with a high degree of proficiency.

Paul considered himself a folk purist. If it wasn't absolutely ethnic and untouched by revisionists, he wasn't interested. He'd heard the Kingstons and "didn't think much of their music." Peter Paul and Mary's first album didn't move him, either.

So, when Frank Fried called saying he represented The Chad Mitchell Trio and was auditioning banjo players, Paul listened to the pitch but didn't plan on leaving Madison to join a group that sang a funny song about an axe murderer.

Frank paid for a plane ticket, though, so Paul flew to Chicago. The Trio was away at a series of engagements at state fairs and colleges. Milt flew from New York to join Frank in their meeting with Paul. Paul had never heard The Trio, so Frank and Milt played a few cuts from their *At the Bitter End* album.

"I like the harmonies," Paul told them. "Obviously they are proficient singers, better than most. But this is hardly folk music. A lot of it is comedy."

"You need to hear the group in concert to understand what they're really about," Milt said. "Their record company is reluctant to record most of their social commentary and political satire."

"But," added Frank quickly, "we're in the process of moving from Kapp to Mercury Records. We think Mercury is willing to let The Trio be who they really are."

They offered to pay for another plane ticket.

Paul caught up with The Trio at the Michigan State Fair. Paul had every intention of walking into rehearsal, wowing them with his instrumental virtuosity, then politely turning down the offer that would surely follow.

———∿———

The Trio was practicing their choreography for *The Twelve Days of Christmas* when the rehearsal room door opened and Milt ushered in a stocky man with dark, thinning hair and a serious demeanor. He sported black horn-rimmed glasses. A Van Dyke beard encircled his lip and chin. He carried both guitar and banjo cases. Chad couldn't help noticing a hint of skepticism evolve to one of surprise, and then delight, as *Twelve Days* proceeded.

Paul had never heard anything like it. The Trio's version of *Twelve Days,* written by Eric Blau, is a scathing satire on the Neo-Nazi movement emerging in Germany during the late fifties and early sixties. While many Americans still didn't understand or realize the extent of the Holocaust and only wanted to set World War II aside, many leftist voices wanted to be sure the world understood what had really happened.

Of all The Trio's hallmark songs, *Twelve Days* suffers most on their recordings. Much of its impact relied on its choreography as the song progresses. At one performance, Chad's Nazi salute was so emphatic that he hit Joe's arm with enough force to dislocate his thumb.

Paul's careful resolve melted as he watched and heard this powerful statement.

My God, he thought, these guys might really be willing to say something.

"Okay, guys," Milt said as the song ended, "let's try something else. I'd like to hear Paul add a second guitar part to *Johnnie.*"

Before that song ended, Paul had changed his mind. He wouldn't pack up his instruments and walk away. Now, he urgently hoped The Trio would want him.

———∿———

The State Fair circuit would also take The Trio to the DuQuoin State Fair where they were on the same bill with George Burns and Carol Channing.

One afternoon, George—cigar in hand and wearing a silk smoking jacket—peered from his dressing room and waved for Chad to join him.

Chad glanced over his shoulder to be sure George was summoning *him*. The elderly Vaudeville legend hadn't said eight words to him so far. In their brief initial meeting at George's hotel, Chad hadn't recognized the wizened old man because George wasn't wearing his toupee.

The walls of George's dressing room were covered with photos from his storied past. A bottle of rye whiskey and a box of cigars decorated his dressing table.

George shook Chad's hand. "You know," he said, "Ever since we met, I've been trying to recall who you remind me of. I finally figured it out."

Chad raised his eyebrows in anticipation.

"You remind me of Greg."

"Greg?"

"Greg Peck."

Chad required a moment to process what he'd just heard. "You mean Gregory Peck?"

"Yes," George smiled, "It's uncanny. And I just wanted you to know that."

"Well . . . um . . . thanks."

George dismissed him with a handshake. They exchanged polite greetings the rest of the engagement, but they didn't share any more conversations.

Burns' assertion mystified him. *What in the world about a 23-year-old blond guy would remind anyone of Gregory Peck?*

Chad found himself puzzling over the mystery for months. On long drives or airplane rides, the conundrum would pop into his mind, like an annoying song he couldn't dismiss.

Later that year, at the behest of Frank Fried, Chad met an agent in Los Angeles, who had close associations with several Hollywood stars. During the conversation, Chad asked the agent, "Do you know Gregory Peck?"

"Yes, I know him well."

"Is there . . . anything about me that remotely reminds you of him?"

The agent laughed. "So, you know George Burns?"

Chad blinked his surprise. "Well . . . yes. The Trio did an engagement with him earlier this year."

"And let me guess. George told you he'd been trying to figure out who you reminded him of?"

"That's right."

"Well," the agent said, "he got you. That's George's favorite joke. Whenever he meets someone new, he'll pick some actor or actress who is 180 degrees their opposite and plant that seed in their heads. He knows it'll drive you crazy."

<hr />

In March of 1963, they finally got the priest off the hook with God.

Ed Sullivan called.

"So, you see, Father," Mike said in a long-distance call, "you didn't lie after all. We really were on our way to New York to perform on The Ed Sullivan Show."

Sullivan was not just another television variety show. Sunday nights with Ed became almost as religious a ritual for North American families as church on Sunday morning. Mike remembered driving for hours to catch the Sullivan show when he was a child and his folks didn't own a television set.

The Sullivan show, consisting of a variety of acts, had to be scripted carefully for live television so it would not come up short or run past its allotted network time slot. During rehearsals, each act was timed and slotted. On Sunday nights, though, often as not, Sullivan went his own way.

His introductions rambled. Fearful that they'd run long, his director would tell Ed to cut the next introduction short. Ed would cut it too short. And as the show unfolded, hitting the right timing became an exercise in crisis management.

For the March 17 show, The Trio was on the bill with The McGuire Sisters, Paul Anka and Sid Caesar, who performed scenes from the Broadway show *Little Me*. The Trio had been slated to sing one song mid-show—the first time *Blowin' in the Wind* would be performed on network television.

On this night Ed came up way short.

For his performance, Caesar sat in a prop wheelchair as he delivered his lines, and Sullivan—who only rarely did anything but introduce acts—was supposed to come on stage and wheel Caesar away when he was done. The cast made it through rehearsal fine, but during the live evening performance when Caesar indulged in a long dramatic pause, Sullivan thought he was finished and rolled him offstage. Sid still had ninety seconds worth of dialogue to deliver, meaning Ed now had to add ninety seconds to the show.

The director came to The Trio and asked if they might have a second song as a contingency to fill time at the end of the show. The Trio huddled with musicians Ander and Prestopino and decided on *Leave Me if You Want To.*

Ed decided to eat up the time by introducing recently crowned NCAA basketball champion Loyola Ramblers. Initially, Ed had the Ramblers stand as the cameras panned the audience. The director signaled for Ed to stretch it out. "Well," Ed said, "come on up here on stage so the people can see you."

The towering basketball team clamored onstage and stood awkwardly as Ed organized them for the camera.

Expecting that the basketball team had become the contingency, Chad watched this spectacle with amusement on the opposite side of the stage from Mike and Joe as the director pointed with both hands to Ed and mouthed: *Now!*

Abruptly, Ed said, "Here to entertain you ladies and gentlemen, "The Chad Mitchell Trio!"

Oh, shit, thought Chad. The only way he could reach the set where Mike and Joe waited was to dash across the stage during the instrumental introduction to *Leave Me if You Want To* in full view of the audience, dodging and winding his way through a redwood forest of basketball players.

The Trio's second appearance on the Sullivan show occurred in December of 1964, just before Christmas. They were to sing *The Virgin Mary,* a lovely song with a Calypso feel they performed often. Because their more controversial material was censored from radio and television airwaves, many fans assumed they sang songs like *The Virgin Mary* as an expression of religious commitment. Ed apparently shared this assumption.

Mike, whose parents had brought their strict Catholic religion with them from the old country, was closest to a practicing Catholic, although he later became estranged from the Church. Chad had no religious commitment, and although Joe had an intense theological curiosity, his liberal leanings would hardly tolerate a rigid structure like Catholicism.

The Trio performed songs like *The Virgin Mary* and *I Feel So Good About It* and *The Cherry Tree Carol*, because they were beautiful compositions with beautiful harmonies and very much in the folk tradition.

After the late-afternoon dress rehearsal and about an hour before show time, Sullivan's director knocked on their dressing room door and announced the show was running long and even though The Trio was only singing one song, it would have to be cut by twenty seconds.

He left.

Mike, Chad and Joe huddled and determined they could save the twenty seconds by eliminating one verse and one chorus. They rehearsed the change to be sure they were all on the same page.

Fifteen minutes later, the director returned and announced, "Mr. Sullivan asks that you dedicate this song during this Christmas season to the Pope, who recently returned from a trip to India."

Chad replied, "We'll talk about it, but, my initial reaction is, I don't think so. We're not comfortable doing dedications."

Mike, who agreed with Chad on very few subjects by this time, didn't need to talk about it. "I don't think that's something we'd be comfortable with," he said.

The director turned to Joe. "Sorry, but no."

Fifteen minutes later, as the live audience entered the studio theater and The Trio waited in their dressing room, the director returned.

"Fellas," he said, "Ed—and I can't stress this enough—*really* wants you to dedicate your song to the Pope."

Chad looked to Mike and Joe, who both offered curt shakes of the head.

"Well, I'm sorry," Chad said, "but we *really* don't want to do that. We have an agreement that all of us must be comfortable with anything we sing and anything we say, or we just don't do it. And we aren't comfortable using this forum to make that kind of religious declaration. Why don't we just let the song speak for itself?"

An unhappy director scurried away.

Mike, Joe and Chad thought they'd made their point, until Ed introduced them on live television.

"Now Chad Mitchell and . . . um . . . and the other fellows come from Spokane, Washington, and like Bing Crosby, graduated from Gonzaga University," Ed said incorrectly as he absently waved a director's wand. "Now in this holy month of December, made particularly memorable by India's reception of Pope Paul, The Mitchell Trio dedicates this lovely song."

Ed glared in the direction of The Trio.

Ed never invited The Trio back.

Chicago's Drake Hotel never booked Chad, Mike and Joe for a second appearance, either. They were to play a two-week engagement in June of 1963, but didn't make it past opening night.

The Drake, known for its elegance, is an iconic Chicago hotel. The Trio performed in the Camelia Room, a popular concert venue, although it didn't have a stage. Singers and musicians performed on a dance floor with their audience seated at tables around them.

The Drake attracted presumably high-class patrons—wearing suits, gowns and furs—older than a typical Chad Mitchell Trio college crowd. This was also prom night for high schools using another of the Drake's venues. As the prom activities broke up, teenage couples were allowed to file into the Camelia Room and stand along one wall, waiting for the second show to begin.

The Trio ended their set with *Alma Mater*, a sharp satire criticizing violence on the University of Mississippi campus as the Kennedy administration attempted to enforce federal laws banning segregation at southern universities. Like Alabama Governor George Wallace, Mississippi Governor Ross Barnett was an outspoken segregationist who declared he would defy federal mandates.

Alma Mater ends with the sarcastic line, *God bless thee, Ross Barnett*. Rising above the crowd's applause came a voice that shouted, "What's wrong with Ross Barnett?"

Okay, thought Chad, *so here, of all places, we have a heckler.*

To enthusiastic applause, The Trio trotted off, waited an obligatory moment, then returned for their encore.

As they were singing *Last Night I Had the Strangest Dream,* Chad saw flickering glints of light emanating from one portion of the darkened room.

Oh, that's nice, he thought to himself. *They've added some kind of strobe effect to the lighting.*

Then he realized the glints were reflections from pennies being thrown at them from a nearby table.

Chad couldn't believe it. This wasn't some southern roadhouse with chicken wire screens to protect the acts. This was the Drake Hotel, for godsake!

They finished. Chad and the musicians went to dressing rooms to change from their performance attire. Mike went to the hotel lounge to enjoy an after-performance cocktail. So, he wasn't present when Joe found Chad in the dressing room and said, "I found the guy who threw the pennies."

"Oh, God," Chad said, "I hope you didn't . . ."

"No," Joe said. "He's just a little jerk, probably four inches shorter than you. I gathered the pennies, took them to his table and told him, 'Here, sir. Perhaps you can use these to buy yourself an education.'"

"What did he do?" Chad asked.

"He said, 'I'm very well-educated, thank you.'"

"What a cretin," Chad said, growing angry.

"I can introduce you, if you want," Joe said.

Chad followed Joe to the Camelia Room.

As they approached, Chad saw a short round man wearing a stylish grey suit, scowling and sitting at a table he shared with a taller, elegantly dressed woman.

Chad felt relief that Joe had not gotten into a physical altercation with the little guy. While Mike was The Trio's tallest member, Joe had an athletic build and a rough childhood to go with it.

As they reached the table, Joe said, "Sir, I'd like you to meet—"

The man leaped from his chair and threw a hard right into Joe's face.

Joe staggered, then—bleeding from the corner of his mouth—drew himself into a picture of outrage, as if acting in some Victorian drama, raised an index finger high above his head and said, "How dare you, sir!"

Chad considered punching the man. Then he noticed high school prom-goers lining the walls in their pastel suits and gowns. He envisioned The Chad Mitchell Trio rolling around on the floor among fur coats and patent leather shoes. He grabbed Joe and pulled him away.

The Trio's accountant, a six-foot-four specimen named Harvey Weinberg, sat at a nearby table as Frank Fried's guest. Frank hadn't attended the show, because he'd injured his back and was home in traction. As Chad restrained Joe, Harvey jumped up and, pointing a boney index finger at Joe's assailant, said, "Hey, you can't—"

The little guy picked up a glass of Coca Cola, dashed the liquid in Harvey's face, then waved his butter knife in a threatening fashion, implying he would either stab or butter the next person who approached.

Chad guided Joe to the Drake's lobby where he demanded that the hotel staff call the night manager, a timid, mincing man whose response was, "What do you want me to do about it?"

"We want the guy removed!" Chad demanded. "Make sure he knows that kind of behavior is not acceptable."

"I don't see why you people are so upset," the night manager said. "We've had instances where guests have thrown camelia pots at female performers, and the women didn't complain."

"Camelia pots?" Chad said.

"So, you're not going to do anything?" Joe asked.

The manager said no.

"Well," Joe said, again striking his theatrical pose, "I've been assaulted! I'm calling the police."

As soon as Joe got off the lobby telephone, Chad used it to call Frank, who told him to call their lawyer. Frank always referred to the man as their "shyster" lawyer.

The Drake had three separate entrances leading into the lobby. Chad and Joe had waited about fifteen minutes when, with uncanny timing, Frank Fried limped into the room from one walkway, their shyster lawyer— wearing a Tyrolian hat featuring a feather in the hatband as if he'd just finished a stroll through the Alps—entered from a second walkway.

And at the third entrance appeared Carmen, a woman well-known among folk acts as someone who always had drugs in her purse. Carmen was followed closely by two police officers.

Chad recalls sitting in his lobby chair, watching this convergence, thinking, *Gee, I wonder how this will work out.*

Carmen said hello to Chad and Joe.

The policeman asked the night manager to take them to the perpetrator, who still sat at his table.

The manager refused.

"Look, all we want is for this guy to leave," Chad said.

Again, the manager refused.

"Well, I'll show you who he is," Joe said, and strode back toward the Camelia Room.

The police, who apparently needed permission of hotel management to enter beyond the lobby, didn't follow. So, when Joe approached the little guy's table for a third time and dramatically declared, "There he is!" he turned to find no backup.

The man grabbed his empty Coke bottle by its neck, raised it over his head like a club, and charged. Joe ran, twisting and dodging among the tables. When he made it back to the lobby at a full sprint, Joe pointed over his shoulder and yelled, "This is the one! This is the one!"

As the police seized him, the man threw his Coke bottle at Joe. He missed, and the bottle shattered on the floor.

"So, you want to press charges?" one of the cops asked Joe.

When Joe, inspired by the presence of his shyster lawyer, said yes, his assailant responded, "Then I'm pressing charges, too. He came to my table three times in a threatening manner. I have a right to defend myself!"

Joe and his assailant shared the back of a paddy wagon on their way to jail.

The next day, hotel honchos met with The Trio.

"We'll issue a formal apology concerning last night's events," one Drake official told them.

"I don't think it needs to be that elaborate," Chad said. "It's enough to admit you should have kicked the guy out."

"No, you don't understand. We're issuing the apology to him and our other patrons, both on behalf of the hotel and The Chad Mitchell Trio."

"Whoa," said Joe. "We're not apologizing to anyone."

"If you don't apologize, you won't perform again at the Drake."

"Then I guess we won't perform," Mike said. "And I'll remind you, we have a contract."

The Drake paid The Trio for a full two-week engagement. The Trio enjoyed a rare two-week vacation.

— CHAPTER FOURTEEN —

ike much of America, The Trio faced 1963 as a year of hope and bright promise.

America was captivated by its charismatic young president, who'd forced the Russians to back down in Cuba just a year before. John Kennedy continued to charm his countrymen, despite dragging his feet while racial tensions boiled in the South and seeds of the Vietnam debacle were being sowed.

On the day John Kennedy was assassinated, The Chad Mitchell Trio struggled through take after take of a commercial for Sterling Beer, a regional Indiana brand.

"We'd never done a commercial," Chad said, "and under most circumstances, we wouldn't. But Frank thought this one wouldn't hurt our image, because the product wasn't national. So, we did it for the money."

They began at nine a.m. on Nov. 22, 1963. The advertising agency had rented a studio on the top floor of a downtown Chicago building. The guys wore coats and ties, and the room was stifling. Frequent touch-ups were required by a makeup lady who spent the rest of her time watching soap operas in a tiny dressing room.

Mike, Joe and Chad found the musical jingle inane and had difficulty taking it seriously. They flubbed lyrics and played with harmonies as many takes dissolved into laughter. Morning dragged into noon. A lunch break neared when the makeup lady staggered from her cubicle and sobbed, "The President's been shot!"

Everyone gathered around her television until Kennedy's death was confirmed.

"What now?" Mike asked. They didn't want to continue

"Sorry, guys," the director told them after conferring with ad agency representatives, "but we've spent a lot of money already. We have to go ahead."

The day ground on.

"We'd make a mistake," Chad said, "or something would be wrong with lighting of the beer glass, or pouring of the beer wouldn't be exactly right, or sound would be out of sync with the film."

Darkness had settled outside when the production team decided everything was finally right. They took one last look at the finished commercial.

"Uh, oh," said the producer.

"What?" Chad asked. "What's wrong now?"

"See those bubbles forming on the side of the glass instead of rising?"

Chad stared, Mike and Joe looking over his shoulder.

"It means there's a fingerprint on the inside of the glass, so bubbles bunch up right there."

Chad looked closer. He didn't see a fingerprint.

"We have to do it over," the producer said.

As did many Americans, Mike, Chad and Joe had mixed feelings about Kennedy prior to his martyrdom. Despite his charisma, they saw Kennedy as a Cold War warrior who brought the world to the brink of nuclear disaster with the Bay of Pigs debacle, then the Cuban Missile Crisis.

Chad remembers Harry Belafonte angrily complaining, "That guy's going to get us into a war yet." Belafonte, who later became much closer to Robert Kennedy than he did Jack, was also unhappy with Kennedy's reluctance to be more aggressive during civil rights confrontations in the American South.

John Kennedy's assassination, though, elevated the president to a higher plane among liberal activists as the loss of a young, vigorous leader galvanized a nation in grief.

The Trio was booked for a Carnegie Hall performance on Nov. 28, and they hoped the show would be canceled. When it was not, they felt they had to speak to the Kennedy tragedy.

Literally within hours of the assassination, Herb Kretzmer and David Lee wrote *In the Summer of His Years*. The popular British Broadcasting

System TV show, *That Was the Week That Was,* which satirized American life and politics, quickly rescripted its November 23 telecast to focus on Kennedy's death. They included the Kretzmer-Lee song:

> *". . . the heart of the world weighs heavy*
> *with the helplessness of tears,*
> *For the man cut down in a Texas town*
> *in the summer of his years . . ."*

"We should do something related to President Kennedy," Milt said as The Trio prepared for their Carnegie Hall date.

"What about the song from *That Was the Week That Was*?" Mike asked.

"Yes, something like that," Chad agreed. "But there's no expression of hope in that song. We need something more uplifting."

Something, Milt agreed, that spoke to resiliency of the American spirit through calamity.

And, typical of Trio rehearsals, the collaboration began to flow.

Chad found Abraham Lincoln's 1864 campaign song. Sung with exuberance in its original version, it looked forward to the end of war and a unified nation. At Carnegie Hall, The Trio sang in somber unison a single verse from *Summer of his Years,* then followed with a quiet, almost prayerful harmony:

> *". . . the Union forever, hurrah boys hurrah,*
> *the union forever and up with the star,*
> *And we'll rally round the flag, we'll rally once again,*
> *shouting the battle cry of freedom."*

That word—freedom—had become a touchstone of controversy in 1962 as Black Southerners, led by Martin Luther King Jr., sought to claim their full rights of citizenship through protest. The demand for civil rights was a ticking bomb as white Southerners sought to perpetuate a long-accustomed way of life.

The Trio welcomed Belafonte's invitation to include them in the Stars for Freedom Concert in St. Jude, Alabama set for March 24 1965. They joined Peter, Paul and Mary, Belafonte, Tony Bennett, Frankie Laine, Sammy Davis Jr., Joan Baez, Nina Simone, Mike Nichols, Anthony Perkins, Leonard Bernstein and others to entertain King's Selma marchers in a muddy Montgomery field.

Chad recalls the experience as being surreal.

When Belafonte's cast de-planed at the Montgomery airport, a voice on a loudspeaker said, "Will the outside agitators meet at their bus near baggage claim."

Belafonte warned the performers not to leave their hotel that night, but if they did, "be sure and go in a group."

Mike, not yet an American citizen, had to leave after the concert to return to Canada so he could renew his U.S. work visa. Chad and Joe stayed the next day to join the thousands of marchers who followed Dr. King to Alabama's capitol building.

Chad came to Alabama with little sympathy for white southerners. He'd braced himself for possible violent reactions to the activists' presence. As they marched, though, he didn't confront an angry, shouting mob. White citizens lining the streets looked on in dead silence.

"They were being invaded," Chad said. He recalled a famous photograph from World War II as a Frenchman with tears streaming down his face watched Germans march past him through the streets of Paris.

"I didn't agree with the white southerners' beliefs," Chad said, "but I found empathy for them. Their whole world was changing. Nothing about the experience was what I expected."

On the final Mitchell Trio album to include Chad, The Trio offered a counterpoint to Southern prejudice in an elegant statement concerning Northern society's struggle with racial integration.

If one had to choose a single song to best represent what The Mitchell Trio stood for both musically and in terms of social conscience, *Which Hat Shall I Wear* by Fred Hellerman and Frank Minkoff, would come closest.

The song tells of a Northern woman who feigns sympathy for the Civil

Rights Movement as she patronizes her Black maid, explaining why she doesn't want her child bussed to schools with Black children. The harmonies are complex. A careful listener will hear three men sing four parts. The Trio had never been, nor ever would be, better than this.

—∿—

Martin Luther King's activism put the Kennedy administration in an untenable position as it slowly applied the weight of federal law to force the integration of southern universities. To the surprise of many, the man who enthusiastically picked up the baton Kennedy only reluctantly carried was his successor, the ultimate Southerner, Lyndon Johnson.

For two decades, Johnson had been a steadfast member of the Southern bloc, voting to stymie civil rights legislation. Even during his presidency—away from cameras and press—he frequently used the 'N' word in referring to blacks, including Thurgood Marshall, whom he appointed as the first black man to hold a seat in the U.S. Supreme Court.

His Southern congressional colleagues regarded Johnson as a traitor when he used national sentiment following Kennedy's death to push the Civil Rights Act of 1964 and the Voting Rights Act of 1965 through Congress.

Journalist and Johnson expert Adam Serwer wrote, "The Civil Rights Act made it possible for Johnson to smash Jim Crow. The Voting Rights Act made the U.S. government accountable to its black citizens and a true democracy for the first time. Johnson lifted racist immigration restrictions designed to preserve a white majority—and by extension white supremacy. He forced FBI Director J. Edgar Hoover, then more concerned with 'Communists' and civil rights activists, to turn his attention to crushing the Ku Klux Klan."

While radio stations had shunned The Trio since *The John Birch Society* and *Johnnie*, the stake was driven into the heart of any remaining hopes they held for commercial acceptance when they rushed to Johnson's aid during the 1964 presidential election by recording *Barry's Boys*.

By now, The Trio sang almost exclusively to college audiences, and June Reizner's wonderful satire poked fun at a conservative movement on campuses in support of Barry Goldwater:

*"We're the bright young men
who want to go back to 1910,
we're Barry's Boys . . ."*

The Trio's only television performance of Barry's Boys occurred on *That Was the Week That Was.*

A radio station in Redding, California, embraced the song, playing it several times over a few days, getting the station in hot water with the Federal Communications Commission.

A United Press International report on July 18, 1964 stated:

> Goldwater forces have apparently won the first "equal time" encounter of the presidential campaign.
>
> A satirical anti-Goldwater folk song called "Barry's Boys" achieved such popularity on a local radio station (KVIP) that supporters of the Republican presidential nominee demanded—and received—equal time for an album of anti-liberal songs.
>
> Station manager Don Chamberlain said, "Barry Boys" was "the hottest tune in our programming right now." The song has been recorded by The Chad Mitchell Trio.
>
> It was doing so well, Chamberlain said, that at least one pro-Goldwater listener urged advertisers to withdraw their accounts from the station.
>
> The album that will be given equal time with "Barry's Boys" is a group of parodies called "Folksongs to Bug Liberals By," performed by the Goldwater Boys of Nashville, Tenn.
>
> Chamberlain said the request for equal time was granted under the Federal Communications Commission "fairness doctrine," in which political candidates must be given equal time on the air.
>
> He said the station's programming was otherwise "middle of the road."

According to a Conelrad Music Blog report published in 2006, The Goldwater Boys were the "warped brainchild" of Nashville-based brothers Mark and Buford Clark, who "recruited four kids with moderate musical skills from nearby colleges. The result was a Republican answer to The Chad Mitchell Trio." The group produced a "nearly unlistenable" album, and then went on the road with the Goldwater campaign.

The Conelrad Blog tracked down Ken Crook, lead singer for The Goldwaters who later became a broadcast news personality in the Southwest.

"Our album wasn't nearly unlistenable," Crook said "It was completely unlistenable . . . I have played the album for very few people. I have had entire relationships, including marriage, where the other person has no idea of this part of my life."

The Trio's support of Johnson earned them an invitation to the White House and an audience with the President and his family in 1965.

By the time Vietnam came to overshadow Johnson's civil rights triumphs and his progressive domestic programs, The Trio's sentiments shifted to support for the peace movement as Johnson led America deeper and deeper into the quagmire of war.

Johnson's chance to be regarded as one of the giants of the Presidency based on his domestic leadership was squandered when he sent thousands of young Americans—including a disproportionate number of economically disadvantaged Black and Hispanic men—to Vietnam.

And as American society lurched into turmoil over both domestic and international events, 1964 and 1965 plunged The Chad Mitchell Trio into an internal dispute that would tear it apart as well.

Before the Kennedy assassination, the fall of 1963 had been a stellar season for The Trio. They'd shed themselves of Kapp and signed with Mercury Records. They released *Singin' Our Mind*, the first of four Mercury albums that represent The Chad Mitchell Trio's best work.

While their popularity on college campuses continued to grow, The

Trio still sought that mainstream hit single that would put them back on the radio and produce some real money.

At long last, they thought they'd found it.

In early November, Mercury released one of *Singing Our Mind's* cuts— Tom Paxton's *The Marvelous Toy*—as a single, thinking it had potential to become a Christmas standard. And, indeed, *The Marvelous Toy* took off.

Paxton held his breath right along with The Trio. Tom and his wife were driving a Volkswagen bug across Texas in the fall of 1963, sorting through the static trying to find a radio station when a sudden burst of clarity revealed The Trio singing *The Marvelous Toy*.

"There we were in the middle of Texas," Tom said, "standing along a highway, shouting our heads off."

Chad, Mike and Joe watched with glee as *Toy* climbed quickly to number fifty on various top one hundred lists and seemed sure to be headed higher.

Until November 22nd.

"When the assassination occurred," Mike said, "the music industry came to a halt. No one was buying records, and certainly not records about toys. That was a somber Christmas."

The Marvelous Toy received enough notice to help Paxton win a contract with Elektra Records the next year. It became one more song The Trio recorded first, only to see someone else reap its commercial fruit. Peter, Paul and Mary had a hit with *Marvelous Toy* when they included it on their 1969 *Peter, Paul and Mommy* children's album.

"A lot of good things happened to me because of that song," Tom Paxton said. "It certainly raised my profile as a songwriter."

— CHAPTER FIFTEEN —

October 1963

"For five years we'd spent more time together
than married people do.
Married people at least have the benefit of sex."

—Chad Mitchell

Milt asked Mike to stay following a recording session.

"That was something, wasn't it?" Mike said with a grin as Chad and Joe departed Mercury Records' Chicago studio.

Milt nodded. "You fellows have never sounded better. The material is great. Mercury is such an improvement . . ."

Milt's voice trailed off. Nothing in his demeanor or tone seemed to match Mike's enthusiasm for the way *Singin' Our Mind* was shaping up.

"So, what's wrong?" Mike asked.

"I . . . I have something I need to share with you," Milt said. "I've puzzled over what I should or shouldn't say, but . . ."

Mike waited.

"Frank and I had a discussion yesterday," Milt said.

Mike, and everyone else for that matter, knew Milt and Frank Fried did not get along. Mostly they avoided each other, but Frank had wanted to sit in on some of the recording sessions.

"A discussion?" Mike asked.

"Well, more of an argument," Milt said. "I won't go into all of it, but Frank became angry and told me Chad is bigger than The Trio, that he's the only one among you who has a future beyond The Trio."

Mike felt his anger rise as old suspicions seemed confirmed. "So, we're back to this solo career thing," Mike said, recalling Frank's plan for Chad to host the ill-fated *Folk Song* television pilot.

Another recent development added to Mike's concern. Frank had made Chad a partner in Triangle Productions, which Mike considered a conflict of interest. Legally, Chad remained a one-third partner in The Trio. Under this new arrangement, Chad's Trio income went to Triangle and Triangle paid Chad a fixed weekly salary. Frank did not provide Mike and Joe with details of Chad's income through Triangle.

As The Trio's management company, Triangle earned fifteen percent of each concert's purse. The booking agency took another fifteen percent off the top. A typical Chad Mitchell Trio campus concert earned between $2,500 and $3,000, leaving $1,750 to $2,000 for The Trio partnership. From that amount, The Trio paid salaries to two backup musicians and covered travel and lodging expenses for everyone. Chad, Mike and Joe split the leftovers equally.

"Triangle's fifteen percent off the top," Mike said, "amounted to more than my thirty percent of what was left."

By 1963, The Trio's base of operations had moved from New York to Chicago. Mike rented an apartment and was engaged to be married. Joe maintained his New York residency and stayed in a hotel when Trio business brought him to Chicago.

Chad gained a further financial advantage when Frank allowed him to share living space in a back room of Triangle's offices.

———— ⁓ ————

"If you're planning to leave The Trio," Mike said, "you need to let us know."

Chad took a moment to absorb the question before he could answer. "Why would you think—?"

"It's pretty clear you've been unhappy," Mike said. "And I don't understand. We're better than we've ever been."

For some weeks now, Chad had felt a growing dissatisfaction he'd tried to deny. But truth revealed itself little by little with each passing day. Some of it had to do with misconceptions regarding his role. He didn't want to do interviews. He didn't like being expected to mingle with fans. He didn't want to spend every waking hour in the company of Mike and Joe. He wanted to rehearse, perform, then be left to a life of his own—whatever that might be.

"I'm tired," Chad told Mike. "I just need a break. Do you realize you and I have been together practically day and night since 1959? We get up, we get on an airplane or a bus. We rehearse, we perform. Then we do it all over again. If we'd just slow down, take some time off, it wouldn't be such a grind."

"To make a living at this," Mike said, "we have to perform."

"The Kingston Trio doesn't perform year-round," Chad argued. "They perform a fall schedule for the campus circuit. They perform a spring schedule for the campus circuit. Maybe they'll do a couple of big events during the summer. But they take breaks."

"They have hit records," Mike said. "They draw bigger audiences than we do. They can afford vacation breaks."

"I'm just asking for some time off!"

Frank's statement to Milt, though, kept ringing in Mike's ears. *Chad's bigger than The Trio.* To Mike, time off meant only one thing. Chad would be pursuing Frank's solo ambitions, while he and Joe waited on the sidelines, not earning a living.

The arguments intensified. None of Chad's denials could shake Mike from his suspicions.

He dug in his heels more than ever. Chad became exasperated at what he viewed as Mike's intransigence.

Through it all, though, rehearsal continued. These sessions became Mike's and Chad's only refuge. The performances glowed. Night after night, college crowds welcomed them with applause and adulation. They began work on the next two albums.

Apart from that, they seldom spoke.

Finally, Chad again brought up his desire for a less stringent schedule. Mike again refused to budge. Joe had the deciding vote but would not cast it. Finally, Milt stepped in. His stand surprised both Mike and Chad.

"Mike," he said, "you're not listening. You need to hear what Chad has to say!"

They agreed to take a break at year-end.

Milt took the opportunity to revisit his suggestion about changing the group's name. He agreed that, at this point, they couldn't abandon Chad's name entirely. "How about dropping the first name, though," he said. "Just *The Mitchell Trio?*"

Mike and Joe agreed. Chad didn't cast a vote.

"I remember going into that break thinking I'd won," Chad recalled. "But when I returned in January, I found we were booked to the same old schedule. I felt like nothing had changed."

~

In retrospect, the point of no return forcing Chad's departure occurred the day Frank told Milt that Chad was bigger than The Trio. More than fifty years later, Mike and Chad still hold different interpretations of that statement.

Mike believes Frank coveted a solo career for Chad, that Frank wanted Chad to leave The Trio all along.

Chad concedes Frank saw his long-term future as a solo singer and actor. Frank thought Chad's talent and charisma offered opportunities beyond the life of The Trio. Chad believes, however, rather than mentally relegating Mike and Joe to the status of back-up singers, Frank was simply taking a realistic view of folk music's fading commercial relevance.

Sitting in the shade of cherry trees during the summer of 2018, Chad said, "I never wanted to be a solo performer. I think Frank wanted that for me. I didn't know how to be a solo performer, though."

"But, Chad," Mike protested, "that's not what you said at the time."

Mike's mother kept extensive scrap books of newspaper accounts regarding every aspect of The Trio. Those scrapbooks—which his mother pronounced in her Russian accent as *crapbooks*—have been a key source in reconstructing details of The Trio's history. Mike produced a copy of a Chicago newspaper article concerning Chad's departure.

"The reporter quotes you," Mike said. "*I felt I was encumbered by the other two, that I wasn't advancing my career according to my ability, and that they were holding me back.*"

Chad, a deeply introspective man, took on a haunted look during a few seconds of silence, then said softly, "If that's what the story says, I can't deny that I said it. But I honestly don't remember ever having felt that way."

Chad doesn't deny that anger afflicted him during the final year of his association with The Trio. The root of his dissatisfaction though, wasn't a sense he'd outgrown The Trio. "I've been singing for six years and I'm honestly tired of it," he told a New York Times reporter.

Chad wanted time away from the hectic pace—night after night of performance before college students, a different campus each night. Day after day of fitful sleep on airplanes and buses.

Mike, though, could not shake his suspicion that Chad wanted time away to advance his own ambitions. Unlike Chad, Mike had a wife and growing family to support. Chad might be perceived as The Trio's front man, but Mike was the steady, responsible one who saw to details, who made sure obligations were met.

Only one aspect of their lives was not tainted by this growing rift. Both Mike and Chad put the music above their differences.

The next stop on their 1964 grind was Spokane.

———— ✿ ————

"Remember, *A prophet is not without honor except in his own town.*" Father Beaver placed a hand on Chad's shoulder and offered a supportive squeeze.

Chad stared at the *Spokane Spokesman-Review* spread before him at a booth in the Davenport Hotel's coffee shop, shook his head, and under his breath said, "Jesus Christ."

"That's correct," the priest answered.

"What?"

"Oh," said the priest. "I'm sorry. I thought you were commenting on the source of scripture I just quoted."

"No, Father, I'm commenting on the imbecility of the guy who wrote this review. He doesn't have a clue what our music is about."

After five years, The Mitchell Trio had returned to its roots. They'd performed before an enthusiastic crowd the evening before at the Spokane

Coliseum. While they'd been away, The Chad Mitchell Trio had forged a role as the voice of an emerging liberal American counterculture among what would become known as the Baby Boom generation. On every campus, people their own age offered thanks for creating an awareness of questions concerning social justice and political deceit they hadn't previously considered.

Reviewer Ed Costello, though, a conservative employee of a conservative newspaper in conservative Spokane, expressed a decidedly establishment view when he took The Trio to task.

Trio Extremely Talented but Somehow Depressing

In light of their great talent as performers, two things about The Chad Mitchell Trio are depressing. The first is that they attracted only 2,383 persons to the Coliseum Wednesday night for a benefit for their old alma mater, Gonzaga University . . . Second, and most distressing, is that The Trio has developed and is apparently being directed by what its press agent calls its "social and political conscience."

Pointing Ridicule

In plainer terms, this means that The Trio has found that by finding something at which to point ridicule (fun is one thing, ridicule another) they can find immediate favor with a certain type of person.

Time was when it was considered great fun to make sport of minorities. This game has been refined and "intellectualized" and people with a "social conscience" sing or listen to songs that give a clever, but cruel barb to new minorities.

Actually, there is no more cause to point the finger of scorn at a defunct political regime (Nazism) or the conservative John Birch Society or Billie Sol Estes than there was to hurling insults at Irish immigrants at the turn of the century. Is this progress?

> Thus, a concert by three fine-looking, fine-sounding young men can have something lacking because of this rather commercial "conscience." Laughter at someone else's expense cannot be completely satisfying.

The songs that offended Costello were staples of The Trio's performances. *The John Birch Society*; *The Ides of Texas* which addressed flamboyant embezzler Billie Sol Estes who had close ties to Lyndon Johnson; and *The Twelve Days of Christmas,* their cutting commentary on a growing neo-Nazi movement in Germany.

"I'll write a letter to the editor," Chad said.

"It's the man's opinion," the priest cautioned.

"I won't tell him he's wrong about whether we were good or bad last night. I'll explain the point of what we do. How could anyone but a social and political dolt compare Irish immigrants just trying to be useful American citizens with graft and fraud surrounding Billie Sol Estes, or fanaticism of the Birchers or Nazi genocide? Folk music should be a forum questioning the political status quo, making fun of social propriety and challenging injustice. Not just pretty songs about highwaymen and English maids."

Rejecting the priest's advice, Chad wrote a letter and managed, he thought, to be civil and constructive. He was not consoled. The world was shifting beneath his feet. The Beatles had arrived. Interest in folk music began to wane. Animosity and suspicion were driving the gulf separating Chad and Mike ever wider.

A tour with Miriam Makeba took them to Sacramento, Edmonton, Vancouver, Seattle, Minneapolis and Philadelphia. They played a week at San Francisco's Hungry i. They appeared four more times on *Hootenanny,* all the while maintaining their college concert schedule.

Chad didn't resume the argument about time off. He slipped back into the grind, stifling his anger. He had recurring dreams about confronting Mike, then feeling bad, waking up almost in tears over a sense that he was treating Mike unfairly. Guilt fed anger. Anger fed guilt.

Ironically, at a time when Mike, Joe, Milt, Frank—as well as critics—felt The Trio was at its peak, "I began to feel that, for me, The Trio had run its course," Chad said.

Mercury followed, *Singin' Our Mind* and *Reflecting* with *Typical American Boys* and *Slightly Irreverent* in the space of two years.

Chad's dissatisfaction gnawed at him. If he couldn't change the schedule, at least he could reduce the time he spent with Mike and Joe outside of rehearsal and performance.

So, he bought a Porsche.

———— ❧ ————

Chad has always been partial to cars that make a statement.

By 1964, Chad hadn't owned a car in years. Single and without financial obligation, he decided he wanted something exciting.

"A sports car," he said. "I asked people what would be a good sports car? Someone said, 'Porsche' so I went to the big Porsche dealer in downtown Chicago."

Two cars, both 1963 models, sat on the showroom floor. These were the last classic bathtub models before Porsche switched to the 911 design.

Initially, the salesman seemed doubtful that someone who looked as young as Chad could afford their product.

Chad pointed to a one of the cars and said, "How much?"

"That car runs $5,000," said the salesman with a sardonic smile.

Chad nodded. "Could I ride in one?"

When the price tag didn't seem to scare his prospective customer, the salesman's smile became more genuine. "Let me get the keys."

Chad recalls the drive. "This guy scared the shit out of me."

Blasting along surface streets, the Porsche's acceleration pinned Chad to his seat. G-forces through the turns sent his stomach churning. The salesman hit a thirty mile-per-hour on-ramp at sixty and accelerated from there along a couple miles of freeway.

Chad hung on and thought to himself, *Oh, yes. This is the car I want.*

They returned to the dealership, and Chad said, "I'll take it."

The salesman said, "Well, this car has a special engine. It's called a Carrera." He pointed to the second Porsche. "*That* one's $5,000. The one we rode in is more expensive."

"How much?" Chad asked.

"Eight thousand."

"I'll take it."

At the age of 82, Chad still wants his car to make a statement. Granted, the issue doesn't come up much anymore. But if the need arises . . .

Sitting in his living room telling Porsche stories, he pointed in the direction of a sedate-looking Audi in his garage. "I know for a fact that car will do 165. I think it would probably do 180, because I had some work done to increase the power by about a hundred horses."

His Porsche, he said, would do "130 all day long." Which offered him an alternative.

"I was so angry that last year, I didn't want to fly with the other guys," he said. "I would drive to concert dates unless they were like, 1,000 miles away."

Chad drove from Chicago for a concert date at Ball State University in Indiana and calculated he might be late. He cranked the Porsche up to 100, all the while keeping an eye on his rear-view mirror where he caught a gleam of reflection off chrome. The glint transformed itself to a car closing fast. A red light came on.

Shit, thought Chad, and slammed on his brakes. Even at 100, the Porsche could stop on a dime. The police car couldn't. The police sedan skidded into a full 360-degree spin as the officer wrestled his American-made tank to a standstill.

Chad expected a ticket. The officer said, "That's not how we do it here. Follow me."

They drove to a Justice of the Peace's office. Chad paid his fine so he could be on his way. As they walked to their cars, the officer told him, "I was about out of gas. If you'd hung on for another ten miles, I never would have caught you."

Knowing there would be no way he could make the concert in time, Chad found a local airport and paid a guy to fly him. He arrived at Ball State a half-hour late. The performance occurred without further complications, but the university booking agent was angry at the delay.

"You're going on the list!" he told Chad.

Universities had formed a network to share information about the acts they booked. The Chad Mitchell Trio would now be listed as a group prone to tardiness. Which they really were not.

The story doesn't end until two decades later when Chad worked for The Delta Queen Steamboat Company. Frank Fried, now the president of Delta Queen, had conceived of a traveling show to help promote the company. He called it *Mississippi Jambalaya* and, Chad said, "It was awful. And of course, I had to be in it. We were booked at Ball State University. I think we had bus trouble. We were late. And would you believe it? That same guy was still the booking agent."

He scowled and told Chad, "I remember you. You're going back on the list."

Chad loved everything about his Porsche until driving to the Chicago airport he encountered a Corvette on a long, straight two-lane road. He pulled alongside the Chevy, exchanged a meaningful glance with its driver, and they were off.

The Corvette left Chad and his Porsche behind.

He found the driver sitting on the Vette's hood at the side of the roadway and pulled over as well.

"You know," the driver said, "if we'd been on a road course, something with turns, no way could I keep up with you. But your car can't compete on a straightaway."

Chad thought about it all the way to the concert performance and back. He recalled a drag racing friend from childhood who told him he'd rigged a system to inject nitrous oxide directly into his car's carburetors to get extra punch off the line. Chad recruited Hans, the mechanic at the Chicago Porsche dealership, to help him. After much research, including securing a special solenoid used in rockets by NASA, they devised a scheme with nitrous oxide tanks under the hood—the rear-engine automobile's trunk—and a dashboard switch to turn the system on and off. Chad mounted another switch under the accelerator. When the system was on, tromping down on the gas pedal released the laughing gas.

Chad departed for a concert date and left his Porsche with Hans to test their device. Chad called Hans from the road.

"How did it work?"

"Great, except for one thing," Hans said, "I stepped on the gas and the wheels didn't stop leaving rubber for two blocks."

"What's the one thing?" Chad asked.

"Well, then the engine burned up."

Turns out old '40s and '50s dragsters could handle the heat of a nitrous oxide injection because the engines had water-cooled iron blocks. The Porsche's air-cooled engine just couldn't take it.

Chad spent $3,500 on a new engine.

"From then on," he said, "I drove the car pretty reasonably."

Which still didn't keep him out of trouble.

Driving from Chicago to a performance in South Carolina Chad was passed by a Dodge Charger—the newest hot American muscle car. When they pulled into the lane ahead of him, Chad thought he was dealing with a farmer and his son. They wore straw hats, and seen from behind, the passenger's head barely cleared the Dodge's front seat.

The Charger put on a burst of speed. As it disappeared over a hill, Chad accepted the challenge. He topped the hill at 130, to find the Charger facing him on the roadside, alternating blue and red grill lights flashing. The "child" turned out to be a trooper who stood about four feet and six inches tall.

On a Sunday afternoon, the Justice of the Peace's office wasn't open. So, they drove to the judge's house where Chad encountered a scene right out of Mayberry. The justice and his family were having Sunday dinner. A cell complete with iron bars occupied one corner of their living room.

"If you don't have money to pay," the justice said, "you can wait in the cell until you make arrangements. Meantime, my wife cooked up this wonderful chicken. Why don't all you fellows join us?"

Chad eventually traded the Carrera for a 911. To this day, he regrets the transaction. "About ten years ago," Chad said, "the Carrera's engine alone would have sold for $80,000. I wonder what it would be worth now?"

— CHAPTER SIXTEEN —

OCTOBER 2007
SPOKANE OPERA HOUSE

The Opera House audience sat silent as Bob Hefferan and Paul Prestopino began playing a slow, classic funeral dirge. Mike faced the microphone with a grim expression, eyes tilted down, while Chad and Joe stood to one side. As the dirge continued, Joe initiated a slow, steady clap of his hands. Chad started to join in, but Joe warned him away with shake of his head.

Finally, Mike spoke in a sorrowful tone.

"Thank you for the applaud."

Chad and Joe joined in on *A Dying Business*, Frank Ebb and Norman Martin's satire on the rising cost of funerals.

Chad waited for applause and laughter to subside, then said, "We have Jessica Mitford to thank for that. She wrote *The High Cost of Dying*. We just took it a little further."

Joe stepped to the microphone to perform his best-known lead, *The Last Thing on My Mind*.

"Are you going away with no word of farewell?. . ."

The Last Thing on My Mind
—Tom Paxton

1964

Though Chad's cycle of anger and guilt churned on, his decision to leave ultimately centered on his dedication to The Trio's excellence. Audiences' delight in their concerts came from a unique combination of musical virtuosity, a balance of humor and poignance, and the clever choreography underscoring the presentation.

One day in mid-1964, to Chad's horror, he found himself "stepping back from the microphone," leaving Mike and Joe to carry the performance.

Fifty years later, Mike expressed surprise at Chad's revelation.

"I never saw that," Mike said to Chad. "In both rehearsal and performance, I've never seen you behave in anything but a completely professional fashion."

So, while Chad's withdrawal might have played out mostly in his mind, he felt he had compromised The Trio. Regardless of his dissatisfaction and an aloofness he'd constructed as a shield, Chad remained intensely proud of what The Trio had accomplished.

This group, these people, he realized, *mean more to me than this. I can't allow myself to do anything to ruin it.*

He gathered Mike, Joe, Milt and the musicians and announced his decision. Mindful of Mike Pugh's abrupt departure, he wanted to give plenty of warning. Mike's recollection is that Chad gave them a year's notice. Chad thinks the span was more like six months. In any case, he knew Mike wanted and needed to continue, as did Joe. Chad would do his best to make the transition seamless.

"Let me know," he said, "when you've found a replacement. You'll need time to rehearse, bring him up to speed."

To ease the transition, Chad agreed Mike could use the Mitchell Trio name so long as Mike or Joe were members of the group.

CHICAGO
JULY 1965

Chad had expected to feel relief. In truth, as he walked a long path to the dressing rooms, he wasn't sure what he felt. As had become his custom, he'd fled the stage quickly, hoping not to cross paths with Mike.

They had retreated to a quiet animosity, had become nodding acquaintances offstage, each in his own way looking forward to this ending. Each, though, feeling an unsettling uncertainty. The final concert was a single evening's booking at Chicago's Ravinia Pavilion, an outdoor venue in which The Trio performed under the stars on a perfect July evening.

As they trotted, smiling and waving, from the spotlight after their final encore, they'd faced each other during an awkward moment. Chad could not bring himself to just turn and go. Neither, it seemed, could Mike.

Mike extended his hand. Chad took it. Mike pulled him into a brief hug, a quick pat on the back. Then a nod.

"A handshake and a hug," Mike recalls. "Then twenty years of silence between us."

Joe, who had made it a practice not to engage in this quiet battle, looked on from a careful distance.

When Mike turned to Joe, Chad made his escape.

As he walked alone to the dressing room, lost deep in a fearful "what now?" Chad realized Mike was speaking to the crowd.

"Many of you may not be aware . . . ," the sound system echoed through the night. Some had risen, starting their journey to the parking lot. Most, though, as crowds tended to do, kept their seats on the vast lawn, hoping for one more song. Those retreating were arrested by Mike's voice. ". . . that tonight was Chad's final performance with The Mitchell Trio."

Chad stopped. He hadn't wanted his departure to be a big deal, hadn't wanted the audience distracted from the music.

"The Trio, however, will continue, and I'd like you to meet the young man who will join us. Please welcome, if you will, John Denver."

Chad heard applause as, he assumed, this Denver fellow had come onto the stage.

Chad knew, of course, that Mike, Joe and Milt were looking for a replacement. They'd listened to some 200 audition tapes. But he had not been involved. He made a point to know nothing about it.

He was vaguely aware they'd been rehearsing with the new guy. The Trio had a favorite little night spot called *Mother Blues* in Chicago where they sometimes took the stage when called from the audience to do a number. And someone had let Chad know they'd done two or three songs there a few nights ago with the new guy.

He'd heard a funny story, in fact, about Joe explaining that Chad would be leaving and adding, "I'd like to introduce you to the new member of The Mitchell Trio. Ladies and gentlemen, here's Bob Denver."

Oh my God, Chad thought to himself when he heard the story, *they've hired Gilligan.*

Chad didn't wait to hear any more. He trotted to the dressing room, grabbed his keys, and roared away in the Porsche.

Scared to death.

He hadn't a clue how to proceed from here.

The Trio, though, didn't miss a beat.

Mike, who had always been the behind-the-scenes de facto leader—the responsible, steady one—now wore an undisputed mantle of control.

The group picked up its hectic college concert tour to find crowds growing smaller, not because The Trio's quality of performance suffered, but because the Beatles had arrived. Their brand of rock & roll would sweep aside the folk era.

PART TWO

1965–1986

— CHAPTER SEVENTEEN —

*"I know that to this day Mike believes I formulated
a plan to go out on my own and have a solo career.
But I never had a plan. I haven't had a plan most of my life.
The only time I made a plan, I ended up in prison."*

—Chad Mitchell

Here's the difference.

Chad Mitchell is a man to whom life happens. Mike Kobluk is a man who makes plans.

Chad never needed a plan. His looks, his talent, his personality—a gift of charisma—created opportunities, and he almost always found a way to make the most of them.

Both Joe Frazier and John Denver pursued membership in The Trio. For Chad and Mike, The Trio just happened.

Along the way, they met two men—Milt Okun and Frank Fried—who gained enormous influence over their enterprise. Had those two chosen common goals, things might have been different. But their visions and their personalities clashed. Okun believed Fried doomed The Trio because he thought Chad's talent eclipsed the others. Milt thought Frank saw dollar signs in the management of Chad as a solo performer and actor. Frank thought Milt was greedy and conflicted for taking on other groups while directing The Trio.

Ironically, a member of The Trio would, indeed, make one of these two rivals a multi-millionaire and a huge force in the music industry. But it wasn't Chad, and it wasn't Frank.

Frank Fried would have a successful career as concert promoter and liberal crusader. Milt Okun would form a long-standing association with John Denver and create Cherry Lane Music, among the most successful music publishers in history.

Following that night when Chad drove away in his Porsche, the fundamental differences between Mike Kobluk and Chad Mitchell played out in dramatic fashion.

During the next three years, Mike recognized the music industry was moving in a direction The Trio couldn't follow. He formed a company to provide income for his growing family when The Trio came to an end. He sold that company, went back to Gonzaga and finished his degree. He went to work for The World's Fair, Expo '74, as Director of Performing and Visual Arts. That evolved into a career managing Spokane's entertainment facilities—a job from which he would retire some thirty years later.

While Mike walked a careful path to his future, Chad's departure was more like a leap off a high ledge, counting once again on circumstance to provide him a safe landing.

He landed in Mexico.

A few months before he joined The Trio, Henry John Deutschendorf had been told by Randy Sparks of the New Christy Minstrels, "You better do something about that last name. It'll never fit on a marquee."

Mike, Joe and Milt had been on the lookout for Chad's replacement for months, and they hadn't really come up with anyone they liked until Mike Kirkland contacted Milt about a young man performing in a Phoenix club called The Lumbermill. Kirkland had left the Brothers Four and moved to Phoenix for health reasons.

Kirkland's recommendation was so glowing, Mike and Joe flew to Phoenix to hear twenty-one-year-old Deutschendorf, the son of a career U.S. Air Force pilot.

They listened to his set, liked his singing and competence as a guitarist. They were more impressed, though, with his exuberance, his complete comfort on stage, and a naïve sort of sincerity pulling the audience into his act.

During a break, they introduced themselves and explained their mission.

"Your name is quite a mouthful," Mike noted.

"Don't worry about that. I'm calling myself John Denver now."

They asked about his career goals.

He grinned and, with neither hesitation nor apology, said, "I'm gonna be bigger than Frank Sinatra. And I'm gonna own a jet airplane and hire my to be my pilot."

Mike told him, "If you're interested, we'd like to bring you to New York for a week. We'll introduce you to our musical director, work on some songs, and see how it goes."

John accepted immediately. After a week's rehearsals, Milt, Mike and Joe remained uncertain. They sent John back to Phoenix so they could think about it and promised to give him a call. The issue, according to Mike, was what had kept Tom Paxton out of the group a few years earlier—vocal blend.

"John had a great voice," Mike said, "but it wasn't a great choral voice," and The Mitchell Trio was a choir.

His range might have matched Chad's, but he couldn't compete with Chad's vocal power or depth.

The blend, Mike says, was not bad—just different.

Chad's physical appearance and demeanor—conveying a youthful, freshly-scrubbed naiveté—was trumped ten times over by John Denver. Chad's dual nature of innocence and flawed human being were both authentic. The complexity of this contradiction made him a full-dimensional stage presence, which, in the context of The Trio, John didn't match.

John was every bit the naïve, bubbly junior partner he appeared to be, and that vanilla image would plague him throughout his storied career.

Finally, John was an accomplished guitarist, particularly adept at the twelve-string. How would his guitar be worked into the act? The Trio had initially been rejected by folk purists, partly because they didn't play instruments. They'd deftly turned that to their advantage, though, creating a stage presence the lack of instruments afforded.

John later said he'd returned to Phoenix thinking he'd failed.

"I sat around waiting for their phone call," John told an interviewer. "I mean I didn't leave the motel at all except to go to the Lumbermill to work at night."

After three days of debate, Mike, Joe and Milt decided positives outweighed negatives. They offered John the job.

During Chad's final weeks, Mike and Joe were rehearsing with John at every opportunity. The owner of *Mother Blues* allowed them to perform with John before small audiences.

"We introduced John that first night as the person who would be replacing Chad," Mike said. "So, John goes up, with Joe and me sitting in the audience, and starts playing his guitar. He was so excited he got carried away and broke a string. Well, he didn't have a replacement guitar, so he's stuck. He reaches into his case and starts putting on a new string.

"Everybody knows this will take some time. But, as he's working on the string, John starts telling stories. And the audience is completely engaged. When he finally got his guitar strung and retuned, the audience gave him a standing ovation. And he hadn't even sung a note yet."

———

When the reconstituted Mitchell Trio made its debut two weeks following Chad's departure, Mike had been performing several times a week for almost six years. Material, harmonies, stage presentation, travel all came naturally as breathing. He couldn't remember the last time he'd been nervous before a show.

He was nervous for this one.

Milt Okun assured Mike, Joe and the musicians that The Trio, featuring John Denver, could thrive. The issue remained, though. How would their fans receive a different sound?

Both sound and presentation *were* different.

On several songs, the choreography changed because John played his twelve-string. Where Chad's gestures, eye movements and reactions were nuanced, John played the role more broadly, as if trying *too* hard.

The best-side-by-side comparison are videos of *The John Birch Society*—a song so popular among their audiences that The Trio couldn't set it aside when Chad left. Musically, *John Birch* emphasized the difference in John's and Chad's voices. John's voice was made for ballads. It didn't have the strength to soar above the others as Chad's could.

They had a little more than a week to prepare for their debut at *The*

Cellar Door in Washington, D.C. Fortunately, Mike recalls, John was a quick study. "He could listen to a song once or twice and know it."

Mike chose *The Cellar Door* because The Trio had played there several times and enjoyed a popular, neighborhood following. So, he expected their audience to be kind. He wasn't sure of the critics.

Following that inaugural performance, Mike had trouble sleeping as he anticipated the morning papers.

Don Hearn of the Washington Daily News wrote:

The Cellar Door has a winner in The Mitchell Trio

This may come as a surprise to followers of this famed folk group now that Chad Mitchell is on his own and, of course, no longer part of the threesome.

Frankly, his absence doesn't bother me.

He's been replaced with an immense talent. Namely, John Denver, who has been with the other members—Mike Kobluk and Joe Frazier—for only a couple of weeks.

After catching this group the other night, I'd say Mr. Denver is a "find." He fits this niche superbly . . .

The Mitchells are supported by seasoned and expert Jacob Ander (guitar) and Paul Prestopino (banjo and mandolin). Happily, everyone concerned will be around through Saturday.

What's more, you're not going to miss Chad.

Another critic wrote:

Usually when a member of a famous folk singing group leaves, the remaining singers fall on collective hard times. But not so with The Mitchell Trio now that Chad Mitchell is on his own.

In fact, John Denver, who has been with The Trio for only thirteen days, fits in quite well. I think he even has a better voice than Mitchell.

The Trio debuted several new songs. They'd put *The Twelve Days of Christmas* to rest, but maintained their satirical assault on neo-Nazism with Norman Martin's brilliant *I Vuz Not a Nazi Polka:*

> *". . . I never shot a Luger, or goosed a single step,*
> *Sing I was not a Nazi Polka . . ."*

They added *That's the Way It's Gonna' Be* by Bob Gibson and Phil Ochs. John sang the lead in a funny spoof on the popular *Long Tall Texan*. And they did a satire on Lyndon Johnson's foreign policy called *Lucy Baines*.

Johnson, whom The Trio had championed with *Barry's Boys* a couple of years earlier, was deep into dismantling his domestic legacy as he waged the Vietnam War.

The critical consensus seemed to be that The Mitchell Trio was different. Different, however, did not imply better or worse. Critics still loved The Trio.

Most of them anyway.

They ran into outspoken disapproval at their next venue.

The Trio went from Washington, D.C., to a nightclub on Huntington Beach in Los Angeles where they shared the bill for two weeks with José Feliciano. Suffering blindness, Feliciano was accompanied on stage and off by his guide dog.

The new trio's funniest and most profound bit of satire, the *I Vuz Not a Nazi Polka*, offered a scathing criticism of Germany's neo-Nazi movement. By 1965, that movement had been toned down, but Mike and Joe still felt strongly that history should not be allowed to paint the German people's willingness to accept Adolph Hitler and the Nazi movement in a softer light.

That first night at Huntington Beach, The Trio struck up the *Polka* and Feliciano's guide dog, back-stage in a dressing room, began to howl. As they continued, the howls were punctuated by fits of barking.

Mike, Joe and John were startled by the ruckus, but pushed ahead without missing a beat.

"Gee, I'm sorry guys," Feliciano said as The Trio hustled off stage, "I've never heard him do that before. He's around music all the time, and he really doesn't pay much attention. I'm sure it won't happen again."

The next night, throughout The Trio's performance, Feliciano's dog remained silent, until the *Polka*. Again, an otherwise perfectly behaved guide dog came unglued. Without the element of surprise, though, Mike noticed the audience's laughter.

When a distraught Feliciano offered to remove his dog before the song came up in the program, Mike told him not to worry about it.

"The audience thinks it's funny." he said, "We'll work it into the act."

The song's introduction came to include a warning that some critics did not care for the number's point of view. And not once during the two weeks did Feliciano's dog fail them.

"Being blind and all," Joe asked Mike one night, "do you think Jose might not fully appreciate the irony?"

"Oh, I'm pretty sure," Mike said, "he knows his dog is a German Shepherd."

From Huntington Beach, The Trio jumped back into the college campus grind—four and five performances a week, constant rehearsal, airplanes and buses. John settled in, and like Chad before him, the enormity of his talent brought him to the forefront on stage. In John's case, though, Mike bore no resentment. Mike wanted The Trio's success. He'd understood all along that Chad's talent was critical to that success. He was glad for John to take up that role, because John was thrilled to be a member of The Mitchell Trio.

The differences between Chad and John made touring more pleasant. During the months of Chad's discontent, after rehearsal or performance, they went their separate ways. When concerts ended, Chad's discomfort with fan adulation forced him to flee, leaving Mike and Joe to sign autographs, pose for photos and listen to student after student offer thanks for awakening their social conscience.

John, though, couldn't get enough. He loved time with the fans. Sometimes, when the bulk of the crowd had gone and only a few diehards lingered, he'd reward them by grabbing his guitar, sitting on the edge of the stage, and inviting them to sing with him.

Concert after-parties, which had been an obligatory appearance, became celebrations to which Mike looked forward. John and Paul Prestopino took their instruments along, and sometimes revelers sang until the dawn.

John maintained these traits even at the height of his fame. Several years later, John and his entourage of backup singers and musicians played a concert date at tiny Eastern New Mexico University. The venue was the university's basketball arena, and one student there had learned a trick of sneaking into obscure seats at the rear of the building so he could listen to the concert artist's sound check.

The student and his younger brother were not only talented singers and musicians themselves, but were huge John Denver fans. They sat slumped in their seats as they listened to tuning of instruments and balancing of mics and amplifiers. John and the band sang snippets of a few songs before going into *Take Me Home Country Roads*. The two fans couldn't contain themselves and joined in on the harmonies. When the band abruptly stopped, the outlaw singers continued for a couple of beats.

John shielded his eyes, peered into the stands and called, "Who's out there?"

The two rose and started to make their escape.

"No," John said. "You guys come on up here."

When they arrived, sheepish, at the stage, John asked, "Do you guys know any more of my songs?"

They said they did.

John ushered them onto the stage and together, they sang for almost an hour.

In October, The Trio staged another Carnegie Hall performance. For Mike, the New York audience's enthusiastic reception of a new Mitchell Trio was final validation. While college students clearly still loved The Trio, Mike sometimes worried the on-campus response was bent more to The Trio's message than to excellence of the music. Carnegie Hall's concert-goers represented an older, more sophisticated crowd.

One member of the audience offered a reassurance that touched Mike more deeply than any other.

Exhausted as usual after a show, he sat before a lighted mirror in his backstage dressing cubicle when Joe poked his head inside.

"Guess who was here tonight?" Joe asked.

Mike didn't care to guess, just shrugged into the mirror.

After a moment of silence, Joe said, "Chad."

Mike turned in his chair, not sure he'd heard correctly. "What did you say?"

"I was talking with some people after the show, and I saw him. He waved, and turned to go, but I jumped down and caught up to him. I asked him to come backstage, but he wouldn't."

"Did he have anything to say?" Mike asked.

"Yeah. He said we were really good. And he meant it."

———— ∿ ————

During the twelve months from July 1965 to July 1966, the new Trio hit its stride. They released *That's the Way It's Gonne Be* early in 1966. For the first time, neither Milt Okun nor any members of The Trio had written or adapted any of the dozen songs. John Denver had yet to try his hand at songwriting.

Clearly, the title song written by Bob Gibson and Phil Ochs, along with a cover of Bob Dylan's *Mr. Tambourine Man,* and *Get Together* by Chet Powers—a song that would become a huge hit for the Yardbirds a year later—showed The Trio drifting toward folk-rock.

Ian Tyson's *Song for Canada* and Shel Silverstein's *Three-Legged Man,* along with *I Vuz Not a Nazi Polka* were true to The Trio's roots. At least one of the Mitchell Trio songs, though, would not have made it onto a Chad Mitchell Trio recording or performance.

The Trio's decision to do any given song had to be unanimous. A few songs fell out of favor as society's threshold of political correctness evolved. One of Tom Paxton's funniest songs recorded on the *Typical American Boys* album—*The Natural Girl for Me*—was written during the Twiggy era and bewailed a chic trend of anorexic models who set standards for fashion that countered a free and natural female hippie style:

> *". . . Show me a pretty little number,*
> *When she walks, she rolls like thunder . . ."*

The 1980's, though, represented a more enlightened era. When The Trio began performing again, one of the musician's daughters objected to *Natural Girl* as offensive to LGBT sensitivities. Chad sympathized, and *Natural Girl* fell by the wayside.

The song that wouldn't have gotten past Chad in 1966 was the satire on Lyndon Johnson's foreign policy aimed at daughter Lucy Baines Johnson, written by Howard Liebling and Marvin Hamlisch. Chad agreed with several critics who called *Lucy Baines* a cheap shot.

"Why make fun of Lucy Baines?" Chad asked. "We met her when we visited the White House. I wouldn't have agreed to that song."

Another song on *That's the Way It's Gonna Be* got The Trio in trouble when a production crew on a daytime television show didn't pay enough attention to The Trio's rehearsal.

The Mike Douglas Show, produced in Philadelphia, was popular afternoon fare syndicated nationally from 1961 to 1982. Tape of the show was distributed to markets throughout the country for re-airing but was presented before a live Philadelphia audience.

The Trio appeared several times on Mike Douglas, but its first appearance late in 1965 was almost its last.

They now took for granted that their most cutting satire would be disallowed for television, so they'd gotten into a routine of singing one of their controversial numbers—like *John Birch* or *Johnnie* or *The Draft Dodger Rag* during rehearsal and watching the director go a little pale as he told them, "You can't sing that song on television."

So, for their rehearsal number for the first Mike Douglas appearance, they sang *The Ecumenical March*, written by Robert Ascher and Patricia Eliran. They waited for someone to rush over in a panic and warn them off.

No one seemed to care, though.

"Do you think we should really do it?" John asked Mike. Mike was the cautious one. John knew what Joe's answer would be. But they all had to agree.

"Well," Mike said with a shrug, "they didn't tell us not to."

Ecumenical March had been inspired by a much-publicized world-wide Ecumenical Council influenced by a liberal Catholic movement under the direction of Pope John XXIII. One action of the Council was an absolution of Jews for the crucifixion of Christ.

The song opens with The Trio singing *Hava Nagila*. John speaks over the music: *"Did you read the newspaper? The Vatican has decided, us Jews didn't kill Jesus.*

Mike Douglas could only look on with stunned silence as phones began to ring. The Trio managed to piss off both Catholic and Jew, along with any number of Protestants outraged that their ecumenical brethren were being berated.

The song ends as John asks, *"Well, wait a minute? If we didn't kill Him, who did?"*

Joe shrugs a question, *"The Puerto Ricans?"*

While reaction was overwhelmingly negative, television producers generally subscribe to the tenant that any publicity is good publicity—so long as you don't chase away sponsors. So, Douglas invited The Trio to return on January 20, 1966, and explain themselves.

Douglas's co-host that day was David Frost, who certainly understood satire. From 1962 through 1964 Frost hosted the smart and caustic *That Was the Week That Was,* a British television show enormously popular in the United States. TW3, as it was known, lampooned both British and American politics and society.

The Trio opened with the title song from the *That's the Way it's Gonna Be*. Then Douglas waved them to the interview set.

"Normally we don't bring groups over here to talk," Douglas said, "but the last time you were on our show, you did some satirical material, and we had a lot of reaction—all of it negative. Why do you do this kind of material? Where do you draw the line? How are you sure you're not offending people when you do these things?"

Both Joe and John offered rambling explanations before Mike said, "In doing this type of material, we know there are people who will disagree with us. We're stating our point of view, and it's not always a popular point of view. But we feel there are people, organizations and ideas in our society that deserve to be laughed at."

Joe said they'd performed Ecumenical March at Catholic schools, including Philadelphia's St. Joseph's College, a Jesuit institution. He said the priests, who have an intellectual understanding of satire, loved the song.

"I think," said Frost, "very often people who object to your songs do so not on behalf of themselves, but on behalf of other people. 'Of course, I understand what you're doing, but while you're doing it, you're not being very kind to Roman Catholics.'"

Joe compared The Trio's choice of songs to the burgeoning folk-rock movement, which abandoned folk music's social conscience for the profits of rock and roll. "But we're singing the same type of satire we've always performed, even though in the beginning we were cautioned not to by our record companies and our managers."

Joe suggested that a reason *The Ecumenical March* had gotten such a negative reaction from Douglas's television audience was, because on television, they didn't have an opportunity to 'set up' the song with the kind of explanatory preamble they'd provide in a concert.

Douglas asked them to do a segment of *The John Birch Society*—only the second time that song would be heard by a television audience—and wondered how they would set it up for a concert audience.

"It needs no setup," Joe said. "We're not concerned about offending the John Birch Society at all."

Next, Douglas asked them to sing a verse from *The Draft Dodger Rag*, another song that would otherwise be hidden from television viewers until Tom and Dick Smothers performed it with George Segal a couple of years later on *The Smothers Brothers Comedy Hour*, but even they sanitized some of the lyrics.

Finally, Douglas asked them to sing their newest song, *Your Friendly, Liberal Neighborhood Ku Klux Klan*, written by one of their most prolific contributors, June Reizner. And the set up?

"We feel the KKK is an immoral organization developed on hate," Mike said. "We feel it shouldn't be a part of American society."

— CHAPTER EIGHTEEN —

". . . Some rebels are commercial, some are not
Some rebels make a million, some get shot . . ."

The Sound of Protest Has Begun to Pay
—Fred Hellerman

The Joe, John and Mike version of The Mitchell Trio would record two albums in 1966. *That's the Way It's Gonna Be* was followed by *Violets of Dawn.* The title songs were two more steps in the direction of folk-rock. But the original Trio style remained alive in Fred Neil's *Another Side of This Life,* and three Paxton songs: *We Didn't Know, One Time and One Time Only*, and *Talking Football.* The album included Joe's solo *Business Goes on as Usual,* The Trio's most powerful anti-war statement since *Johnnie,* as well as Reizner's *Your Friendly, Liberal Neighborhood Ku Klux Klan.*

The album showcased John's first songwriting effort, *For Bobbi.* And finally, a song written by The Weaver's Fred Hellerman as a satire on the folk-rock movement, *The Sound of Protest Has Begun to Pay.*

The Trio directed Hellerman's satire more specifically, aiming at their old friend, Roger McGuinn, who was now on top of all the charts with The Byrds. The Trio's arrangement, with John Denver's guitar, perfectly mimics the Byrd's 12-string electric sound.

"I'm not sure," Mike said with a chuckle, "that Fred appreciated our adaptation of his song."

The third and final Mitchell Trio album, *The Mitchell Trio Alive,* was recorded in 1967. It did not, however, include Joe Frazier.

—⁓—

DUKE UNIVERSITY
July 1967

Anger churning, Mike stood at the entrance to a tent serving as his dressing room as he peered at rows and rows of students, who sat waiting on folding chairs along a vast green expanse of lawn at Duke University.

Joe had missed the flight from Chicago. Mike could only hope he'd made other travel arrangements.

To some extent, sixties concert crowds had become accustomed to being abused by artists' lack of punctuality. Peter, Paul and Mary were notorious for late arrivals on stage. For some rock bands, making their audience wait seemed a banner of distinction.

Not The Mitchell Trio. Not when Mike was in charge.

They'd canceled a concert a few weeks earlier. The promoters were not happy, but an excuse about a trio member falling ill was accepted. The Trio was not paid. But the fallout had been managed.

That scenario wouldn't play a second time, though. Certainly not at a venue like Duke. University booking agencies communicated with each other. This failure would damage The Trio's reputation and could cost them future bookings.

Almost an hour into the delay, Mike turned to John. "I'll tell the musicians we're done. Can you bring your guitar and see if we can't placate the crowd a little before we send them home?"

Mike confronted the patrons on a beautiful Carolina summer evening. A surge of applause greeted him as his audience thought its wait was over. Their happy response quickly died, though, as people understood what was happening.

"I'm sorry," Mike said to an odd silence. There would be no makeshift excuse tonight. "Unfortunately, we have to cancel our show this evening because one of The Trio members has not arrived. Your admission fee will be refunded. Before you go, though, let me introduce the newest member of The Mitchell Trio, a talented young man who would like to sing a few songs for you. John Denver."

Most of the audience began their exit as John bounded onto the stage.

As initial chords rang from John's guitar, Mike heard the drone of a small plane passing overhead.

Almost everyone had left when Joe came running toward the stage.

"I... I'm sorry..." he said as he attempted to catch his breath. "I chartered a private plane..."

Mike said nothing, just turned and walked away.

Joe had always been The Trio's liberal firebrand. Chad described him as the "social butterfly" of the three. "Mike was like a father," Chad said, "the adult. Even though we were all the same age, Mike just seemed older, more mature."

Neither Mike nor Chad nor John came to The Trio with a political or social agenda. Joe was all about social and political causes.

"I remember telling my father on my 28th birthday," Joe explained for The Chad Mitchell Trio website, "that I was *never going to work like you do* as his dad was leaving for his job as a welder in a Philadelphia steel mill."

Unable to afford college, Joe enlisted in the U.S. Air Force to qualify for the GI Bill.

"Within a few months I was singing with the chorus at Sampson Air Force Base in New York and, after an audition," Joe told his website biographer, "I was scheduled to join the *Singing Sergeants* in Washington, D.C. It never happened. I soon found out that the OSI—the military FBI— was investigating me because of my political opinions and I ended up in the stockade, where I was incarcerated and intensely questioned for three months. Apparently, reading the 'wrong books,' listening to Pete Seeger, and talking about it were frowned upon. Military prisons were then (and still are) not very nice places. If I wasn't a radical when I went in, I was certainly one when I left."

Labeled a security risk, Joe was offered an honorable discharge, along with eligibility for the GI Bill.

Joe met his wife Charlotte at Lebanon Valley College and followed her to New York where she found work as a singer and dancer in Broadway choruses. Joining The Trio was a godsend for him.

Although The Trio's most outgoing member, Joe revealed little of his personal life. Neither Chad nor Mike can remember when he and Charlotte divorced. Their assumption is that with two demanding schedules, the couple drifted apart. As the rift between Mike and Chad played itself out, Joe did his best to maintain a cordial relationship with everyone. At times, as in the Bertha Case-Frank Fried argument, he was forced to take one side over the other. He did so reluctantly.

Even after Jim McGuinn left The Trio, Joe maintained a relationship, smoking pot with McGuinn and other stars of the emerging folk-rock scene at Jim's house in Laurel Canyon.

Soon after Chad's departure from The Trio, Joe invited Chad to join him on an LSD trip at a time when the hallucinogen was still legal.

"I don't think I'd even tried marijuana yet," Chad said.

They met at Chad's New York apartment. They recruited a mutual woman friend named Nancy to be their *guide*—to make sure they didn't jump out of any windows or murder anyone.

"Joe and I really connected that evening," Chad said. "We talked and talked and talked. Finally, Nancy got bored and went home."

Joe also maintained a relationship with John Denver. He told friends stories of visiting John in Colorado and flying in his biplane.

Joe's struggle, though, Mike believes, was not with grass, LSD or hard drugs. Mike believes he became addicted to amphetamines.

"With our pace," Mike said, "we were sometimes so tired before a concert that we had to take something." Mike remembers a pill called eskatrol that gave him the boost he needed to get through a performance.

Amphetamines can significantly alter the brain's pleasure response, destroying pleasure receptors and decreasing the ability for the body to feel pleasure without using the drug. Normally taken by mouth in pill form, the drug can be snorted, injected, or smoked to get a more intense high. Experts say amphetamine addiction is extremely difficult to overcome.

Another factor in Joe's crisis, Mike and Chad believe, was an ongoing struggle with his sexual identity. Although he would joke occasionally with Chad about "being attracted to the boys," he was married to a beautiful woman. He was masculine in appearance and manner. He enjoyed flirting with female fans and, his colleagues assumed, he sometimes shared clandestine assignations with women he met on tour.

John Denver, in his biography *Take Me Home,* says, "... Joe got increasingly difficult to work with. He started wearing his hair like Prince Valiant and being gratuitously flamboyant, if not outright provocative."

When Joe entered their attorney's Chicago office following the Duke debacle, Mike could see in Joe's eyes that he knew what was coming.

"Guys, I'm so sorry. I'll..."

Mike raised a hand to cut him off. "We can't function this way, Joe. Being late for rehearsals is one thing. Forcing us to cancel concerts is another."

Joe's shoulders sagged. He placed his hands on a conference table, separating himself from the others, and stared at his feet. "I ... I know," he finally said. "I guess I'm a little surprised you've put up with it this long."

"What's going on?" John demanded in a tone that seemed to take Joe even further aback. John seldom expressed anger, but he did now.

Joe responded with a blank stare.

"We have to find a replacement," Mike said, reaching to offer a check. "This is what we can give you for your share of the partnership."

The amount was $10,000, a hefty sum in 1967. Joe pocketed his check without looking at it. Mike read desperation in Joe's face.

"I ... I ..." Joe began but choked on his emotions.

He turned and walked away.

The period between July of 1967 and January 1970 is a blank space in Joe Frazier's history. He told one interviewer he was "into marijuana." The only thing Joe ever said to Mike about those missing years is, "I hit rock bottom."

He spent some of the time with acquaintances from the California folk scene, probably including Roger McGuinn and Barry McGuire. At some point he made his way to the East Coast, where he was introduced into a group of writers and artists who were on their way to becoming leading voices among an emerging gay intelligentsia in American society.

At that lowest point of his life, he found himself in Key West, Florida in the company of James Herlihy and Tennessee Williams. Williams, one of America's greatest playwrights, was deep into his own struggle with alcohol and drugs.

Herlihy, another enormous literary talent, regarded Williams as a mentor.

Herlihy was on top of his game. The adaptation of his novel *Midnight Cowboy* had been named best picture of 1968 by the Motion Picture Academy Association. His other works included the play and subsequent movie *Blue Denim*, *All Fall Down* and *Season of the Witch*.

By 1968, Herlihy had become a passionate opponent of the Vietnam War, so he certainly would have known of The Mitchell Trio. Whatever the circumstances of their meeting, Herlihy's adoption of a down-and-out singer struggling with drugs, religious faith and sexual identity is certainly plausible.

Herlihy lived a hedonistic existence in his Key West enclave, but Chad believes Herlihy is also the man who steered Joe back to the foundations of his faith. Williams also may have played a role. While Williams' father ridiculed his young son for his effeminacy, the boy found love and acceptance from his maternal grandfather, the Reverend Walter Dakin, an Episcopal priest.

Despite the demons plaguing both Herlihy and Williams, they saw something in Joe that made them suggest he consider studying theology. Through their connections, they found someone who had the influence to engineer Joe's acceptance into the School of Divinity at Yale University in 1970.

He was ordained to the diaconate in 1972, and to the priesthood on January 13, 1973. He spent a year with a monastic order—the Society of St. John the Evangelist—in Cambridge, Massachusetts, before taking a position at the Cathedral of St. John in Wilmington, Delaware.

Of this tumultuous time, Joe told interviewer Doug Bight that Mike and John's decision to fire him was the best thing that could have happened.

"My mind (was) sort of falling apart," Joe said, "so I turned back to my religion, and immediately people came into my life. I'm grateful, since then I was forced into a change which led me . . . to the Episcopal priesthood."

The Episcopal Church allowed Joe his role as liberal crusader. He described himself as "the radical priest who comes to get you released" that Paul Simon sings about in *Me and Julio Down by the Schoolyard*.

"If you are going to apply what you believe, in terms of your spirituality, to what goes on in life and what goes on in the world," Joe said in an interview recorded during The Trio's reunion years, "you are required to work for justice, to work for peace, to work to better the way of life of people everywhere."

Joe told Chad of Herlihy's advice to him: "Beware of the pygmies. Small-minded people will eat you up."

Joe remained close to Herlihy throughout the troubled writer's life. Joe and his life partner, John Tveit, lived in Herlihy's California home at times during the eighties and nineties, and remained there for a time after Herlihy's 1993 suicide.

———— ✳ ————

With Joe's dismissal, Mike and John had to move quickly to find a replacement. After the loss of income from the Duke fiasco, they could not afford to cancel more dates. John suggested a Texas singer-guitarist named David Boise, whose enthusiasm and personality were similar to John's.

Boise's assimilation was more seamless than John's, according to Mike, because his voice was closer to Joe's than John's had been to Chad. After only a few days of rehearsal, The Trio headed to Columbus, Ohio, where they played a week-long booking at a small bistro. They traveled from there to Philadelphia to record what would be The Mitchell Trio's final album.

They recorded for Reprise Records, still working with Milt Okun as musical director.

The Mitchell Trio Alive! declared the album's cover, followed by an explanation in the cover notes:

Alive in a time when folk music is fast becoming passé, when the airwaves and concert halls are being flooded with the big beat, electronic sounds of rock-and-roll and rhythm and blues. Alive and living. Not content, as most, to drift off into the psychedelia of pot and LSD, but talking and doing, listening and speaking out about things that concern us as people and Americans.

As a performing group—both in concert and in albums— our first purpose is (and always will be) to entertain. But we feel it isn't necessary to limit ourselves to love ballads and nonsense ditties in order to fulfill this obligation. We can include in our show songs of a little more substance, songs that need to be listened to a little more intently, and still have an entertaining program.

One of the finest Americans the world has ever known once said, "There are three things in life that concern us as human beings: Life, Death and Laughter. We have no control over the first two so we must do what we can with the third." This, then, is our aim, to do what we can with the third.

If, by including in our program both social and political satire, we can entertain you and make you laugh, our first purpose is accomplished. If we can also present a point of view common to the younger generation, good. And if we can be just a bit provocative and stimulating, so much the better. Though we may seem slightly irreverent in our attitude, in what we do and by what we say, as long as we can continue with this unique idea of entertainment, The Mitchell Trio will be very much alive for a long time to come.

In a sense, that lengthy explanation of purpose is an admission of defeat. Sort of like having to explain a joke. For almost a decade, The Mitchell Trio had been entertaining, provocative, irreverent, satirical while offering meaningful commentary on American society and politics. They had done so at a level of musical excellence unmatched during the folk era.

They'd never previously felt a need to explain themselves.

Ironically, they answered their own question.

The Mitchell Trio didn't survive much longer.

The *Alive* album certainly had its moments. It opened with a spoken parody of a White House staff person trying to teach Lyndon Johnson how to properly pronounce the word Negro—a skit that would surely not survive the political correctness standards of its era—then jumped into the prescient *What This Country Really Needs is Another Movie Star* by June Reizner. It included satires on Congressman Adam Clayton Powell and Alabama pseudo-governor Lurleen Wallace, along with a brief theological commentary called *God is Dead*, in which guitarist Paul Prestopino—after years of accompanying The Trio in silence—finally was assigned a lyric: "No, I'm not!"

The traditional *Coal Tattoo* is the only cut genuinely representative of The Trio's folk roots.

John Denver's second and third attempts at songwriting made the album. One, *I Like to Deal with the Ladies*, is forgettable. The other, Oh Babe, I Hate to Go—renamed at Milt's suggestion *Leavin' on a Jet Plane*—became one more instance of a song The Trio recorded first that would become a mega-hit when Milt's other clients, Peter, Paul and Mary, got their hands on it. *Jet Plane* would be the foundation of Milt's relationship with John, and they would build on that foundation to become wealthy, powerful men within the music industry.

"In order to pay the bills, we had to be on the road ten months of the year. That meant Clare was home by herself with three small kids. I knew that just wasn't going to work."

—Mike Kobluk

While Chad's departure invigorated Mike's commitment to The Trio, it also posed an unsettling reality. The day would come when demands of a growing family would force a choice, and Mike knew what he would choose.

So, he began to think about constructing a landing spot.

As an employee of the Chicago booking agency to which The Trio was assigned, Tom Mallow handled most of The Trio's scheduling. Mallow had confided in Mike several times that he'd like to establish a company of his own.

"But it wouldn't be booking concert performers," Mallow said. "What I'd love to do is Broadway. Take Broadway shows on the road to second-tier cities like Memphis or Minneapolis or Des Moines or—"

"Spokane," Mike said. "Cities big enough to have quality performing venues, but not big enough to sustain major theater companies locally."

"Exactly," said Mallow.

"And no one's doing that now?"

"Not really."

"Well, why haven't you done it?" Mike asked.

Mallow confided he didn't have access to the financial resources needed to get his idea off the ground.

"What would it take?"

Mallow told him $50,000.

"If you had a backer," Mike said, "do you think you could put something together that would pay the investor and make a profit?"

"Absolutely," Mallow said.

Mindful of his resentment when Chad became Frank Fried's partner in Triangle Productions, Mike explained his plan to John and Joe, the latter still a member of The Trio at the time. "This company wouldn't have anything to do with The Trio," he assured them.

He invited them to join the partnership. He would put up $20,000 if they wanted to invest $15,000 each.

They passed. "I don't think," Mike said, "either Joe or John had $15,000 to spare."

So, Mike gave Tom Mallow a check for $50,000 and became fifty-one percent owner of American Theater Productions.

They called the shows bus and truck tours. The first production Mallow sent out was a play called *Absence of a Cello* starring Hans Conried. Two weeks of touring produced enough capital to pay the bills for six months.

After ATP produced two more tours with similar success, Mallow told Mike he wanted to move to New York.

"That's where the producers are," Mallow said. "Sure, I can make deals over the phone. But we'd be so much more successful if I dealt with them in person."

Mallow made the move, and, in 1967, Mike and Clare followed. They bought a house in Pound Ridge, New York. "That way," Mike said, "when The Trio had a couple of days off, I could go into the office and learn the business."

John, who had just married Annie Martel, leased Mike and Clare's Chicago apartment.

Mike and Clare had just celebrated their daughter Lydia's first birthday, and Clare was almost nine months pregnant. They planned to make the move, then return to Chicago so the baby could be delivered by Caesarian section.

"And that's when we found out there were two babies, not one," Mike said, "so Clare was grounded so she could incubate." They no longer had a home in Chicago, though, and with her doctors there, she stayed with neighbors next door to John and Annie for another month.

Mike took charge of one-year-old Lydia.

The Trio was booked into a nightclub the first evening Mike had Lydia on his own. David and John were surprised to see him appear with Lydia in her baby carrier.

"I couldn't find a sitter," he said.

A sympathetic bartender, the father of several, told Mike he'd watch Lydia during The Trio's set.

"Just park her here on the bar," he told Mike. "I'll look after her and everyone will get a kick out of it."

Mike wasn't sure what Clare would think about her daughter spending the evening in the care of a bartender, but Lydia was a hit among the nightclub crowd.

"He said she didn't fuss," Mike recalls, "and when she heard my voice coming over the speaker system, she laughed and smiled."

That nightclub performance was the first of a week on the road. Artie Mogul, who had replaced Frank Fried as The Trio's manager, and his wife took charge of Lydia when The Trio performed over the next few weeks.

Mike and Clare's identical twin sons, Justin and Gerald, were finally born on July 24 1967.

Mike's experience with Lydia made him acutely aware of his growing responsibilities as a father while, despite assertions on the *Alive* album liner notes, The Trio struggled to find a foothold in an evolving music landscape.

The only way to survive, Mike knew, was to embrace the change and hope to finally find the hit single that had eluded them for so long. *Violets of Dawn*, their next album, was a clear concession to folk rock. They released a single with *Dark Shadows and Empty Hallways* by Willett Enzel on one side, and John's *Stay with Me* on the other. They recorded a second single of John's *Take Me to Tomorrow*.

The versions of these songs are hardly recognizable as The Mitchell Trio.

They went so far as to hire an orchestra for the first time. As they worked on a single of John's *I Like to Deal with the Ladies*, Paul Prestopino observed, "This sounds like a song you'd sing in the shower."

Since *Ladies* is gimmicky anyway, Milt put together an arrangement with orchestration and shower sound effects and called it, *I Like to Deal with the Ladies, As Sung in the Shower by The Mitchell Trio Accompanied by a Twenty-Seven Piece Band.*

None of their attempts made headway on the charts.

Their college audiences grew smaller.

Late in 1968, Mike told John and David he was done. He told them he'd stay long enough for them to find a replacement and help get the new guy up to speed. They chose Michael Johnson, a veteran singer-songwriter on the folk scene.

Mike invited John, David and Michael to his home in Pound Ridge to rehearse and integrate Johnson into the group.

CHAPTER NINETEEN

*". . . You're paid to stop a bullet, that's a soldier's job they say
And so, you stop the bullet. Then they stop your pay.
Should I write a letter to my Congressman?*

*Each Congressman has two ends.
A sitting, and a thinking end.
And since his success depends on his seat
Why bother, friend . . ."*

Rhymes for the Irreverent
—E.Y. Harburg

**Spokane
October 2007**

"We had the privilege a long time ago to meet somebody else who was a fantastic lyricist," Joe told the Spokane Opera House audience. "His name was Yip Harburg. Now, you may not have heard of Yip Harburg—he was another one who was blacklisted— nevertheless, he wrote magnificent things like all the lyrics to *The Wizard of Oz, Somewhere Over the Rainbow, Brother Can You Spare a Dime?* He'd written this little book of poems he called *Rhymes for the Irreverent*. And he allowed us to take those poems and incorporate them into one of our albums. Very meaningful poems . . . Maybe the names have changed a little bit, but the issues have remained the same."

Chad and Mike each recited one of Harburg's brief ditties, leading to Joe's recitation as preface to *The Draft Dodger Rag*:

*"We've licked pneumonia and T.B.
and the plagues that used to mock us.*

*We've got the onus on the sun.
The smallpox cannot pock us.*

*We've found the antibodies to the staphylo streptococcus.
But, oh the universal curse from Vietnam to Korea.*

*The bug of bugs that bugs us still
and begs for panacea.*

Oh, who will find the antidote for Pentagonaria?"

———

Chad and Mike have both given thought to factors that thwarted The Trio's success while groups with lesser talent thrived.

Was the mistake Milt Okun's as Milt encouraged them toward controversial material—like *The Draft Dodger Rag* and *What Did You Learn in School*?

Was the villain Bob Bollard who, by choosing *Lizzie Borden* for their first KAPP album, set them on the path to *The John Birch Society,* a song that defined The Trio in concert but alienated most radio station executives? Bollard who then denied them *Blowin' In the Wind*, the singularity that might have changed everything?

Or did the priest commit the original sin by naming them The Chad Mitchell Trio?

Chad and Mike both believe the name became a root cause of their internal turmoil. It forced a publicly perceived status and responsibility on Chad which he did not want, and which Mike took pains to counter. It led to more bad feeling and confusion when they reduced the name to The Mitchell Trio in the months before Chad departed.

And finally, when Mike left, it created an ultimately insurmountable barrier for John Denver, David Boise and Michael Johnson.

"Why do we have to change the name?" John asked when he and Mike sorted through the details of his withdrawal.

"Our agreement with Chad," Mike said, "is that the group could continue to use the name only as long as one of the original members remained."

"But we'll need the name recognition to get bookings," John said.

Mike understood his concern. John made the same argument Mike had made years earlier when Milt Okun suggested they abandon The Chad Mitchell Trio for something that wasn't tied to one of the members.

"It would be like starting over," Mike had told Milt.

During the 1970's, John Denver attained the star status he'd predicted for himself when he told Mike in 1966 that he would be "bigger than Frank Sinatra." His fame as a singer, songwriter and actor prompted newspaper and magazine articles dissecting his roots, including his time with The Trio. Some stories suggested that Mike and John had not gotten along, and that Mike and Joe never appreciated John's talent.

Why else, one journalist wondered, would The Trio have refused to record *Leavin' on a Jet Plane*? The Trio, in fact, recorded two different versions of *Jet Plane*.

Another article charged that Mike had walked away, leaving The Trio with a $40,000 debt.

"That simply wasn't true," Mike says. "When I left, we had bills amounting to ten or eleven thousand dollars. John and I were the two partners, so half that debt belonged to each of us. I owed about $5,000, which The Trio forgave in exchange for my agreement that I wouldn't seek additional payment."

A 1975 interview with John touched on several of these points. Without quoting John directly, the writer said Mike and John had a "tense stage relationship" and that John suggested one of them should leave. Mike adamantly denies this. The interviewer also states that Chad sued the group to keep it from using The Mitchell Trio name.

Chad didn't sue anyone.

He and John had met once. Early in Chad's attempts at a solo career, he played a week at *The Bitter End*, coinciding with a Trio performance at a different New York venue. One evening, John came to Chad's show and sought Chad out during a break.

"We sat and had a drink," Chad said, "and he proceeded to critique my performance. He focused on one song in particular and made suggestions about how I should do it."

John was only a few months into his work with The Trio, and Chad was tempted to think *who are you to tell me how to sing*?

"But here was this young man, so enthusiastic and so completely sincere," Chad said, "I just couldn't be mad at him."

John called Chad in 1968 to ask him about continued use of The Mitchell Trio name and invited him to listen to the group rehearse.

"I'd known Michael Johnson for years," Chad said, "so I was glad to do it."

"Our agreement that when the last original Trio member left, the name left with him, was made for a good reason," Chad said. So long as one original member remained, he explained, the integrity of what The Trio stood for, along with musical direction and quality, would be protected. "The Mitchell Trio wouldn't become owned by some agent or manager, who would just use the name to do anything they wanted to."

Chad trusted that Milt wouldn't allow Denver, Boise and Johnson to violate that integrity, "But what if Milt was no longer involved?"

Frank Fried advised Chad he should enforce the agreement, because Chad Mitchell was attempting to establish himself as a solo performer. That task would be more difficult with the presence of another Mitchell entity.

"So, I went and listened to them, and I told them they were terrific," Chad said. "But I asked them why they wanted to be The Mitchell Trio. Why not be Denver, Boise and Johnson?"

Ultimately, Chad granted John permission to use the name for a limited time—long enough to get a few bookings and establish themselves with promoters. Soon, though, the group took the name Denver, Boise and Johnson and toured for almost a year.

They recorded only three songs, but two were gems. John's so-so *Take Me to Tomorrow* was the A side of a Reprise single. The B side was June

Reizner's final contribution to The Trio: *The '68 Nixon,* a smart and funny parody of Richard Nixon's efforts to reinvent himself as a man for all political seasons:

> *". . . The Reagan can ramble, the Rocky can race,*
> *But Dick can jump from left to right and not lose his place."*

Milt Okun produced an outstanding three-record set in 1968, *Something to Sing About,* including songs from most major folk acts. The Denver, Boise and Johnson contribution was Tom Paxton's clever Forest Lawn, a second Trio satire on the high cost of dying.

The record set also includes the Joe Frazier version of The Chad Mitchell Trio singing *The Battle Hymn of the Republic Brought Down to Date,* Mark Twain's devastating parody of Teddy Roosevelt's American imperialism in the wake of the Philippine-American War.

Although Milt's project was assembled in 1968, three years after Chad left, The Trio recorded the song years earlier. Mike recalls that Joe discovered the song. He is not sure why it lay dormant all those years. So, Chad sings on this recording, not John.

It represents Twain at his most controversial. In fact, the poem remained unpublished in Twain's lifetime and did not appear in print until 1958. Sung to the tune of *The Battle Hymn of the Republic,* the final verse goes:

> *. . . In sordid slime harmonious Greed was born in yonder ditch,*
> *With a longing in his bosom—and for others' goods an itch.*
> *As Christ died to make men holy, let men die to make us rich—*
> *Our god is marching on . . .*

> —Mark Twain

Whether the final incarnation of The Trio could have survived any longer under The Mitchell Trio name is questionable. The folk era was over. Before

1967 ended, John waved a white flag and laid The Trio to rest.

"That makes two favors I did for John Denver," Chad said. "The first was leaving The Trio so he could join."

By granting John only a couple of months' extension to use the Mitchell name, though, Chad said, "The biggest favor was forcing him to go out on his own."

~

Mike worked in the office of American Theater Productions as his company sent *Hello Dolly* and *Hair* on the road. Then he found himself touring again, away from family, acting as business manager for a two-week tour by Robert Goulet. He knew other road assignments would follow.

When he was home, the commute between Pound Ridge and the city took an hour and a half each way.

The whole point of leaving The Trio had been to focus on his role as husband and father. And on a morning in 1969, he walked into his office and sat down with Mallow.

"Tom, this situation isn't working for my family," Mike said. "I'm selling my share of the company and you certainly deserve a right of first refusal."

Tom appeared surprised for only a moment.

"What do want for your share?" he asked.

"I'd like to recover what I put into ATP, plus a modest profit."

"What's modest?"

Mike told him.

"Come by Tuesday," Tom said. "I'll have a check for you."

Mike took the twins, Gerry and Justin, to Spokane, leaving Clare to sell their home in Pound Ridge, then make the cross-country drive with daughter Lydia and their dog.

A decade earlier, on a whim, he'd accompanied Father Beaver, Chad Mitchell, Mike Pugh and Dennis Collins for a summer vacation in New York. He'd fully intended to return and finish school. He re-enrolled as a senior at Gonzaga in the fall of 1968, graduating with a BA in English literature and mathematics in 1969.

Now, he needed a job.

Artie Mogul, who became The Trio's business manager after Chad's departure, had moved to Los Angeles to become president of Bill Cosby's record company. When he left the East Coast, Mogul told Mike to look him up if he ever needed a job.

Mike called Mogul and was hired over the phone. Within a week, the Kobluks were headed for Beverly Hills where Mike's job was to develop new talent for the record label. They faced California sticker shock, though, when they began to look for houses. The only affordable homes in suitable family neighborhoods put Mike right back into a ninety-minute commute each way. After only six weeks in Los Angeles, they returned to Spokane where Mike was hired as director of alumni for Gonzaga.

The city of Spokane had embarked on a massive project to replace its downtown rail yards with an elegant park that would host a world's fair exposition in 1974. A world's fair certainly had to include entertainment. The redevelopment included a new 2,700-seat opera house and convention center, smaller entertainment venues throughout the site, and the nearby 7,500-seat Spokane Veterans Coliseum.

Mike had an impressive résumé. He'd been a touring entertainer himself. He'd owned a nationally recognized entertainment booking and touring company, and he had his Gonzaga degree.

Mike was named entertainment director for Expo '74, and contributed significantly to success of the project that reshaped Spokane both physically and culturally.

He confronted a woefully naïve World's Fair Board of Directors, who gave him a budget of $100,000 to book acts for the six-months run of Expo '74. He asked if that figure could be supplemented with ticket revenue. When told it could not, Mike presented them with a difficult reality.

Bob Hope's one-night appearance fee would be $50,000. When the costs of stagehands, ushers, security, facility rental, insurance and other fees were added, that single show would exhaust the budget. Mike told the board that, if he had ticket revenues to work with, he could hire acts like Hope throughout the run of the fair and show a profit.

The Royal Shakespeare Theatre performed, featuring Sir Michael

Redgrave and Dame Peggy Ashcroft. Mike booked Harry Belafonte to three shows in the Opera House. He booked a Glen Yarbrough and the Limeliters reunion concert, Gordon Lightfoot, Kris Kristofferson and Helen Reddy. Other acts included Jack Benny, Liberace, Ella Fitzgerald, Isaac Stern, Itzhak Perlman, Van Cliburn, The Carpenters and more.

Mike's goal was not just to provide the best entertainment to fairgoers, but to do so without losing money. In additional to the paid acts, Mike said, "We ended up with over 1,200 groups who paid their own way to travel to Spokane to perform free of charge to Expo visitors. We ended up with over 4,500 performances at no cost to Expo '74.

When the fair closed, Mike's department showed a profit of $320,000.

"Congratulations on the great entertainment program are in order for Expo officials in general and in particular for Michael D. Kobluk, director of visual and performing arts, and Michael Vokchok, manager of performing arts," the Spokane Daily Chronicle editorialized in February of 1974."

Based on that success, the city offered Mike the job of managing all its entertainment facilities. The qualifier was that he "could not risk taxpayers' dollars" on guarantees to any artists. Which meant he had to find promoters to bear the financial risk for each performance.

Mike created relationships with backers and made the system work.

In 1986, a critical opportunity presented itself. The Broadway cast of *Cats* was planning to tour and would be available to Spokane if Mike could guarantee a full week of eight performances and $400,000. Mike was sure he could sell out eight performances and show a profit, but none of his promoters could handle the $400,000 guarantee. He asked the City Council to underwrite the show. They refused.

Barbieri Enterprises, which owned two major Spokane hotels, had just won the contract to sell computerized tickets for all events at the city-owned entertainment venues, so Mike approached Don Barbieri. Barbieri was intrigued when he saw the numbers Mike presented. He then did his own research, which included a trip to New York.

He returned and told Mike he would not only underwrite the *Cats* run, but that he would establish the Spokane Broadway Series to bring in similar events. The Broadway Series has been a huge success for thirty-six years.

When Jack Lucas retired as president of the Broadway Series in 2019, he was replaced by Mike's son, Justin Kobluk.

Among the most elusive acts Mike pursued for Expo '74 was John Denver. By 1974, John had become the biggest act in show business. *Annie's Song* topped the charts that summer. *Sunshine on My Shoulders* had hit number one in March. *Back Home Again* was on the rise. During the next few years, John would have eighteen top-ten hits. Nine would go to number one.

Mike desperately wanted John to appear in Spokane. The issue for John was making time in his schedule. They finally settled on an August 23 date.

"John, thanks so much for working this out."

Mike met John at the Spokane Coliseum where roadies were setting up sound equipment. The backup musicians milled around the floor, now lined with row upon row of folding chairs, where either a basketball court or a hockey rink hosted sports fans during those seasons.

"Our pleasure, Mike. Our pleasure. The World's Fair, man. How could I miss this? It's far out."

They spent a few minutes catching up.

"Do you need anything else?" Mike asked.

"We have a couple of hours before we're ready for sound check," John said. "Let's go see the fair."

They drove a short distance to the fairgrounds and used a back entrance. Mike hoped they could maintain a low profile. That didn't happen. Someone recognized John and soon adoring crowds—most of them women— were crushing them on all sides.

John tried signing autographs and shaking hands, but the throng threatened to become overwhelming.

"Sorry, Mike," John said, "but we have to get out of here."

That wasn't the only time adoring fans stymied one of John's Spokane visits.

Mike Kobluk is a man of principle to whom setting the record straight is of extreme importance. He bristled at entertainment journalists' accounts that repeated allegations of discord between Mike and John during their time together in The Trio.

In his new job as Spokane's Director of Entertainment Facilities, the criticism threatened to damage his credibility within the entertainment industry and limit his effectiveness.

He wrote a letter to John dated March 31, 1977:

John,

I feel we know each other well enough to be candid, and rather than hold things inside, I'd rather unload on you, looking for a suitable explanation. I want to protect our friendship the best way I can.

I've been very disturbed about portions of a syndicated series of articles that are presently appearing in newspapers across the country. I feel personally ridiculed and humiliated by many of the false and misleading statements about me and about the Trio in general.

A number of the written comments have put me in an awkward and embarrassing position in some of my dealings with others, locally and nationally, and I feel I've lost some effectiveness and credibility.

It seems no matter how one answers articles such as these, the fact they're in print makes them true to many readers. No matter how one attempts to reply, many continue to believe the falsehoods presented.

I assume the articles are authorized by you or by your publicity people. In the least, I assume the content was taken from personal interviews.

Although there are many minor inaccuracies concerning the origins of the Trio, there are two major points I must bring to your attention:

1. Great emphasis is placed on the claim that Kobluk and Frazier "turned down" Leaving on a Jet Plane,

and further, the Trio never recorded the song. Actually, as you remember, it's one of the few songs the Trio ever recorded twice—in two completely different versions—one with Joe and a large band, released as a single; and one with David Boise released on The Mitchell Trio Alive.

2. Much is made of a $40,000 debt "saddled" on Denver by Kobluk. John, before I left the Trio, I asked Nathan for the total of outstanding Trio bills. He told me we owed approximately $1,000 to Paul Prestopino, approximately $3,000 to Milt Okun, and approximately $6,000 to $7,000 to travel agents for airline fares. It totaled between $10,000 and $11,000. At that point, John, the partnership consisted of you and me. In essence, one half of the outstanding debt was yours, and one half mine. When I left, you agreed by letter to assume my half interest, or between $5,000 and $6,000. I suggest that if there was a $40,000 debt, the majority of it was amassed after I left, when sole ownership was yours (or whatever partnership arrangement you had with Boise and Johnson.)

All of this may sound trivial to a person in your position, but I am proud of the accomplishments of the Trio. I value my experiences with Joe, with Chad, with Paul, with Milt, with Hal, with you, and with the many people we worked with over the nine years I was with the group. Yes, there were difficulties, but there were far more good times to remember. I learned a lot during that period of my life. I am who I am today because of the influences that you and others had on me. I appreciate that. I wouldn't trade those experiences for anything, and I resent gossipy articles passing as fact, downgrading others to make someone look better.

What's going on?

Mike

John responded a few weeks later.

On a weekday morning, Mike answered his doorbell to find a limousine parked in front of his Spokane South Hill home and John Denver on his doorstep.

"Mike, I'm sorry I haven't been able to get back to you sooner," John said, offering the now world-famous grin, "but I've been touring, and I didn't want to just send a letter. I don't know where that stuff comes from, but it's not from me. We should go talk about this on a golf course somewhere."

John had taken up the game during his days with The Trio. Guitarist Bob Hefferan, who had replaced Jacob Ander as The Trio's second guitarist soon after Chad departed, was a scratch golfer. He, Mike and John played whenever The Trio's schedule allowed.

"The Manito Country Club," Mike told John, "is just around the corner. Let me call and see if I can get us on."

Mike called a club member he knew through his connections at City Hall. The club member, considerably older than Mike, was reluctant to intervene.

"John Denver? He's one of those rock-n-rollers, isn't he? I don't know if we want one of those guys on our course. I've read about how they tear up hotels."

"No, John's not like that," Mike assured. "He's quite well behaved. I promise I won't let anything get out of hand."

The man finally agreed to make the call. "But I'm holding you responsible for any damage," he warned Mike.

The Denver-Kobluk group teed off without incident. On the third hole, though, they met a half dozen people waiting at the green. John signed autographs and posed for pictures. By the sixth hole, this gallery had grown to twenty. John signed more autographs. They pushed on. When they faced a crowd of thirty at the fourteenth, John gave up.

"I can't do this," he said. "I'll make too many people mad if I don't sign. Sorry, Mike. I'll call the limo to meet us out front."

The limousine returned them to Mike's home. John sent the car and driver away, saying he'd call when he was ready to leave. A half hour later, Mike peered through a window to his front yard.

"It was like the Pope on Easter Sunday," Mike said. "There must have been sixty people on my lawn."

Mike confronted them. "What are you people doing here?"

"We're here to see John Denver. Can you ask him to come out?"

"He's not here," Mike lied.

"Yes, he is. People saw him. He came in a limousine."

"And he left in the limousine," Mike told them. "He's not here."

After a couple of hours, the crowd dispersed, and John snuck away. During the course of that visit, Mike said the misunderstandings between them were resolved.

Mike and John shared one other Spokane-area golf adventure.

Mike booked John for a return concert during the summer of 1980. When Mike met John and his entourage the day before the event, John told him how much he'd heard about the new Coeur d'Alene Resort Golf Course.

"Let me make a call," Mike said. "I'll see if I can get us on."

Coeur d'Alene, Idaho is just across the Washington-Idaho border, forty miles from Spokane. The resort's course, while not particularly difficult, enjoys a spectacular setting. Its signature feature is the fourteenth hole's green that floats on Lake Coeur d'Alene. The green can be moved so the hole never plays quite the same. After hitting their tee shots, golfers are ferried from tee to green on beautiful antique wooden motorboats piloted by attractive young women.

"No, sir," a scheduler told Mike by phone. "That would be impossible. A foursome on Saturday morning? We've been booked for weeks."

"I'm making the request on behalf of John Denver," Mike explained. "He's performing in Spokane Saturday evening, and he's heard about the resort course. He really would like to play."

"John Denver?"

"Yes."

"*The* John Denver?"

The scheduler made a brief consultation.

"Come out whenever you like," he said. "We'll work your group in."

Unlike those at the Manito Country Club, the resort staff practiced careful discretion. Their group, which included Mike and Clare, didn't draw crowds. Their round proceeded without incident until they reached the fourteenth hole.

The boat's pilot—a young woman who should have checked every box in a typical description of John Denver's fan base—gave no sign of recognizing John. Mike could see that John seemed a little miffed at this slight. He appeared more miffed when he hit two shots into the water. As they motored to the green, it had become clear the young lady wasn't being discreet. She hadn't any idea who John was.

When a group completes play at the fourteenth, a second task of the boat pilot is to issue souvenir certificates to each golfer proclaiming, "*Name Here* shot a *Score Here* on the Coeur d'Alene Resort Golf Course's signature floating green."

"Your name, ma'am?" she asked Clare, filling out the certificate with a beautiful script. "And you shot?"

"A four."

Mike reported his five and was awarded his certificate.

"And you, sir," she asked John.

"A seven," he replied with a snip in his voice.

"And your name?"

John glared. "Glen Campbell."

The young woman dutifully recorded his answers and gave him his certificate.

A month later, Mike received a call.

"Mike, this is John. Just wanted to let you know, I played a round of golf with Glen Campbell today. He was really happy when I gave him his certificate for shooting a seven on the fourteenth hole in Couer d'Alene."

— CHAPTER TWENTY —

"What this country really needs is another movie star . . ."

—June Reizner

Mike had fully settled into his life working for the City of Spokane by the summer of 1979. His three children, entering their teen years, had some vague awareness their dad had once been a performer of sorts, but they'd never seen that side of him.

"We didn't play The Trio's records at home," Mike says. "That part of my life was over, and I didn't talk about it much, either with my kids or the people I worked with."

Through John, Mike knew of Joe Frazier's rebirth as an Episcopal priest, but he hadn't talked with or seen Joe since that grim 1968 morning when Joe was fired.

So, Mike was taken completely by surprise when the call came.

"Mike? This is Joe Frazier. I have a favor to ask."

Joe led a church in Wilmington, Delaware. He and other priests in his diocese had been asked to suggest fundraising events for the Episcopal Bishop's Relief Fund. Joe created quite a stir when he said, "Well, I know John Denver."

John and Joe had remained close. Joe had visited John on several occasions at John's compound in Aspen. He told a story of flying in John's open-cockpit biplane on one visit, praying for survival as John swooped into valleys with mountain peaks towering above them, howling with the sheer joy of having wings.

When Joe called John to ask if he'd perform a benefit concert for the church's charities, John said no.

"I'll tell you what I will do, though," John said. "If you can talk Mike into it, we'll do a Mitchell Trio reunion concert in Denver and donate the proceeds to your fund."

Mike surprised himself.

Joe's voice on the phone didn't recall the anger of their parting. It didn't spark a request for explanations of past behavior. Rather, it ignited warm memories of a past he thought he'd put away.

Neither did he take a moment to wonder whether he was even capable of performing again. John, of course, was among the world's most accomplished performers. Joe, he assumed, sang frequently in the course of his religious duties. Besides singing along with the radio occasionally or humming around the house, Mike hadn't sung in almost a decade.

His response, though, was immediate. "I'd be glad to do it, Joe. Now, how will this work?"

"John will have his people book a venue in Denver," Joe said. "He wants us to come to Aspen for a week and rehearse."

Bob Hefferan and Paul Prestopino both agreed to make time in their schedules to join the event. Bob had returned to his job in Phoenix-area real estate. Paul had kept busy touring with Peter, Paul and Mary for the past decade.

They gathered at John's compound, Starwood, in Aspen five days before the concert date, and rehearsed several hours each day. They spent evenings around a roaring campfire, sharing memories and discussing world events.

Mike and Joe were taken aback the first evening when John said, "I want to run something by you guys. I've been thinking about this, and, well, not to be immodest, but right now, I'm one of the most well-known and popular people in the world. With all this stuff that's going on, I think I could be elected President of the United States if I decided to run."

Mike gave a chuckle, thinking John was joking. When Mike looked at Annie, who had covered her eyes with her hand, he realized John was serious.

"John," Mike said, "that's the dumbest thing I ever heard. What do you know about being President? When you joined us in The Trio, you didn't even know how to pronounce *politics*."

John expressed surprise. "Just think of all the good I could do. The environment, shutting down the arms race."

The Cold War ran full bore in 1979. The Soviet Union and United

States stood toe-to-toe at the nuclear brink as they had for decades. Jimmy Carter's presidency was sinking under the weight of an inflated economy. Republican hopefuls included California Governor Ronald Reagan, former CIA director George Bush, and GOP stalwarts like Howard Baker and John Connally.

"I could get in this thing, and I could win," John insisted.

As the evening ended, Annie took Mike aside. "You and Joe have got to talk some sense into him," she said. "He brought this up a few weeks ago and everyone around here is encouraging him."

"Encouraging him?" Mike said. "Who could possibly . . ."

Annie shook her head. "Just look around." She waved toward buildings that made up the Denver compound. "John has these people who do one thing or another for him, all on the payroll. They're just a bunch of sycophants who aren't about to tell John that anything he comes up with is a bad idea."

Mike and Joe sought to dissuade John at every opportunity. Jimmy Carter campaigned on his status as a Washington outsider and learned how little he knew about the political practicalities of getting things accomplished in D.C. Presidents can't change anything on their own. They need to understand the machinations of the political process to work with Congress. Mike understood this on a much smaller scale through his day-to-day dealings with Spokane city government.

While his time with The Trio might have sparked John's social awareness and launched him on some meaningful crusades, popular or not, he remained a babe in the political woods.

John's résumé had gone beyond the concert stage and recording studio. He'd starred in *Oh, God,!* one of 1977's most successful movies. He appeared ever more frequently on national television.

"You know what worries me most?" Mike told John one day following rehearsal. "The way things are going, the day may come when someone with no political skill or understanding gets elected based solely on the strength of celebrity. That person could do a lot of damage, whether he intended to or not."

The first cut on the final Mitchell Trio album—John's third album with the group—was June Reizner's satire on an evolving political landscape, including Ronald Regan's election to the California governorship. When John raised the issue of his presidential possibilities a final time that week, Mike and Joe offered a quick comment in acapella harmony: *"What this country really needs is another movie star . . ."*

John decided not to run for president.

———— ❧ ————

When they weren't arguing about the presidency, Mike, Joe, Paul, Bob and John rehearsed diligently for four days leading to the concert. Mike easily fell into rehearsal rhythm and found he enjoyed the process as much as he ever had.

Because none of The Trio's arrangements had been written down, they first had to remember harmonies on old songs and build arrangements for new material. Mike felt relief to realize that with a little vocal exercise he recaptured his range and timbre.

They prepared several Trio songs: *Can't Help but Wonder Where I'm Bound, We Didn't Know at All, What Did You Learn in School Today?* from Tom Paxton; *Friendly, Liberal Neighborhood Ku Klux Klan* from June Reizner.

A resident of Atlanta when she wrote the song during the sixties, June thought better of using her real name. The album credits identify her as Bernie Cross.

The concert program included John's *For Bobbie* and *Jet Plane* as well. Mike soloed on *Adios Mi Corazon*. Joe sang *Lord of the Starfield*. And they added several of John's hits: *Annie's Song, Country Roads,* and *Grandma's Feather Bed*.

Mike savored every moment.

"I found out performing was fun again," he said. "Of course, I was pretty much in the background. John was the center of attention. And Joe, on stage with his clerical collar representing the Episcopal Church and charities the concert was aiding, drew a lot of attention. I was just there, enjoying the heck out of it."

Although they didn't attend, the idea of the concert was an eye opener for Mike's daughter and twin sons. Mike estimates the credibility he gained with the three teens lasted at least a couple of weeks before he was just Dad again.

They played to a sold-out house, and the presiding bishop took the stage to thank them.

"This has been one heaven of an evening," he told the audience. "This has been a more effective night of preaching than the rest of us could do all week long. I want to thank the gentlemen who volunteered to make this reunion of The Mitchell Trio possible."

He introduced Paul and Bob, then "First, John Denver," he paused for the ovation, "Father Joe Frazier," another pause, "and of course Mike Kobluk.

"And, by the way, who the hell is Mitchell?"

Mike and Clare flew to Spokane the next day. While the concert might have been news in Denver, it didn't cause a ripple in Mike's office. He settled back into home and work, thinking once again his life on the stage was over.

Until a call came from Washington, D.C. seven years later.

— CHAPTER TWENTY-ONE —

October 21, 1973
San Antonio, Texas

". . . But that's another side of this life I've been leading . . ."

—Fred Neil

The hard part was over.

Although he'd hardly stuck to Chad's carefully orchestrated plan, David's driver had succeeded in getting the pickup and camper shell safely across the border.

Now, there it sat, all by itself in a deserted Holiday Inn parking lot on the outskirts of San Antonio. Maybe twenty or thirty thousand dollars just sitting there. Chad took a table by a window at the hotel's restaurant and ordered dinner.

All through his meal, nothing stirred. The parking lot abutted a busy street, a stand of shrubbery separating the two. This scene was so absent of life, it might have been on the moon.

Finally satisfied, Chad went to his room to retrieve Sam the Basset Hound. He left Sam in the camper, then drove to a rental car agency where he deposited the Buick and called a cab.

The cab returned him to the parking lot where Chad again was struck by a dearth of activity. He wanted to appreciate this moment—the culmination of months of sacrifice and preparation—before he and Sam drove off into the sunset, although technically, they'd be driving east.

As Chad unlocked the camper shell, Sam—elderly and nearly blind—waited for instructions.

"It was like crocuses blooming in springtime," Chad said. "They came from everywhere."

Out of bushes, from the hotel, from cars driving along the street. A helicopter hovered above. Vehicles roared from two different directions, tires squealing across the asphalt.

And they had guns. All of them.

"Hands where we can see 'em! Hands where we can see 'em! Now!"

Sam, startled from his old dog lethargy, made a break for it. He leapt from the camper on a beeline for the shrubbery and street traffic beyond. Accustomed to chasing after Sam to protect the hard-luck canine from one peril after another, Chad took off after him.

"Stop!" came a chorus of voices. "Stop right now!"

"Hang on a minute," Chad called over his shoulder. "I have to get my dog."

Fortunately, Sam was no longer fleet of paw, and Chad required only ten strides or so to grab him.

Now the screams were louder as gunmen advanced on all sides.

"Put down the dog! Show us your hands!"

In that moment, realization struck Chad. He carefully placed Sam on the ground and raised his arms high. In a blur of sound and fury, he found himself face down on the asphalt. Someone twisted his arms behind him. He heard the metallic snap of handcuffs.

Sam got in a couple of sloppy licks to Chad's face before they arrested the dog, too. His captors hauled Chad to his feet.

"You idiot," said an agent who tugged at Chad's elbow, directing him toward the hotel, "don't you understand how stupid it was to run? We could have shot you!"

"I wasn't running," Chad said. "I was trying to get my dog. That dog's been through a lot. I didn't want him to get hit by a car."

They took Chad into a hotel room where a bevy of DEA agents and local authorities crowded around him.

"Okay," one agent said, "you want to tell us what's going on? What's in the camper?"

"I'd really like to help you," said Chad, "but I have no idea. I'm just being paid to drive this pickup back east. Um . . . is somebody looking after my dog?"

"Yeah," growled a local cop, "he's fine. Although he may not be for long if we don't get some answers."

The DEA guy rolled his eyes and asked again, "What's in the camper?"

———

JULY 1965

"Okay, Frank. What now?"

A couple of days after Chad's final performance, he and Frank Fried sat in the Dearborn Parkway apartment they shared. When Chad left The Trio, Mike fired Frank as the group's manager.

"Now, you go out and be a star," Frank told him. The unspoken implication being that Chad needed to replace income Triangle productions had realized through Frank's management of The Trio.

For all the animosity generated regarding Mike's suspicions that Chad had coveted a solo career, "I didn't have a clue how to be a solo performer," Chad said. "I'd always been a group singer. The prospect of being on a stage by myself terrified me."

To get things started, Frank dispatched Chad to Los Angeles to recruit more clients for Triangle. "You can talk to these people, performer to performer," Frank said. "You speak their language."

Frank named Roger Miller as Chad's first target. Miller's *King of the Road* topped all the charts in early 1965.

"I didn't know him," Chad said. "I'd never even been introduced. He was performing in an L.A. nightclub, and I just sat there and thought, 'how am I supposed to do this?' Approach this guy and tout Frank Fried as a great manager? That's the last thing I wanted to do."

Chad met Miller during a break, introduced himself, told Miller how much he enjoyed his music and left.

Next, Frank asked Chad to listen to an audition of an unknown performer who aspired to sing folk songs. Chad listened to Louis Gossett Jr.

sing two songs acapella.

"He had a good-enough voice," Chad recalls. "But what else could I say?"

Frank booked Bill Cosby for an appearance at a McCormick Place, one of Chicago's largest venues. As the concert promoter, he assigned Chad as the opening act.

That experience convinced Chad he needed to research the art of solo performance in more depth.

He traveled to Las Vegas to hear Frank Sinatra and Bobby Darin. Sinatra was such a presence, he didn't have to do anything but sing to connect with his audience. No frills. Count Basie's orchestra backed him. Sinatra sang song after song, offering little or no introduction. During instrumental breaks, Sinatra would stand at the piano and leaf through music scores. He followed with twenty minutes of Rat Pack stories. His audience was thoroughly captivated.

Bobby Darin was trying to make a leap from lounge singer to protest singer. For the first half of his show, dressed in a tuxedo and backed by an orchestra, he was *Mac the Knife*. After the break, he reappeared in a Belafonte calypso shirt, and sang *Simple Song of Freedom*, backed by Jim McGuinn on guitar.

Chad didn't take the opportunity to talk over old times with McGuinn.

What he came to realize was that he enjoyed the drama of performance rather than just singing. He'd always found folk groups, who stood before microphones and strummed guitars, lacking in their presentation.

"What I wanted to be," he said, "was an actor who performed through music."

He also learned a lesson about Las Vegas and relationships.

Despite his dalliance with Miriam Makeba a few years earlier, Chad remained a sexual neophyte. That would eventually change as he discovered that solo performers had more time on their hands than did a trio constantly rehearsing and rushing from venue to venue.

He hadn't wanted to make the Las Vegas trip alone. Through a friend, he'd gotten to know a woman from Los Angeles whose company he enjoyed in a platonic sort of way. He asked her to meet him in Vegas.

At their hotel check-in, Chad paid for two rooms. He soon became aware that Ann's interest ran deeper than friendship. Which led to an awkward hallway scene that evening as he tried to decide what to do.

"Finally, I just said, 'Good night, see you in the morning,'" Chad recalled. "After I gave it some thought, I felt really bad. So, next morning I called."

"Listen, I feel dumb about last night. I didn't handle it well, and I'm sorry," he said.

"Oh, no. It's all right. Really."

"No, no, it's not.," Chad said. "What are you doing now?"

"Well, I'm writing a letter to my mother."

Chad thought for a moment. *Her mother? Ann's mother is dead. Oh, no. I've dialed the wrong room.*

"And I realized, that in a Las Vegas hotel, you could dial practically any number, apologize about last night, and whatever woman answered would understand."

～

Before Chad had a chance to hone a singing act, Frank pushed him into acting—something in which Chad had an interest. He would have preferred, though, to dip a toe into the water, maybe some obscure little play in an obscure little theater. Instead, Frank shoved him off the deep end and onto Broadway.

Robert Nemiroff, who produced *A Raisin in the Sun*, knew Frank from their pre-war radical days as members of the International Workers of the World. In fall of 1965, Nemiroff prepared a play called *Postmark Zero*. Frank invested in the production and arranged for Chad to be cast as one of the principal actors.

The subject matter of *Postmark Zero* was grim. When Hitler refused to allow German forces to retreat from Leningrad, though his army was being decimated, Germany's propaganda ministry offered each soldier the chance to write a letter to their loved ones, which would be transported on the last plane to depart before the German Army fell. The idea was to show the German people that, even in these most difficult of circumstances, German soldiers were thinking of their homeland and remained committed to their cause.

These letters all carried the postmark zero.

The letters, though, didn't convey that heroic message at all, and some poor minion in the propaganda ministry was probably strung up by his heels. After the war, bundles of these letters were discovered and published as a book.

Postmark Zero consisted of a series of scenes depicting stories told in those letters.

Chad had his reservations about both the play's concept and his ability to perform to the standards of Broadway theater.

"I have no experience at this," Chad told director Peter Yates. "I'm depending on you to work with me because, obviously, I'll need help."

Yates, whose films included *Bullitt*, *Breaking Away* and *The Deep*, assured Chad that he understood.

Two weeks into rehearsals, though, Yates bowed out to direct a movie. Peter Coe replaced Yates.

"Okay, folks," Coe told his troop as he introduced himself, "let's read through this so I can get an idea where we are."

Chad listened to actress Viveca Lindfors offer a reading that she could have taken directly to opening night, and he thought, *Oh, God, what am I doing here?*

As rehearsals continued, German actor Hardy Kruger became less and less satisfied with Chad's efforts and went to Coe, demanding Chad be replaced.

Chad departed with relief. He stayed around long enough to attend opening night and, "I realized I was thankful I wasn't in this play." *Postmark Zero* closed five days later.

Following his Broadway debacle, Chad relocated from Chicago to New

York. He rented an apartment at One Christopher Street and set out trying to create a solo singing act. Frank landed Chad a recording contract with Warner Brothers, and in the final months of 1965, they produced *Chad Mitchell Himself.*

Ironically, this album contained two tracks The Mitchell Trio recorded at about the same time: Fred Neil's *Another Side of This Life*, and *Violets of Dawn*, the title cut of the second album recorded by The Trio's John Denver incarnation.

The duplication was entirely coincidental. Those songs, though, were not what Chad enjoyed singing most. *Brother, Can You Spare a Dime,* and *Somewhere Over the Rainbow*, both with lyrics by E.Y. Harburg; and *She Was Too Good to Me,* by Rogers and Hart, became cornerstones of his solo act.

"Most of the time during those first three or four years," Chad said, "I wasn't connecting with the audience. Sometimes, with those three songs, I felt I did connect, but in the way an actor connects with his own emotions as he is reciting lines."

Much of the time, though, he felt lost.

"The Trio always had a party going on stage," Chad said, "and if our audience didn't like what we were doing, then somehow we got through it because we were good, and we sang to be good—in a sense, for our own satisfaction. We knew we were doing a good job, even if the audience didn't get it."

The critics liked this new Chad Mitchell well enough. Both the album and Chad's solo persona were well received. Reviewers initially gave him the benefit of the doubt, realizing he was trying to adopt the style of performers like Jacques Brel or Charles Aznavour. They heard a more formal vocal style than the previous Chad Mitchell. "The albums are good," one critic wrote, "but more suited for fans of Bobby Darin than Chad Mitchell."

Chad Mitchell Himself provided a base upon which Chad constructed a solo act. His arranger, Walter Raim, recruited guitarist Stu Scharf and pianist Bob Dorough to back him. When they had a large enough audience to warrant the expense, Chad also hired bassist Bill Lee, father of Spike Lee, to join them. Raim reminded Chad on more than one occasion, "Do you realize who you're performing with? Sometimes, I think you don't understand how good these guys really are."

"What I understood," Chad said, "was they were so much better, more sophisticated musically, than I was. I was intimidated by them."

While the album cover listed Frank as producer on Chad's second Warner Brothers release, *Love, a Feeling Of,* Scharf and Dorough were the real producers. Released in 1967, the album pushed Chad further from his folk roots. It included Paul Simon's *Poem on an Underground Wall*, Herman Hupfeld's *As Time Goes By*, and Leonard Cohen's *Suzanne*. The album received less notice than its predecessor.

Warner Brothers dropped Chad, and his final attempt, under a Bell Records label, entitled *Chad,* was released in 1969. Like The Trio, now manned by John Denver, David Boise and Michael Johnson, Chad struggled to find a niche in a new market reality.

Frank's grand plan to make Chad Mitchell Triangle's centerpiece was foundering. "Obviously, I wasn't becoming a star, and I was sucking up a lot of money."

As a last effort, Frank conceived of a tour entitled *Chad Mitchell, Songs of the New Renaissance.* "Whatever the fuck that meant," Chad said. "That whole show was a dumb idea."

The presentation attempted to interpret the late sixties music scene for those who just couldn't make the leap from the big band era. "It's like I was saying, 'You people won't listen to Dylan because he can't sing, or Paul Simon because, whatever. Well, I'm here to interpret those songs for you, because they are really great writers, by God.'"

He wore a dark turtleneck sweater for half the show and a Nehru jacket for the other. "I think that jacket went down to my knees," he said. Frank booked him at *The Happy Medium* in Chicago, then Chad took his show to New York's aptly named *The Bitter End*.

As he performed opening night, he noticed the New York Times critic's eyes glaze over before he left. The critic reported he gave Chad's show ten minutes, "but nothing was happening."

The last gasp occurred back in Chicago at *Punchinello's East* where Frank informed Chad he wasn't holding up his end of their partnership. "Maybe he thought I wasn't trying," Chad said. "I didn't know what trying meant. Nothing seemed right for me. In retrospect, there just wasn't a slot for me in the pop music world."

Frank bought Chad's share of the partnership for $80,000. Chad's separation from Triangle left him without an income source for the first time since his 1958 arrival in New York.

During his time at *Punchinello's* though, he met a dark-haired waitress named Karen Webb. These circumstances set Chad on a path leading to that camper in the San Antonio parking lot four years later.

— CHAPTER TWENTY-TWO —

". . . I went on uptown, to see a man,
I heard he had a little stuff on hand . . ."

The Hip Song (Sometimes it Doesn't Pay to be Too Hip)
—Shel Silverstein

"I always considered myself out of sync with my own generation.
I was on college campuses for ten years and ended up way
behind in dealing with society. I was incredibly naïve.
I didn't find out about sex until I was 23, or drugs until
I was 28. I didn't get married until I was 34."

—Chad Mitchell

As the 1970's dawned, teens and young adults held a different perception of drugs like LSD, marijuana and even cocaine than broader American society. These were the sex, drugs and rock-and-roll kids, who questioned things like a double standard represented by grass and alcohol. Until the late '60s LSD wasn't a controlled substance. Cocaine emerged as THE party drug. The "hip" culture wasn't scared of it yet.

Chad may have been thirty-four in 1970, but, as he explained to a Texas judge at his sentencing hearing three years later, his whole world had been defined by sixties college student audiences.

He'd had a single experimentation with LSD, had begun to use marijuana in his post-Trio experience and didn't encounter the demons Richard Nixon's silent majority warned about.

His final days of performance at *Punchinello's* were a chore, fraught with concern over what was next. His anxiety was tempered, though, by Karen. This beautiful, smart and funny woman softened all the sharp edges, and Chad fell in love.

When the Chicago gig ended, Chad took Karen to New York so she could complete a master's degree. They married in 1971. Karen found a job. Chad didn't. For the first time in his life, he had no creative outlet. Money wasn't a problem yet. His bank account still reflected saved earnings through both The Trio and Triangle.

Boredom became the issue.

"I was embarrassed when people would ask me at parties, 'What are you doing now?'

My answer? 'Nothing. I was killed in an unfortunate mishap.'"

He considered trying the real world. "But I'd been too independent for too long. I couldn't imagine a life structured by an office."

In full flight from the clean-cut image he'd projected as both a teenager and member of The Trio, Chad grew his beard and hair. He gravitated toward social circles comprised of hip young New Yorkers, who smoked grass recreationally. One of them told Chad about a California friend who had a couple pounds of weed she didn't know how to unload.

Seeing an entrepreneurial opportunity, Chad agreed to take the grass off her hands. He discovered that selling wasn't as easy as he'd anticipated. He had the stuff for two months before he found a middle-man—who cost Chad most of his profits.

Sam the Basset Hound entered the scene years before Chad met Karen.

Chad had been dating a member of the Second City performance group in Chicago. She aspired to the Broadway stage. Chad was going on tour with his solo act. Circumstances had come between them, but Chad wasn't ready to give up on their relationship.

Maybe, Chad thought, she would like a dog. A dog might keep me in her thoughts.

He saw an ad in the back of a newspaper:

CONEY ISLAND!

Alligator Wrestling and Trained Dogs

All the better, Chad decided. *A trained dog.*

Dogs represent something more to Chad than they might to the casual pet owner. For Chad, dogs epitomize commitment, and commitment is a powerful talisman in his psyche. Chad spent his childhood in a world where commitment was a vague promise, at best.

An absent father would have been less painful than a father who dropped in and out of his life on a whim. While his mother's commitment was beyond question, it was bestowed by an obsessive perfectionist who doted on her son.

"Chad hasn't always been able to count on people," his wife Chris said. "But he could always count on the dogs."

"My affinity for dogs and theirs for me is one of my earliest memories," he said.

His first dog chose him rather than the other way around.

His family lived in Portland during the war. Chad's father worked in the shipyards and drank heavily.

"A dog on our block was named Sniffy and his owners weren't there all the time, so Sniffy would come down the street to see me," Chad said. "He was my pal. They finally had to give Sniffy to me, because he just wouldn't come home."

So, of course,Chad took the newspaper ad and drove to Coney Island. He found a tent—with a picture of an alligator—and a nine-month-old basset hound sitting in front.

A man stepped through the tent flap and stood next to the basset.

"Is this one of the trained dogs for sale?" Chad asked.

The man looked at the dog, then back to Chad. "Sure."

The dog appeared relieved to be getting into the back seat of his Porsche. Maybe because there weren't any alligators there.

Noticing an uncanny facial resemblance to his piano player, Chad named the basset "Sam".

While she appreciated the gesture, the girlfriend didn't have room in her life for a dog—or Chad. He lost the girl, but Sam became his constant companion for the next twelve years. During their time together, Sam suffered several maladies, including a heart murmur. "I'd take him to the vet for his checkups," Chad said. "The vet would listen to Sam's heart and say, 'I don't know why Sam's still with us.'"

Only prison separated them. The saddest moment of Chad's incarceration was the day Karen called to say Sam had died.

On the back of His second solo album, *Love, a Feeling Of*, is a photo of Chad and Sam—Chad with jacket thrown over his shoulder á la Sinatra, Sam at his heel—walking away from the camera.

Among the members of Chad and Karen's New York social circle was piano player Barry Flast, later a member of Poco. He had connections at a recording company called The Record Plant, and he and Chad recorded a demo tape of Barry's compositions. Chad said they needed to present their act to some audiences first to determine what would and wouldn't work.

"I know a guy," Chad said, "who can book stuff for us around Minneapolis."

"Yeah, I can do that," the agent said, "but I'll warn you, you'll hate every place I book you."

"Why?" Chad asked.

"Because they're shitty places."

The shitty places were bars, mostly. Bar owners were thrilled to book Chad Mitchell for peanuts. At first. They became less thrilled when Chad Mitchell sang Barry's songs instead of Trio material. The worst shitty place was in Des Moines where Chad and Barry were to perform for a week.

After a couple of songs, the crowd lost interest, reducing Chad and Barry to background noise accompanying drunken conversations. The first two nights, Chad managed to get through the sets. On the third night, though, some of Barry's friends stopped by—people who wanted to hear the music.

Part way through the first set, Chad shouted into his microphone, "If you'd just shut the fuck up, other people could hear."

Chad and Barry didn't survive to the second set. The owner called them to his office and told Chad, "You have an uncanny ability to alienate our customers." He wrote a check for the whole gig and told them not to show up again.

Despite this rough beginning, Chad liked Minneapolis. Although they kept Chad's New York apartment—it was rent controlled, so Chad didn't dare give it up—he and Karen moved to Minneapolis briefly where Chad and other out-of-work performers formed a group called *Childe. Childe* barely had enough bookings to pay the rent, so Chad found work singing jingles for local commercials. During the Minneapolis period, Chad also played triangle and occasionally sang in a "folky hoohaw band."

Finally, Chad took stock and said to himself, "I was Chad Mitchell of The Chad Mitchell Trio. Now I'm doing zip squat."

He and Karen returned to New York where Chad and Barry completed their demo tape.

Chad considered the first smuggling gig a lark.

Looking back on his previous crimes—gas siphoning and stealing the Chevy from a Spokane used car lot, shoplifting in New York City, and his minor marijuana enterprise—Chad viewed smuggling grass as an adventure rather than a crime against society. Fulfilling a need. Thumbing an enlightened nose at mainstream sensibilities. Respectable New York friends who used drugs were not felons. They didn't steal or rob to support any sort of addiction. So, where's the harm?

And, as always, getting caught wasn't a part of the equation.

Chad's initial encounter with smuggling came via his association with sculptor Harry Bouras. Frank hired Bouras to develop the *Songs of the New Renaissance* fiasco. Despite its failure, Chad and Boruas hit it off. Bouras introduced Chad to cigars, educated him in the same way he'd later be educated about wine.

"You know what JFK did?" Bouras asked him. "Right before he cut off trade with Cuba, he had 2,000 Cuban cigars shipped to him at the White House."

So, again, where's the crime?

When Chad performed in Detroit a few weeks later, he and Sam drove to Canada and bought half a dozen boxes of Cubans. He secreted the cigars behind the Porsche's door panels and motored back to New York. Someone stole half his stash, though, when he left the car unlocked on the street while he unpacked.

———— ∾ ————

Back in New York, once again jobless and without purpose, Chad's funk returned. Karen suggested a vacation. They decided on Mexico, but not touristy places. Chad gave up his Porsche and bought a 1972 Chevy Blazer, bright yellow with a black top, that they christened "Tweety." Chad, Karen and Sam set about exploring back roads south of the border.

They met a hippie couple, Rick and Tic, along the way and traveled together to Oaxaca. There they met an American expatriate, who called himself Henry. He had a small compound housing a commune. He offered Chad and Karen lodging. He also offered marijuana.

"Where do you get it?" Chad asked as he and Henry shared a joint.

"Villagers grow it in the mountains.".

"Really?" Chad asked. "And you can just buy it?"

"It's easy," Henry told him, "but you need money. Everything has to be a cash transaction."

"And how would I get it across the border?"

"You hire people for that. I know a chick named Cindy who will do it for you."

During the drive from New York, Chad held out hope that the demo tape he and Barry made would turn into something more. A friend of Barry's who also worked at The Record Plant, said he wanted to produce the album and was working on a deal. Soon after meeting Henry, Chad received word the record deal had fallen through.

The idea of a drug smuggling adventure became more enticing.

"And Henry knows someone who could get it across the border?" Karen asked him.

"Yeah, but the more people we involve, the more people we have to pay. And you gotta' hide at least a hundred pounds of grass somewhere in your car to make it worthwhile. A pound of cocaine would probably be worth more, and we could put it in the door panels."

But, they wondered, how much would a pound of cocaine cost? They didn't bring all that much cash with them. Chad arranged for his bank in New York to transfer $17,000 to a San Antonio bank.

They drove to Mexico City, where Chad caught a plane to San Antonio. Armed with cash, they headed back to Oaxaca where Henry directed them to José who lived in Zihuantanejo.

Chad and Karen rented a room in a hotel several stars below a Motel Six. Ever security conscious, Chad taped an envelope bearing the $17,000 to the underside of a dresser drawer, and then went to find Jose.

"Cocaïne. Si, si," Jose told them. "Is not problem."

José brought them everything *but* cocaine. He produced scraggly marijuana plants, mushrooms, peyote caps, even unrefined black tar heroin. All of which Chad refused, finally giving up on José.

They were about a hundred miles out of Zihuantanejo headed back to Oaxaca when Chad slammed on the brakes, rested his head against the steering wheel and told Karen, "Oh, my God. I left the $17,000 taped under the drawer."

Back in Zihuantanejo, Chad told the desk guy they needed to check the room because they'd left something behind.

"We cleaned already," the guy told them. "We didn't find anything."

Chad doubted that telling a Zihuantanejo desk clerk he'd left $17,000 taped under a drawer would be a smart thing to do.

"Oh well," Chad said, "it wasn't that important. We really enjoyed that room, though. We'd like to take it for another night."

A suspicious desk clerk gave them the key.

Holding his breath, Chad slid the drawer from its chest where he found his $17,000 undisturbed.

———❧———

Back in Oaxaca, Chad told Henry that José was a bust. Henry knew another guy, an Indian named Feliz. Feliz told Chad cocaine was scarce, but he would spread word in the mountains and help Chad assemble a shipment of grass.

Chad accompanied Feliz night after night to a field thirty kilometers from town where they met Indians bearing scraggly, molding, wilted marijuana specimens.

"Feliz, I can't use this," Chad said.

"But these people have walked three days to come here," Feliz answered.

Chad felt sorry for these impoverished folks, paid them and sent them on their way.

In this manner, Chad gathered three hundred pounds of grass, much of which would be unsellable to a New York clientele. But it barely put a dent in Chad's $17,000.

Now the marijuana had to be compressed into bricks. They took the weed to Henry's compound where Henry provided a garage. They spread the grass across the floor to dry out some of the mold, and rigged a press using a car jack.

"The process was slow-going," Chad said. "You had to put a lot of weight on that sucker to compress the bricks. We wrapped them in cellophane and then aluminum foil."

———❧———

Previously in New York, when smuggling grass was just a germ of an idea, Chad sought legal counsel. He'd become acquainted with a neighbor who was an attorney.

"I'd like to buy an hour of your time," Chad told Joel Steinberg. "I need to know about the legal issues someone might face if they decide to smuggle marijuana."

"My first advice," Joel said, "is don't do it. If you do, though, and you should get arrested, be cooperative. Tell the cops you'd like to help them as much as you can, but first, you have to talk to your attorney."

Joel confided to Chad that he had another client in that same business who traveled frequently to Mexico.

Taking a break one evening from traveling to the sticks to buy moldy grass, Chad accompanied Henry to a vegetarian restaurant popular among Oaxaca's hippie community. There, Henry introduced him to Ralph—the other drug smuggling client Joel had told Chad about.

"So, I'm new at this," Chad told Ralph. "Can I pick your brain?"

Ralph laughed. "Depends."

"How do you get it across the border?"

Ralph considered Chad a long moment before finally saying, "I have a camper on a pickup truck. I put the grass in the truck bed, then set the camper down on top of it."

"And then you just drive the camper across?" Chad asked.

"No way. I hire people to drive it from here to San Antonio. Then I drive it to New York."

"What do you do when you get it to New York?"

"I wholesale it," Ralph said.

"See, that's what I'd like to do," Chad said. "Would you be willing to handle the stuff we bring across?"

Ralph adopted a disdainful expression. "Yeah, if you manage to get anything out of Mexico. But I don't think the odds of that happening are very good."

"Why don't you—?"

"Because you stand out like the biggest gringo drug smuggler in the world!" Ralph said. "Look at you. Blond. Beard. Long hair. And you drive a bright yellow truck. When I'm down here, I do everything I can to blend in."

Indeed, Ralph's outfit included a battered straw hat, worn jeans, dirty boots, plain long-sleeved shirt. His deep tan and dark hair could pass for native.

"If you do get it across the border," Ralph added, "here's my phone number. Call me, and I'll move it for you."

———～———

"Okay, we can't use the Blazer," Chad told Karen. "We have to find something more non-descript. I'm thinking a Volkswagen Camper."

"Isn't a Volkswagen Camper a hippie-mobile?" she asked.

"We won't be the ones driving it across."

"We won't?"

"No. We'll find Cindy. She's who Henry told me about."

Cindy lived on the U.S. side of the border. Henry didn't know how to get in touch with her directly, but he gave them the address of Cindy's grandmother's house in McAllen.

Dressed and coiffed like Republicans, Chad and Karen drove the Blazer. Sam hung his head out a backseat seat window at the border crossing and began to howl his basset hound howl as they neared the inspection point.

"Jesus," Chad said. "So much for keeping a low profile."

Whether the U.S. border agent didn't like the yellow Blazer, didn't like Sam, or was suspicious of young Republicans, Chad has never been sure. But he directed Chad to pull over for an inspection.

"What's this?" the agent asked.

Chad's stomach fell as he remembered the money.

"It's . . . it's our traveling cash."

"Looks like a lot," the agent said as he thumbed the rubber-banded bills. "How much cash?"

"Um . . . just short of $17,000, I think."

"Why are you leaving Mexico with $17,000?"

"We . . . we brought it into Mexico, but we didn't spend it."

"Why did you need $17,000 in Mexico?" the agent asked.

"We're opening an import shop in New York," Chad improvised. "We wanted some Mexican stuff. Art, pottery . . . you know."

"Did you buy some things?"

"Well, yes. But we shipped them on ahead."

"And you have $17,000 left over." A statement, not a question.

"We didn't see that much we liked."

The agent told them to wait. Sam continued to howl.

A half-hour later, he sent them on their way.

In McAllen, as they searched for Cindy's grandmother's house, Chad noticed that a black sedan seemed to be following them.

Cindy was not at her grandmother's house. The grandmother asked if Chad wanted to leave a message. Not wanting to out Cindy to her grandmother, Chad hemmed and hawed until Cindy's grandmother said, "Is this about grass?"

Chad didn't answer.

"If it is," the grandmother said, "Cindy's your gal. She knows what she's doing. She's really cool."

The grandmother took Chad's phone number and said Cindy would call.

Chad and Karen saddled up the Blazer and embarked on a marathon drive to Karen's home in Benton, Illinois where they bought a VW camper. They drove both vehicles back to Oaxaca.

Cindy called to arrange a meeting in a restaurant across the border in Reynosa. She told them to dress conservatively to avoid suspicion in such a "hot" area. Disguised again as young Republicans, Chad and Karen seated themselves and waited. When Cindy showed up, Chad couldn't believe it.

Cindy and her boyfriend were accompanied by Cindy's sixteen-year-old sister. The three couldn't look any more hippie. Cindy had long, straight hair. She wore a shirt decorated with leather fringe and a big peace sign embroidered on the back. Her boyfriend sported an unkept beard and shoulder-length hair. The little sister wore dreadlocks.

Cindy flashed a peace sign as Chad stood to wave them over.

They shared obligatory small talk before getting down to business.

"How much you got?" Cindy asked.

"A couple hundred-pound garbage bags."

"Okay, I'll move it for ten percent of the load. Where is it?"

"Hidden in a VW camper," Chad said. "You want to get it now?"

"No," Cindy said. "We can't drive it across."

Chad was taken aback. "Why not?"

"Because some idiot drove through the border near McAllen a week ago with $17,000 bucks, and the Feds have had my grandmother's place staked out for the past week."

"Um . . . Oh," Chad said. "So, what do we . . ."

"It's a small load," she said. "We can get it across. We'll use the river. But you'll have to help."

Chad agreed to meet Cindy on the Mexican side near Reynosa the next day.

———∿———

Chad and Karen drove their marijuana to the drop location. Cindy appeared on time, carrying a towel. She was alone and told Karen to take the VW bus elsewhere.

"Your guys are late," Chad noted.

"What guys?" Cindy asked.

"Your grandmother said you had guys who helped . . ."

"Yeah, but we don't need guys for just a couple of bags. My boyfriend will help us on the other side."

"Us?" Chad asked.

"Yeah. I can't handle swimming two bags across by myself."

Chad understood why Cindy had brought a towel.

"I . . . I don't have a bathing suit," he said.

Cindy winked. "Neither do I."

She peeled off her clothes—all of them—and pulled one garbage bag toward the water, calling over her shoulder, "We don't have all day."

Chad stripped, hopping a little on one foot to get out of his underwear, grabbed the other bag, and—heart pounding—followed Cindy into the Rio Grande.

The bales floated through a gentle current, making them easy to steer. As they neared the U.S. shore, Cindy's boyfriend appeared from some shrubbery. Chad and Cindy waded ashore long enough for Cindy to kiss her guy. He shook Chad's hand and said, "I've got it from here."

Chad followed Cindy back to Mexico where her towel awaited.

As Cindy glistened in the sunshine, Chad finally relaxed enough to notice. *God, this is quite an attractive woman.*

Cindy handed the towel to Chad. She asked, "You wanna get my back?"

When she turned and began putting on her clothing, she noted Chad's response.

She winked again. "I was beginning to think," she said, "you didn't like me."

"We have a place to stash the stuff," Cindy told Chad as they drove to meet Karen. "You guys wait for my call. A couple of days. Then come and load it up."

Two days later, they met Cindy and followed her to a vacant lot where two black plastic bags of marijuana sat among the weeds.

"I thought you said you were putting it in a secure spot," Chad said.

"Nobody bothered it," she said.

"But anyone could have come by and—"

"The only people who come around here are neighborhood kids," Cindy said. "They don't take much."

Crossing the border was only the first obstacle. Several miles past the border was a U.S. immigration checkpoint. The officers there were looking for people entering the country illegally. If, however, they discovered marijuana during their vehicle searches, they detained the smugglers and called the DEA.

As they finished loading, Chad offered the VW keys to Cindy and said, "Do we switch cars and just follow you through the immigration checkpoint?"

"Yeah, well, about that," Cindy said, refusing the keys. "Sorry, but the guy who drives for me got busted last night. I'm afraid you're on your own from here."

Chad looked on, speechless, as Cindy walked to her car, waved goodbye, and drove away.

"Jesus, what do we do now?" Karen asked.

"I don't know," Chad said. "We'll have to think about this."

They drove to a Holiday Inn and spent the day transferring their grass into cardboard boxes which they packed into the van's storage area.

Filled with trepidation, they debated long into the night whether to go through with it.

"We've gotten this far," Chad said. "The immigration guys aren't even looking for drugs. They'll probably just wave us through."

"Yeah," Karen said. "Probably."

The next morning, dressed in their Republican disguises, they traveled to the point of no return, took deep breaths, shared a hug and drove into the checkpoint.

The officer asked if they had any agricultural products and peered into the van.

"No," Chad said.

He told them to have a nice day.

———∿———

Chad and Karen were giddy with their success. In New York, Ralph handled distribution, and they realized a $20,000 profit. Tales of their exploits made them the toast of their friends.

"Home and safe, the whole thing was exciting," Chad said. "It had been an adventure. We were too naïve to understand all that could have gone wrong, all the ways we could have been caught. And now, I held the self-image of a shrewd desperado."

Karen made plans to study pottery-making at a school in California. Chad once again confronted the question of his own career during those party conversations. "What are you doing now?"

He wasn't at all sure he wanted to again confront the confounding puzzle of constructing a solo career.

And now, considering himself the ever vigilant, ever cunning, wily outlaw, the thing that kept running through his head? *Just think how much I could make in Mexico, now that I know what I'm doing.*

— CHAPTER TWENTY-THREE —

C had approached this new calling with far more self-assurance and enthusiasm than he had during his solo performance career. Here was an enterprise all his own. He didn't have to argue with Mike whether this was a direction The Trio should take. This wasn't like leaving The Trio and leaping into the unknown. He'd tested the waters—he and Cindy—and discovered he could swim.

"Here was something I could be good at," Chad said, adding with an ironic chuckle. "After all, I've always considered myself a clever fellow."

The logistical challenges intrigued him.

Karen, while willing to invest her portion of the previous adventure's profits in Chad's new plan, didn't approve. She saw an uncomfortable difference between bumbling their way through a spur-of-the-moment slapstick adventure, and a carefully premeditated plan.

Chad's new scheme involved more than merely sneaking a load of grass across the border. He envisioned a sort of Peace Corps for poor, struggling third-world marijuana farmers. He would study cultivation, supply seeds, offer agrarian advice and eventually build a reliable source of quality weed.

He would invest in his own transport vehicle, modified to secrete the cargo.

He devised a plan for recruitment of drivers by placing an ad in appropriate publications. "Driver wanted." The driver wouldn't know who he or she worked for, or vice versa. All personal contact would be via telephone. Through the mail, the driver would get a set of keys, partial payment and location of a vehicle in Mexico. The driver would leave the vehicle at a specified San Antonio location. If stopped, the driver could truthfully say he didn't know he was delivering anything but a vehicle. And, Chad believed, you didn't want to short-change the driver. He settled on a fee of $5,000 to ferry the stash into the United States.

Chad's plan read like a business model someone might study in a college economics class, except, of course, smuggling is a criminal enterprise. Sooner or later, such an endeavor tends to attract people who are dishonest.

———～———

Chad put everything in motion during the last half of 1972.

He'd worked with a drummer named Jerry during his solo endeavors. Chad called Jerry "a smart guy from the East Coast," who lived on the edge of respectability. When he wasn't drumming, he always had a scheme working.

"I live by my wits," Jerry was fond of saying.

Chad found Jerry in Cincinnati where he was producing and selling pirated CD's. Jerry was mechanically inclined. Chad asked if he could modify a truck bed to conceal cargo between the bed and a camper shell.

Jerry said he could.

Chad gave Jerry $2,000.

Chad headed back to Mexico and Oaxaca where he renewed his acquaintance with Henry. Together with their guide Feliz, Chad and Henry resumed nightly treks to the middle of nowhere, meeting peasant farmers who hiked down from the mountains.

Chad became frustrated with the process.

"Going out night after night and seeing some poor, exhausted farmer and his wife bringing this stuff was the most horrible experience," he said. "And it was taking forever."

Nights became weeks. Weeks became months. Finally, they'd managed to gather and press about a hundred quality pounds into bricks.

Chad called Jerry, to see if the modified truck was ready.

"No," Jerry said.

"Why?" Chad asked."

"Because I spent the $2,000."

"Why would you do that?" Chad demanded.

Chad heard Jerry shrug over the phone. "I told you I live by my wits."

"I tried to be mad at him," Chad said, "but I couldn't. Giving him $2,000 was just so stupid."

His transportation issue brought Chad back to Ralph, the New York distributor of Chad's first haul.

"I've already got something going this spring," Ralph told him. "And besides, a hundred pounds isn't worth the risk. If you can wait until fall and get a few hundred more pounds in the meantime, I'll send my truck back."

Ralph said he'd used Chad's blind ad scheme to recruit a driver to ferry the camper across the border to San Antonio in his current project.

Given the delay, Chad drove to California to surprise Karen.

When he and Sam knocked on Karen's door, a man answered and introduced himself as Mark, Karen's pottery instructor.

"We're in love," Mark said. "We're going away together."

In their calls and letters, Karen had given Chad no inkling of the affair. She wasn't happy that Mark had taken it upon himself to inform Chad.

"Why?" he asked her.

"I don't know," she said. "It just happened."

"And you're in love with him?"

She shrugged. "I don't know that, either."

Mark envisioned a life in which he and Karen sailed off into a pottery sunset. They didn't. Karen returned to Chad's rent-controlled New York apartment to sort herself out. Chad drove back to Mexico in a state of shock.

If he'd been determined to be a successful smuggler before his marriage began to dissolve, now he'd become obsessive. No obstacle would deter him.

He'd been in Oaxaca only a few days when a more immediate solution to his transportation problem presented itself.

"Hey, Bro! Can you tell me where I can find Henry?"

The big Texan wearing aviator sunglasses with a toothpick in his mouth grinned and extended his hand.

Chad had never heard the term 'bro' as a form of address, but that's what this Texan called everyone. Chad isn't sure he ever knew the guy's real name. He and Henry referred to him as Hey Bro. Chad shook Hey Bro's hand and directed him to the house.

The Texan and another man, introduced as Jimmy, had arrived in a huge self-contained RV. Hey Bro had known Henry in the past as someone who knew how to get in touch with Feliz. As he did for Chad, Feliz served as go-between for Hey Bro and the farmers.

Always interested in learning the business, Chad asked Hey Bro how he planned to get his load across the border.

Hey Bro grinned. "I've got an airplane."

He pointed to Chad's yellow Blazer parked beside Henry's house. "Look, you help me find an airstrip and get my load together, I'll buy your stuff and we'll fly it out. Then, when you're ready, I'll send the plane back for your next load."

An airplane.

An airplane would make everything easy. Chad saw roots of a potential partnership and agreed to the deal.

Chad took a break from his night-time sojourns and followed Hey Bro's RV in his Blazer as they drove north to Monterey to begin searching the desert for a remote landing strip.

During all this time—from the previous year's jerry-rigged adventure to his plan to create an orderly ongoing initiative—Chad had not viewed the business as a criminal enterprise. Rather, he saw himself as a Robin Hood-like desperado, flaunting societal convention in order to provide a harmless service to a needy counterculture.

His time spent with Hey Bro and Jimmy, though, began to chip away at that illusion.

Through snippets of conversation, Chad realized that Hey Bro and Jimmy took their crime more seriously.

The reality hit home one afternoon as they were taking a break in the desert. Since resources concerning economics of the drug business were not otherwise available, Chad had asked Hey Bro what the grass would be wholesaled for across the border. Jimmy wasn't present for this discussion. When Chad broached the subject again as the three of them stopped to rest the next afternoon, Hey Bro pointedly cut off the conversation.

When Jimmy went back to the RV, Hey Bro shot Chad a hostile glare. "Don't ever do that."

"Do what?"

"Discuss what I'm selling this stuff for in front of Jimmy."

"Okay. Why?"

Hey Bro took a quick glance over his shoulder. "Because if he finds out, I'll have to kill him."

Not quite sure if Hey Bro was making one of those because-if-I told-you-I'd-have-to-kill-you jokes, Chad said, "Um . . . why would you . . ."

"I'd have to do it before he killed me."

———

They eventually located a paved air strip with no sign of human activity for miles. The runway likely was one of several maintained by Petroleos Mexicanos, or PeMex, a state-owned petroleum company formed in 1938 via expropriation of all private, foreign and domestic oil companies by the Mexican government. Their strips were used for inspecting and servicing pipelines and equipment operating in remote desert areas.

Hey Bro made some calls.

The Monterey region is flat and brown, pocked with deep, twisting gullies carved out by flash floods that race through canyon bottoms when rains pelt the distant mountains. These dry washes provide off-road vehicle access to this wilderness, but cars and trucks can be swept away when water comes roaring through these streambeds without warning. The coming rainy season lent an urgency to their search. They'd already been caught in one rainstorm that rendered much of the desert impassable even to the Blazer.

On this day, though, a cloudless blue sky and scorching sun greeted Chad as he faced north, listening for the sound of an airplane engine.

The surrounding desert growth consisted of cactus, grasses and mesquite trees large enough to conceal Chad's Blazer. A rutted dirt road accessed one end of the landing strip. The Blazer was hidden among thick mesquite bushes at the opposite end.

A barbed wire fence separated the desert from the airstrip where Chad and Hey Bro waited. They'd piled plastic bags containing bricks of grass next to the Blazer.

Finally, they heard a distant whine.

"Where is he?" Chad asked. "I can't see him."

"He's coming in low," Hey Bro said. "He won't pop up until he gets in position to land."

A few moments later, a high wing single engine craft roared by, paralleling the strip a scant twenty feet above the ground. The pilot gained altitude as he flew a mile or so past, then turned back for the base leg of his approach. The engine whine died as the pilot throttled back.

The craft touched down as soon as pavement allowed, and Chad wondered momentarily if the strip was long enough. Leaning hard on the brakes, the pilot stopped his craft where the pavement ended, twenty yards from the barbed-wire and marijuana. The pilot turned the plane to face the opposite direction, set his brakes, and, without killing the engine, jumped out long enough to open a cargo bay hatch. He motioned for Chad and Hey Bro to start loading.

Hey Bro handed bags over the fence to Chad two at a time and Chad ran them to the plane.

Only a couple of bags were left beyond the fence when Chad saw a dust cloud tracking through the desert towards the runway's opposite end.

"What's that?" he shouted to the pilot.

"Oh, shit! I'm outta here!" The pilot slammed the hatch and jumped into the cabin.

"Wait, wait," Chad yelled. "We've got two more bags!"

"No way—"

"Goddammit, wait! I'll get 'em."

Chad sprinted toward the Blazer, clearing the fence with a hurdle.

Over Hey Bro's protests, he grabbed the last two bags, threw them over the fence, then used a fence post for leverage as he vaulted the wires.

A truck had appeared at the far end of the runway.

Chad grabbed the bags and sprinted. The plane's engine roared. Because he had limited runway length to work with, the pilot had to lock his brakes while the engine came up to speed.

Chad saw uniformed men standing behind the truck cab. They appeared to be armed.

The pilot pushed his passenger door open. Fighting the prop wash, Chad tossed the last two bags inside. The door slammed closed, and the plane leapt forward. Now the truck gathered speed as it came toward them. Chad turned to see Hey Bro waving frantically. Chad leaped the fence again, then checked over his shoulder.

Plane and truck seemed on a collision course. At the last instant, the truck veered. Chad believes the plane's landing gear kissed the truck's roof as soldiers threw themselves to the truck bed.

"Come on, come on!" Hey Bro screamed.

He'd pulled the Blazer from its hiding place.

As the plane gained altitude and banked into the distance, the armed troop turned their attention to the Blazer.

Hey Bro took a jarring cross-desert route paralleling the runway toward the access road. The truck's awkward maneuvering to turn on the narrow landing strip gave the Blazer the advantage it needed.

Chad estimates they hit a hundred miles an hour on the straightaways as they fled.

Hey Bro headed stateside to handle his shipment on that end of the food chain, advising Chad to contact him when he was ready to transport another load.

Now, Chad had to begin assembling his own load again. This task remained tedious with journeys into the desert every night, but the flow of marijuana improved as word spread concerning Chad's enterprise. By the end of September, Chad and Henry had assembled three hundred pounds, dried it and compressed it into bricks.

Chad placed a call to Hey Bro.

"Can't help you, man," came the reply. "My pilot got arrested."

Okay. That left Ralph back in New York City.

They struck a deal giving Ralph a percentage of the load. Ralph dispatched Marlene, his girlfriend, to Oaxaca to inspect Chad's operation. Marlene didn't like what she found.

Chad calculated he needed an additional hundred pounds to offset the cost of Ralph's share.

"You're just being greedy," Marlene complained as the truck and camper shell were due to arrive in four days. "You can't get the additional stuff pressed into bricks by then."

Chad persisted in gathering more grass, working himself to the point of exhaustion.

———&———

Chad's preference for driving the camper and marijuana across the border had been Rick and Tic, the hippie couple he and Karen had met on their tour of Mexico last year. On his way to the fateful California meeting with Karen, he'd stopped off to see Rick and Tic. He informed them of his plan and offered $5,000.

They agreed.

Ralph, though, vetoed that plan.

"We'll use the guy who drove my last load," he said. "The one I found using your idea about the ad in a paper. He's done it before. He knows the routine."

The camper appeared at the appointed location in San Antonio, keys locked inside. Chad used the keys Ralph had mailed him and drove the camper into Mexico.

Henry's compound didn't include a garage large enough to handle the process of loading the camper. Chad solved that problem by renting a place nearby and convincing the landlord to allow him to modify a building.

"It has to be big enough that I can park my camper inside," Chad said. "I don't want any of my stuff stolen."

He didn't explain what exactly his stuff was, but the landlord agreed.

Loading involved raising the camper shell, stashing bricks of marijuana on the pickup bed, then lowering the camper into place. That job accomplished, Chad and the camper headed to Matamoros, Mexico.

———&———

Marlene was right. Chad had waited too long gathering and pressing bricks.

He didn't make the initial rendezvous on time. He headed for Matamoros thinking, if he drove straight through, he could make it. The rainy season, though, showed up with a vengeance, washing out sections of roadway. When Ralph's driver arrived, Chad was still on the road. The driver, identified in legal documents only as Mancuso, flew home. Ralph was furious at the delay.

When Chad finally reached Matamoros, he learned his driver wouldn't be back for three days. Nervous about hanging around with a camper full of marijuana, Chad drove to a small village twenty miles away, rented a hotel room and spent three days watching Spanish language broadcasts of the Oakland A's defeating the New York Mets in the World Series. Chad didn't care much for baseball, but the alternative was Mexican soap operas or masked wrestlers.

On October 20, Chad drove the camper into the Matamoros hotel parking lot, then taxied to a rental car agency where he acquired a Buick under the name Robin J. Kitchner—the identification under which the pickup camper was registered. He arranged to drop the Buick at an agency in San Antonio the next day.

The plan called for Ralph's driver to pick up the camper on October 21. Chad left Sam in their hotel room early that morning and walked to a vantage point to watch the camper crossing into the United States. Ralph had stressed the importance of observing the camper as it negotiated both the border and the immigration checkpoint further north.

"You want to know if the guy gets caught at either place," Ralph said.

When Chad returned to the hotel lot, however, the camper was already gone.

In a panic, Chad hurried to his room, bundled Sam into the Buick, and raced to the border crossing where he found no sign of the camper. Who he did encounter, though, was the same border guard who had discovered the $17,000 when Chad, Karen and Sam had crossed the border looking for Cindy the year before.

"I see you still got your dog," the guard told him.

"Yeah," Chad said. He felt certain the guard would direct him into the inspection lane. Curiously, though, the guard waved them through.

Chad caught up to the camper at the INS checkpoint. He followed at a comfortable distance to the Holiday Inn parking lot in San Antonio.

———— ∾ ————

Chad's mistake, well, one of them anyway, was laboring under the delusion that Ralph had inspired loyalty in his anonymous driver by Chad's offer of $5,000. One problem with having an anonymous associate is the inability to check his most recent résumé.

Sometime between his previous employment by Ralph in April and his October trip, the driver had screwed up. Because the details of federal informants' criminal histories are seldom made public, Chad is not sure exactly what the guy did to get himself arrested by the FBI or DEA.

But imagining what happened after his indiscretion isn't difficult.

The driver—Mancuso—accompanied by his attorney, sits in a holding cell, accused of some nefarious deed for which he faces years of imprisonment.

"Can we work something out here?" asks his attorney.

"No," says the agent. "He's going away for a long time."

"What if he's aware of a more serious pending crime?" asks his attorney.

"Like what?"

"Well, he doesn't know for sure, but he thinks it's something really big."

"Why does he think that?"

"They're paying him $5,000 just to drive across the Mexican border and park a truck in San Antonio."

The agent's arching eyebrows betray his poker face. "Lemme' talk to someone."

So, when Mancuso crosses the border and heads to San Antonio, he's not working for Chad anymore. He's working for the United States government. He parks the pickup at the Holiday Inn, puts his hands in his pockets, and whistles a happy tune as he heads for the highway.

The $5,000 is why a team of fifteen federal agents—equipped with five cars, an airplane, a helicopter and a starlight scope for surveilling the truck by moonlight—descended on Chad the moment he opened the camper door to retrieve Sam.

The Feds were expecting the motherlode. All Chad could do was pretend he and Sam, like Mancuso, were just two more ignorant employees hired to drive this truck to another destination.

When they searched the camper, the Feds found nothing hidden in the pickup cab, engine compartment, camper shell or door panels. They didn't have the correct equipment to raise the camper from the pickup bed, but finally managed to pry it up far enough to find the grass.

Chad spent most of the night handcuffed in a hotel room.

Sam was detained at a different location.

Agents came and went until one said to Chad, "Let's go have a cup of coffee."

As they walked to the hotel restaurant, he said, "If I take these cuffs off, you wouldn't try to escape, would you? Because I wouldn't want to hurt you."

"I'm not going anywhere," Chad assured the agent. "Can you be sure someone takes care of my dog? He didn't do anything wrong."

"He ran."

"That's what dog's do."

"And you ran after him."

"Listen," Chad said again, "that dog's been through a lot. I couldn't let him get hit by a car."

When they finally found the grass well after midnight, the next agent Chad talked to was more judgmental. "You're an idiot," he told Chad. "Nobody pays someone $5,000 to drive a few hundred pounds of marijuana across the border."

Finally afforded his phone call, Chad contacted Joel in New York, who repeated his advice to be as cooperative as he could without telling them anything. Joel immediately called Ralph—also Joel's client—and told him of Chad's arrest. "We don't know what Chad will say to anyone," Joel told Ralph, "but I think you'd better be prepared for the worst."

At his booking, Chad identified himself using only his first and last name: William Mitchell. He hoped no one would know he was *that* William Mitchell, but a night beat reporter for the San Antonio Express-News was not fooled. The next morning, the world knew Spokane's golden boy had been busted for running drugs.

Chad transferred from city to county jail where he was handed a uniform, blankets, then placed in a holding cell with bunk beds and ten other people. Most of his cellmates were Mexican. They watched Chad as he approached an unoccupied lower bunk.

As he started to spread his blankets, he felt a presence looming over him. The man shook his head, pointing to the top bunk.

"Okay," Chad said. "Fine with me. Just let me know if . . ."

But the inmate—along with most of the others—had directed his attention to another prisoner being ushered into the cell. They glared at the newcomer, who looked to the guard with desperation. The guard paid no attention. As soon as the guard was out of sight, a half-dozen of Chad's cellmates descended on the new guy and beat him bloody.

The man who'd directed Chad to the top bunk, pointed a finger and shook his head.

"Right," Chad said, more to himself than anyone else. "None of my affair."

— CHAPTER TWENTY-FOUR —

The arraigning judge set Chad's bail at half a million dollars, meaning he had to produce $50,000 cash to remain free while awaiting trial. Most of the profit from Chad's first smuggling adventure had been reinvested in the failed scheme. Chad hadn't performed in months, so his legitimate bank account had dwindled.

In New York, Karen scrambled to put together $50,000. She managed to do so, but Chad's assets were tapped out.

Chad spent a couple more weeks in the county jail before his early December release on bail. He'd kept out of trouble by acting as scribe for the Hispanic inmates, writing letters for them to their girlfriends and families. Even in jail, everyone liked Chad Mitchell.

Chad returned to New York. Joel told him what to expect.

"My fee," Joel told him, "is $25,000 . . ."

Chad closed his eyes and shook his head as he calculated how he might get the money.

". . . but that covers everything, start to finish."

"Why so much?" Chad asked.

"I have to find someone in Texas to represent you at trial," Joel said. "I'm not licensed to practice there. I'll make sure he's someone good."

"Then why aren't I paying him $25,000?"

"He'll try the case," Joel said, "but I'll supervise from here. He'll do what I tell him to do."

"Okay, what else?"

"You'll be convicted, no question about that," Joel said. "But we'll have a strong case on appeal."

Conviction, Joel assured Chad, wouldn't be so bad. Chad had no previous criminal record. Four hundred pounds of marijuana was insignificant by DEA standards. He'd get a minimal sentence, maybe not have to do prison time at all.

When Chad returned to New York to await trial and work in order to pay his legal fees, Karen moved out of Chad's apartment and kept her distance. They did not divorce until 1980. Despite their estrangement, Chad and Karen remained friends, even after she remarried, until her death from cancer in 2012.

He hoped he might find work in voice acting for commercials. Advertising agencies, though, were reluctant to hire an accused felon to represent their accounts.

Chad didn't want to resume his career as a solo performer, but when owners of The Ballroom, then one of New York City's pre-eminent night clubs, approached him about joining their slate of cabaret performers, he had little alternative.

During 1975, New York's cabaret scene had experienced a revival.

The mixture of music, dance, stand-up and skit comedy offered an alternative to rock music performers, trending by this time toward heavy metal.

Greg Dawson, co-owner and manager of The Ballroom, described cabaret as an art form applying to "any entertainment that removes what has been called 'the fourth wall' separating audience and performer. What matters isn't the size or type of entertainment, but the relationship of the performer to that audience."

Ironically, one of the reasons Chad was a reluctant solo performer was his unease with that relationship. Now, in addition, his audience would know of his smuggling adventures and pending trial.

A common theme throughout Chad's life had been his difficulty with intimacy. As a child, he preferred the emotional safety of his dog-pal Sniffy. He was awkward in his responses to the adulation of admirers for his natural athletic and vocal abilities as a teenager—a discomfort magnified many times over by what felt like cloying adoration heaped on The Trio by fans.

During his late thirties and early forties, Chad realized his romantic relationships couldn't get past a certain point emotionally, and he sought professional help. Some of the therapy focused on the obvious—his dysfunctional relationship with an alcoholic father. But none of that ever solved the riddle of his inability to deeply connect with someone else.

An answer finally came one morning in the summer of 2019 as he worked through a first draft of this manuscript. The writer had nibbled around the edges of this question but had gotten it wrong when he wrote that Chad's sins had finally been laid bare and he didn't have to wear the golden boy image anymore.

"For the first time in 82 years," he said, "I know why I'm uncomfortable with adulation, with adoration. It's because my mother adored me.'"

He summarizes this way: "My mom had a difficult childhood and, as a single mother, struggled to raise me. She had many outstanding qualities, but her world view was limited. I couldn't talk with her about anything that didn't conform to her viewpoint without reducing her to tears. I was not who she thought I was. So, I developed a façade of perfection that turned into the golden boy persona. She adored that façade. But it caused me to keep her at arm's length.

"With The Trio it wasn't that I was uncomfortable with applause after a good show, because we *were* good and had worked hard to achieve it. I was uncomfortable with who or what people assumed I was because of the celebrity. They didn't know me. They adored the image. I was too immature to know how to respond appropriately, so I retreated—as I did with my mom.

"Getting busted was a relief because people would know once and for all I wasn't perfect. I wasn't some idealized image. And if they were going to enjoy one of my shows, it would be because of the artistry. I didn't feel the pressure any longer to maintain some façade. I could allow myself to develop an intimacy with the audience that successful cabaret required. It was an intimacy based on my authenticity as a person.

"All of this is my way of explaining things to myself, not blaming my mom for how I turned out. I look at it as the luck of the draw. If I had had a sibling, he or she probably would have reacted completely differently to the same parenting."

In any case, when Chad returned to the New York stage while awaiting his appeal, something had changed.

And everything clicked.

One critic wrote of Chad's performance:

> After Mr. Mitchell went out on his own, he evolved tentatively in a continental cabaret direction, but the time wasn't right. He didn't feel comfortable with audiences, either, and he realizes now that the discomfort showed.
>
> "I really didn't have an openness on stage," he said the other day. "With a trio, the energy starts between the members onstage. Alone, all your openness has to be right there. The other problem was that it was the wrong time to do what I was doing. Rock music was really heavy, and there were few places to play. It was only when the cabaret scene came back that I could work. I didn't really know where I fit."
>
> Before and after his arrest, Mr. Mitchell spent time in Minneapolis working sporadically. He was offered one-shot dates (in New York), but it was only when he was given an extended run at the Ballroom that he decided to get back into his music in earnest.
>
> It's good that he did. Mr. Mitchell has a warm, easy tenor with a nice vibrato, one that is equally effective in both soft and up-tempo material. And he is clearly correct that his time has come.
>
> Audiences are ready now for folky cabaret artists, and Mr. Mitchell is about the best this observer has heard on that circuit. He tempers the artificiality of the genre with a folkish naturalness yet delivers his set with an engaging professionalism and style, ably backed by a pianist and percussionist. If there is still a hint of self-consciousness, it is far less bothersome than with most of his competitors and far more redeemed by musical excellence.
>
> Given his legal situation, Mr. Mitchell is not making long-range career plans. But he happily admits to feeling better than ever about performing.

"I think I still have a lot of work to do," he said. "I honestly can say that, even including The Trio, I feel better at the Ballroom than I've ever felt before."

⚬

Chad's trial—heard without jury by U.S. District Court Judge Adrian A. Spears—lasted a single day. The government called one witness—Mancuso. Chad's Texas attorney, Roy Barerra, wasn't about to allow his client to testify. In his summation to the jury, Barerra argued that Chad was an unwitting participant in someone else's smuggling scheme.

The judge didn't buy it. On January 14, 1975, Spears found Chad guilty of possessing with intent to distribute four hundred pounds of marijuana. Chad accepted the verdict and, comforted by Joel's optimism concerning first-time offenders, thought the only question was whether he'd be assessed any prison time at all.

Probation officers who prepared a pre-sentence report saw a well-known 38-year-old with no previous criminal history. They both recommended probation. Joel's expectations, though, failed to account for a Texas judge who didn't care for liberal folk singers. Judge Spears was a hawk on marijuana, which he considered a gateway drug.

"I realize you are known all over the country," Spears told Chad at sentencing. "I've never heard you sing, but I'm sure you have an excellent voice. I think, though, you had more to do with this than what you're telling us." Spears sentenced Chad to five years, the maximum term he could assess, with a five-year special parole term to follow.

Chad and Barerra were dumbfounded. Career criminals who had gotten caught with literally tons of marijuana had been sentenced to only three years prison time by other federal judges.

Joel immediately filed an appeal.

Chad was released on his existing appearance bond, pending the outcome, and returned to New York where Joel requested another $25,000. Chad was livid. "You said the first $25,000 would cover the whole thing," Chad told him.

"Yeah, the trial," Joel said. "Not an appeal."

"The trial lasted one day," Chad said. "We didn't call any witnesses."

Chad consulted with Michael Standard, an attorney whom he'd met during some of his civil rights activities. Standard put him in touch with an associate, Eric Lieberman, who handled the appeal.

Standard made it clear he was to be paid up front. Although he was working again, Chad's resources were almost exhausted. He called his accountant, who also happened to be Ralph's accountant. Ralph's drug operations were still going strong. Chad asked the accountant to point out to Ralph that he had consistently kept quiet about Ralph's involvement.

Money to pay for Chad's appeal appeared a few days later.

———⁓———

The issue on appeal was warrantless search.

"An appeals court will be troubled by the fact they searched your vehicle without a warrant," Joel said. "They'll know you're guilty as hell, but they'll be making bad case law if you don't get off."

A legal presumption that police could search automobiles without a warrant dated to Prohibition. If Feds had to get a warrant to search a moonshiner's vehicle, the moonshiner and his car would be long gone by the time a judge acted. So, an exception to the Constitution's Fourth Amendment guaranteeing protection against unreasonable search and seizure had evolved. The Automobile Search Doctrine, recognized by many state courts, held that a warrant wasn't required unless the vehicle is parked on private property.

Other courts had held, though, that the Fourth Amendment requires a warrant unless *exigent circumstances* make it impractical to obtain one.

Chad's attorney argued no exigent circumstances existed. The Feds tracked Chad's truck from the time Mancuso picked it up in Mexico. The truck was under their control from the time Mancuso left it in the San Antonio parking lot. Agents planned their stakeout and arrest well in advance. The truck traveled three hundred miles into the United States before Chad's arrest. Chad and Sam entered the truck seven hours after its border crossing. Chad's attorneys argued that the Feds had plenty of time to get a warrant.

In his pre-trial motions, Barerra asked Spears to declare marijuana found in the truck inadmissible. Judge Spears ruled no warrant was required.

On Jan. 20, 1976, a three-judge panel of the Fifth U.S. Circuit Court agreed with Chad's argument. The three federal appeals court judges said Spears should have suppressed the evidence.

The New York Times caught up with him at the *Ballroom*.

"*I didn't really care how I won,*" Chad told the reporter. "*I just didn't want to go to jail.*" *Mr. Mitchell, 39 years old, refused to discuss what he was doing in the truck or his connection with the man who drove it from Mexico, described by the court decision as an informer for the Drug Enforcement Agency,*" the article added.

———∾———

During his time at the Ballroom, the Times had twice named Chad New York City's cabaret performer of the year. A couple of weeks after the court decision declaring him a free man, an advertising agency executive approached Chad.

Paul Anka had recorded a jingle for Kodak—*These are the Times of Your Life*—and the agency was looking for someone to replace Anka.

"I've been a fan of yours forever," the ad executive told him.

"Well," Chad said, "I'd love to do it, but I have to remind you that I'm a convicted felon and Kodak is pretty vanilla."

"Yeah," the executive told him, "but you won the case."

"Not exactly," Chad said. "The government could still appeal."

And they did.

A U.S. attorney appealed the three-judge panel's decision to the full Fifth Circuit court. The full court, with four dissents, considered the exigent circumstances issue and said essentially, "Yeah, but we all know you did it."

Standard and Lieberman immediately appealed to the U.S. Supreme Court.

Kodak didn't offer Chad the Paul Anka gig.

By May of 1977, Chad had avoided prison by process of various appeals for more than two years while living and working in New York. Tony O'Hare, his parole officer, was a veteran babysitter of federal parolees and informed Chad of the rules.

"I don't have to make appointments," he said. "I will show up at your home any time of the day or night. I want to see if you're smoking grass or using drugs. I'll stop by your place of employment without notification, so if you say you're working, you'd better be working. And if I tell you to come to my office, you'd better be on time."

Parole officers, though, are just as subject to a compelling personality as anyone else.

"We got along great," Chad recalls. "He was a nice guy. He was straight with me, and I was straight with him."

In May of 1977 Chad asked Tony for permission to travel to Chicago to perform June 3 at the annual Chicago Midwest Emmy Awards. Tony allowed the trip.

Judge Spears, though, was displeased when he settled down to watch television one evening and saw Steve Allen introducing Chad Mitchell who sang *Marieke,* leading into the presentation for Outstanding Achievement in a Children's Program Series.

Spears ordered Chad placed in custody when he returned to New York. Chad was booked into the New York city jail. Spears' plan was for Chad to remain in custody until Chad's appeal of the appeal of the appeal was settled. His attorneys, however, again arranged for him to remain free, pending resolution of his case.

Although Chad's attorneys felt they had a shot at getting his conviction overturned by the Supreme Court, while he was at the Emmy awards show in Chicago a friend of a friend warned him otherwise.

During The Trio's visit to Montgomery in 1965, Chad spent time talking with Mary Travers of Peter, Paul and Mary, about benefit concerts. Often, the promoters of these benefits were inexperienced and didn't know how to fill the venues. So, rather than doing hit-or-miss benefit concerts before small crowds, Frank Fried and Chad conceived of an alternative. They proposed a nonprofit organization they called ACRAF, The Artists' Civil

Rights Assistance Foundation. They asked artists to donate proceeds of performances on or near Lincoln's birthday.

Mary was chosen chairman of the foundation.

Mary also performed at the Emmy Awards event in Chicago, accompanied by her date, attorney Richard Ben-Veniste, who had risen to prominence as a special investigator during the Watergate scandal.

Mary introduced Chad.

"I've been following your case," Ben-Veniste told Chad. "Warrantless search is an interesting question. Would you like a bit of free legal advice?"

"Sure," Chad said.

"Tell your lawyer to focus on finding you a good prison," Ben-Veniste said. "I don't see the Supreme Court agreeing to hear this case."

Chad took him at his word. As a result, when the U.S. Supreme Court refused to hear his appeal, Chad was destined for "what they called a country-club prison."

Chad reported to San Antonio in June to begin a five-year sentence at a minimum-security federal prison at Eglin Air Force Base in Florida. Other than the whole going-to-prison thing, Chad enjoyed his journey from Texas to Florida.

"I learned that, at any given time, twenty-five percent of the federal prison population is in transit," Chad said. "They rent space in county jails, so they don't have to build more federal prisons, and they drive you around on buses."

Dressed in a prison traveling suit, with a chain around his waist and shackles on his hands and feet, Chad and the others were handed lunch—a sandwich and a cookie in a brown paper bag—then shuffled onto a bus. They made stops along the way while some prisoners disembarked, and others climbed on. They stopped somewhere new each evening.

A medium security prison at Texarkana was Chad's first overnight visit.

He and his bus-mates were given dinner, assigned a cell and told to shower, where they mixed with local inmates. Chad struck up a conversation with a sociable fellow. Not until the guy showed up to visit Chad in his cell did Chad realize his mistake.

"I was only trying to be friendly," he explained when this veteran inmate's intentions became clear.

"By speaking to me, you were leading me on," the guy said.

Chad apologized.

"Okay, I'll let you off this time. But you can get yourself in a lot of trouble that way."

For the remainder of his journey, Chad didn't engage the locals.

The penitentiary in Atlanta—granddaddy of all federal prisons—was next. Built in 1899 as the largest federal prison, this three-story edifice of bricks and iron bars has hosted mobsters like Al Capone, Whitey Bulger and Mickey Cohen; former major league baseball players Denny McLain and Willie Akins. Eugene Debs, founder of the International Workers of the World—whose membership once included Frank Fried—served a term there for sedition during World War I. Chad had seen the prison's forbidding entrance in several Jimmy Cagney movies. He felt like a guest at a historical bed and breakfast.

The trip from San Antonio to Eglin required a week of travel.

The last stop before Eglin Air Force Base was the federal prison at Maxwell Air Force Base in Montgomery. A decade earlier, Chad had accompanied Martin Luther King's march on Montgomery. As the prisoners waited on the bus, Chad peered out his window to see another famous inmate named Mitchell.

Former U.S. Attorney General John Mitchell, beginning his sentence for his role in the Watergate scandal, walked past wearing his orange jumpsuit, carrying a set of blankets.

Eglin Federal Prison Camp—located in pine woods of the Florida Panhandle on the fringe of Eglin Air Force Base—hosts white-collar tax cheats, embezzlers, Medicaid-cheating doctors, shady lawyers, crooked politicians and low-level drug dealers.

When he finally arrived at Eglin, Chad confronted incarceration with neither bricks nor bars. Guards escorted new prisoners to a paved road with a solid white stripe painted across it. "If you step over this line," they explained, "we'll call the FBI."

Anywhere else, Chad said, most of the Eglin guards would have become examples of Darwin's theory of natural selection. "Inmates who had been in real prisons before coming to Eglin said all these guys would be dead in a high-security situation."

The inmates lived in a dormitory, each with their own half-walled cubicle containing a bed and a desk. They had tennis courts and a weight-lifting area. They didn't have an oval track to run on, but they could still run, so long as they didn't cross any lines.

Almost all prisoners were well behaved because Eglin had a waiting list of guys seeking transfers from more serious prisons. No one wanted to be sent elsewhere to make room. "The guards really had nothing to do but be picky," Chad said. "It was like boot camp. The books on our desks in our cubicles had to be all lined up. Our beds had to be made."

Every inmate was assigned a job. Chad was placed among a crew of four who mowed bunkers. Each day, a sergeant from the base picked up Chad and his crew and drove them to an area featuring row upon row of concrete bunkers covered by dirt and grass.

"Each bunker was like a hill," Chad said. "They only gave us one lawnmower, so we would trade off pushing the mower uphill, then wrestling it down the other side. Not an easy job in Florida during summer."

Often as not, bunker doors were open, revealing every kind of armament the U.S. Air Force possessed.

"The sergeant would just leave us there, unsupervised," Chad said. "We could have taken a bomb."

Once he settled in, friends wrote letters expressing sympathy and asking what they could do to help. Chad wrote back, saying, "Send me a good book."

Soon, thanks to friends on the outside, he'd assembled a library of fine literature. He looked forward to three years of uninterrupted reading, maybe even some writing of his own, while he waited to be eligible for parole.

Five months into it, though, the warden stopped by his cubicle.

"Mitchell, I'd like to see you in my office."

Chad thought, *Oh, shit.*

Other men had been called into the warden's office to be informed they'd broken some rule and were being dispatched to a real prison.

Chad followed the warden on the edge of panic. He felt worse when the warden closed his door and sat behind a broad desk. He didn't offer Chad the opportunity to sit.

He stared at Chad for a moment and then said, "You're outta' here."

"Why? What . . . what did I do . . . ?"

"Don't know."

"Can . . . can I take my books?"

"Take whatever you want. You're out."

"I . . . I don't understand."

"The judge let you go. It'll take a few days to process the paperwork."

———— ❧ ————

Although Joel was no longer Chad's attorney, one of Judge Spears' clerks had contacted Joel Steinberg once Chad was incarcerated and suggested Chad might consider writing a letter to the judge, apologizing for his crime and expressing remorse.

Chad didn't feel particularly remorseful, but what could it hurt?

Apparently, that's what Judge Spears had wanted all along: an admission that Chad had done what the DEA agents said he'd done, and an expression of regret.

Chad still doesn't feel remorse. In an age when state after state is decriminalizing marijuana, he looks back on those events as an adventure rather than a crime against society. Others felt the same way. When he ran his smuggling scheme past Frank Fried, Frank said, "I would advise you not to do it."

"Yeah," Chad said, "but I think I'd be good at it."

Frank shrugged. "Well, if you get caught, I wouldn't look at what you'd done as being anything immoral. I would just consider it a failed business."

Although he remains disappointed that he didn't get to read all those books, prison is, after all, prison, so he wasn't about to volunteer to stay on. His final few days at Eglin, though, became testy.

Chad did not share the good news with friends and acquaintances at

Eglin, but he realized, given the prison rumor mill, inmates and guards would quickly know of his good fortune. A prisoner's release materializing out of thin-air usually meant one thing. That prisoner had informed on someone to earn it.

Chad felt suspicious looks and cold shoulders of people who had formerly been friendly as they separated themselves from someone who might be toxic. He kept his head down, made himself as scarce as possible, and held his breath until November 1977, when he left Eglin and boarded an airplane for New York.

"I have to admit, looking back, I have no ill will toward the judge or the police," Chad said. "I was as guilty as sin, according to the law at that time."

The one thing Chad does regret is the effect his arrest and conviction had on his mother. "I didn't expect to be caught so I didn't let myself think about that. In retrospect, I do feel bad. I know it was very hard on her."

Florence Mitchell planned for her son to be a doctor. She disapproved of his heading off to New York that summer of 1959 to sing and make records. Eventually, as her friends and neighbors spoke enviously to her about Chad's success, she made her peace with his choice, although she never forgave Father Beaver for luring Chad away that summer.

The publicity surrounding his arrest also affected Chad's father. Chad does not, however, feel similar regret where William Mitchell is concerned.

Chad's family moved from Portland to Spokane when he was seven. William, who suffered from alcoholism, left the family a couple of years after the move and subsequently dropped in and out of their lives.

"My mother spoke of him as being a cripple," Chad said. "She never objected to him seeing me, but he never gave her a dime for child support. We were not well off."

Chad remembers his father showing up one night when Chad was at Boy Scout camp. The counselor told Chad his father had come to pick him up. "I couldn't figure out why. We were lurching all over the road, and he hit a car when he tried to park."

Chad's mother divorced his father during one of his extended absences. He remarried, divorced again, then returned to Spokane. "When I was just out of high school, he finally got on the wagon," Chad said. "He converted to Catholicism and a priest at Gonzaga took him under his wing. Once he'd stopped drinking, that priest advised him there was no longer an impediment to resuming the marriage."

Chad's mother, though, wanted nothing to do with him.

As The Trio's success grew in the early sixties, "My dad took a certain amount of pride in telling people he was Chad Mitchell's father." Whatever relationship remained, though, was irreparably broken following Chad's arrest. William had resumed drinking. He contacted Karen as she scrambled to put together $50,000 for Chad's bail.

"He said he was broke and needed money for food," Chad said. "He couldn't ask people in Spokane for help, he told her, because 'I just can't face anybody with all this stuff about Chad being in the paper.'"

Karen rebuffed him. Chad never spoke to his father again.

— CHAPTER TWENTY-FIVE —

C had's New York residency came to an end when he decided in 1979 to buy a new Volkswagen Scirocco and take a trip west.

He hadn't owned a vehicle since his 1973 arrest. The Blazer was still at Henry's compound outside Oaxaca. In 1976, while Chad anticipated the outcome of his federal appeal, he received a letter from Mexico.

"Chad, this is Henry. Man, I'm sorry, but I got arrested and I didn't have enough money to bribe my way out. So, I had to give your Blazer to my attorney."

Chad's attorneys warned him not to respond to or acknowledge the letter. "I didn't begrudge Henry giving away the car," Chad said. "I liked that car, but I wouldn't wish a Mexican jail on anyone."

Initially following his release, Chad didn't have money to spend on a car, and, living in New York City, he got around without a vehicle. He'd returned to his cabaret performances and had appeared in two stage productions. The first, called *Island,* written by Peter Link, the author of the musical *King of Hearts*, was staged in Milwaukee. *He Lived the Good Life,* staged at the Guthrie Theatre in Minneapolis, presented the Biblical life of Christ through a series of songs. Chad played Jesus. Frank Fried tried raising money to take that show to Broadway. *Jesus Christ Superstar,* however, pretty much owned the Savior market.

New Volkswagen Scirocco in hand—and having cleared the journey with his probation officer—Chad headed west to see his mother in Spokane, then south along the Pacific coast. He was derailed in Eugene, Oregon where he discovered grapes and a woman who was "a dead ringer for Candice Bergen."

Chad had intended Eugene as a stopover on his way south. He wanted to visit a couple of days with Wally, whom he'd met during his freshman year at Stanford. Wally introduced Chad to the Candice look-alike.

Candice motivated Chad to hang around. She had a son. Sons were a new experience for Chad. Recalling his Sam strategy, Chad gave the boy a basset hound puppy whom they named Beaumont. The dog tended to hang with Chad more than the son.

Chad and Candice lasted a couple of years, during which time Chad embarked on his second agrarian adventure.

Though his criminal days were behind him, Chad remained disappointed that his smuggling career was cut short before he had a chance to apply the full scope of his ingenuity to the cultivation and marketing of marijuana.

Oregon vineyards at that time were focused on production of white wines, because the climate is similar to German grape-growing regions. Chad met a man at a party, though, who argued Oregon should be producing Pinot Noir grapes. Chad was intrigued.

"He did a whole study, showed me spreadsheets on what we could do with forty acres," Chad said. One of his suggestions was drip irrigation. Chad bought cuttings from Pinot Noir vines and performed drip irrigation experiments, which worked. He found a guy who sold area cheeses and wines at a community market, who agreed to partner with Chad in a retail outlet.

None of them, though, had any money.

Frank Fried declined to invest.

So, Chad researched the sort of folks who typically backed vineyards and wine making—doctors, lawyers and corporate executives. This was an era of rampant inflation, though. Doctors, lawyers and corporate executives could put their money in a savings account and earn a ten or twelve percent return or realize an even higher return with CD's. So why risk fooling around with introducing a new grape variety into Oregon? Reluctantly, Chad bid his grape fantasy adieu at about the same time his relationship with the faux Candice turned sour.

During his time in Eugene, the five-year probation Judge Spears had tacked onto his prison sentence came to an end.

Despite his setbacks, Chad remained someone whom most people found interesting and likable—even, apparently, jaded veterans of the criminal justice system. When he settled in Eugene, Chad's supervision had to be transferred to a parole officer there.

On Nov. 16, 1982, Chad received the following letter:

Dear Chad,

Well, your expiration date has arrived. We appreciate your cooperation during the supervision term. Sorry the District of Texas did not see fit to terminate your case early.

Don't be a stranger and keep us posted on your vineyard progress.

Keith R. Stewart
U.S. Probation officer

P.S. Love to Beaumont.

———✹———

A few weeks after his breakup with Candice, Chad reluctantly accompanied Wally to a party. As is still his preference at social gatherings, he settled into a spot away from the center of activity and became a polite observer. Interested non-participation is an introvert's version of a good time.

A professor in the University of Oregon's Planning Department had invited several female graduate students to a Trivial Pursuit party at her home. One of the graduate students, Chris Johns, was being introduced around when she noticed Chad sitting by himself in the living room. She knelt in front of him and asked, "So, who are you?"

Confident and athletic, Chris was an inch taller than Chad. He didn't find her particularly attractive until he stared into intelligent blue eyes.

"Those eyes just got to me," he said.

Chad and Chris were paired as partners in the Trivial Pursuit game. Chris answered scientific questions. Chad answered for other categories. They ended the night unbeaten.

The next day Chad asked Chris to dinner.

The demands of her master's program had her scheduled every half-hour into the next week.

"Dinner is fine," she told Chad, "but would you mind calling back next Wednesday after 4:30?"

That dinner nearly sunk the relationship.

Things were going fine until Chris, who'd been raised in a rural Southern Illinois town, began to tell Chad of the summers she'd spent in France with her French-born mother. Chad, recalling perhaps an early Trio song called *Putting on the Style,* suggested she was an elitist.

Chris saw nothing funny in his accusation. Chad scrambled to apologize. Chris finished the meal only because she hadn't driven her car and didn't want to pay for a cab ride home. Comfortable in her own skin, Chris didn't know and didn't care who Chad Mitchell was. After a failed marriage in her twenties, she had no interest in marrying again.

But those eyes . . .

Chad persisted. He courted her with short trips to the majestic Oregon coast and picnics beside wild rivers in the lush Oregon forest. He cooked extravagant meals to break the monotony of her rigid study schedule.

Their relationship developed slowly, organically. She found Chad to be kind and genuine. She got his jokes. By the time Frank Fried called, they were making love twice a day and Chad had forgotten all about Candice.

"Guess what?" Frank asked over a long-distance phone line.

"What?" Chad said.

"I've been named president of The Delta Queen Steamboat Company."

Chad didn't know steamboat companies still existed.

"Would you be interested," Frank asked, "in coming to work for us?"

"I can't imagine why," Chad said.

"Why not?"

"I don't have any interest in working for a corporation."

"We don't make widgets," Frank said.

Frank came to his position as president of a steamboat company through his association with legendary entrepreneur and billionaire real estate developer, Sam Zell. Among other things, Zell, who was called a "grave dancer," resurrected failing companies.

"What does a steamboat company do?" Chad asked.

"We have two boats," Frank said, "the Delta Queen and the Mississippi Queen. We do cruises up and down the Mississippi. I need someone to handle our entertainment."

So, in 1984 Chad, who needed the money, moved to New Orleans to become director of entertainment for The Delta Queen Steamboat Company.

Frank knew nothing about cruise ship entertainment or the aquatic tourism industry. Chad thought he'd be working in a nice New Orleans office. Instead, he was assigned to sail as cruise director for the Mississippi Queen.

The Mississippi Queen was the second-largest paddlewheel-driven river steamboat ever built. Constructed in 1976, she was a seven-deck recreation of a classic Mississippi riverboat. She had 206 state rooms for a capacity of 412 guests and a crew of 157. Her paddlewheel measured twenty-two feet in diameter and was 36 feet wide. She also featured a 44-whistle steam calliope.

The Delta Queen, built in 1927, originally plied her trade on the Sacramento River between Sacramento and San Francisco. She reached the Mississippi—after being towed through the Panama Canal—in 1948. An oil-fired boiler produced steam that turned her paddle wheel and gave life to her three-octave calliope. Everything about her required constant attention and repair.

Unlike big cruise lines that hire entertainers only to entertain, The Delta Queen Steamboat Company's entertainment staff had other duties as well. They stuffed themselves into the least-desirable passenger cabins and staffed various activities during the day.

"We had a red-hot-momma singer," Chad said. "She'd headline our evening show and the audience would walk away perceiving her as a star. The next morning she'd be calling 'G-15, that's G-15' at the bingo game."

Chad's innovations were met with predictable, "*that's not the way we do it*" attitudes from both staff and management. Since most of their tourist clientele were in their 60's and 70's, they tailored their entertainment to that crowd. Chad found the entertainment boring and unimaginative. He coaxed his staff into collaborative sessions to write a Vaudeville show, drawing on the jazz era appropriate to the Delta Queen's earlier history. They created a show patterned on World War II-era USO shows. A '40s-era Big Band radio show provided the basis for another Delta Queen production. These sessions reminded Chad of Milt Okun and The Trio's rehearsals, during which everyone fed on everyone else in contribution to the creative process.

The day-to-day reality of living and working on these vessels, though, was grueling. Chad worked a schedule of six weeks on and three weeks off.

"I'd fly to Eugene to spend my time off with Chris," Chad said. "I'd look like death when I got there. For the first week, I didn't do much other than sleep and recover. The second week we'd have fun. Then the third week I'd be preoccupied thinking about the guy who filled in for me, and how much he'd screwed everything up."

After touring for twenty-four months, Chad offered Frank an ultimatum. "I've done my two years before the mast," Chad told him. "Now it's someone else's turn. Either bring me to the New Orleans office, or I'm out of here."

On the boats, Chad had discovered the replication of a pattern. Just as Mike had come to represent The Trio's voice of authority, the front office now represented a collective authoritarianism with Delta Queen. Chad's issue with authority created an animosity he could not suppress. Just as he'd spent a year or more confronting his anger at Mike, "I found I was always angry when I was on the boat."

Chris, in the meantime, had gone to work for a cross-country ski consulting firm in Eugene. Chad's pursuit continued, and if the relationship was to endure, someone needed to move. In January of 1986, Chris packed her car and headed south to New Orleans where Chad had gotten his wish to get off the river and into an office.

Part of Frank's mandate at Delta Queen was to expand the two-boat company into a larger recreational and entertainment presence. After Frank got to know Chris, he hired her to conduct feasibility studies to consider things like luxury rail travel or gambling boats. They settled on construction of a third smaller paddle wheeler that could reach markets the larger boats couldn't. Chris oversaw the project through the engineering drawing phase—one step from the shipyard—when Zell killed the venture.

Chad believes he and Chris are the only couple ever married on a *flotant* in the Atchafalaya Swamp.

"We discovered this swamp tour," Chad said, "and this guy had a small boat with a special propeller housing that could go over logs and other obstructions." The modifications allowed him to take people to parts of the Atchafalaya that most guides couldn't. "You'd get miles and miles back in there, and the setting was just beautiful. We didn't have any church affiliation, so we decided to get married in the swamp."

The Atchafalaya is the United States' largest wetland. Located in south central Louisiana, it's a combination of wetland and river delta area where the Atchafalaya River converges with the Gulf of Mexico.

Clearings within the swamp are pocked with *flotants*. When trees and plants collapse into the swamp's placid water, they sink and deteriorate. Detritus floats to the surface, creating small islands of organic material. Birds and insects transport seeds producing plants and forming lush floating biological structures. Their guide had discovered the largest flotant any of the locals had ever seen—large enough, albeit squishy, to support the weight of two people. Chris's best friend, now a Presbyterian minister, performed the 1986 ceremony from the boat.

Their daughter, Anne-Claire, was born exactly one year later, November 29,1987. She was christened with crystal clear swamp water at the same flotant.

"The ship of state has sprung a leak, she's sinking slowly down.
Well there ain't no need for panic my boys,
we haven't run aground.

And the captain says the ship is sound
and she's headed for the shore.
But the water keeps on rising. I fear for all on board."

Ship of State
—Chad Mitchell

Chris Mitchell always hoped she would have a recording of Chad and Anne-Claire singing together. Chris didn't care what song. Even a rendition of Happy Birthday. But her husband and daughter always seemed to resist the notion, Anne-Claire in the fashion of teenagers who might resist their parents' plea to pose for a photograph, and Chad because he sensed his daughter's discomfort—whatever the reason might be.

Chad's perfectionism allowed him to empathize with a daughter, who might not want to put herself on any kind of a public display, particularly alongside someone so skilled and accomplished as her father.

Chad and Chris both knew their daughter had a pleasant-enough voice, because she'd participated for several years in the Spokane Area Children's Chorus.

"But we hadn't heard her sing a note since then," Chris said.

Anne-Claire was in her twenties when she walked into a conversation her parents shared concerning a request for Chad to contribute a song to an album being produced at Mission Control Studios in Spokane to raise money for the Honor Flight Network, an organization that transports American war veterans to Washington, D.C. for reunions at their memorials.

Chad had never recorded the song he'd written during the seventies inspired by the Watergate scandal. He'd performed *Ship of State* with his piano player, Shelly Markham, during his solo career. Markham, who went on to an impressive run as a composer, arranger, and musical director, sang harmony on the chorus.

Chad decided the Honor Flight project offered the opportunity to finally record *Ship of State*, but only if he could find a second voice to sing Shelly's part.

"What are you guys talking about?" Anne-Claire asked as she walked in on her parents' conversation.

"Your dad wants to record *Ship of State* for the Honor Flight album," Chris said, "but he needs to find a second voice for it."

Anne-Claire said, "I can sing that."

Chad regarded his daughter and smiled, "No, not for a recording. That's a complex harmony."

"I know," Anne-Claire said. "I've listened to the demo tape you and Shelly made. I know the part."

Chad laughed and started singing acapella. She joined in—perfectly.

Chad and Chris could not believe what they heard. "We were stunned," Chris said. "We knew she could sing, but we didn't know she could, you know, *Sing*."

"She sings in the middle of the note," Chad said.

"Chad only says that," Chris added, "when he's really impressed with the singer."

During the recording process, complications with other musicians arose and it became clear to Chad they wouldn't meet the deadline for the Honor Flight album. He offered his recording of *Somewhere Over the Rainbow* for the album instead.

Later, studio owner Karl Bingle invited Chad and Anne-Claire to finish *Ship of State*. It's listed on Amazon as *Ship of State featuring Anne-Claire Mitchell*.

"Chad was so proud," Chris said.

PART THREE

1985–2020

— CHAPTER TWENTY-SIX —

OCTOBER 2007
SPOKANE OPERA HOUSE

"We were often criticized because we sang too many topical songs,
and not enough songs of antiquity.
We're no longer guilty of that crime. It's fifty years later.
Now every song we do is a song of antiquity."

—Chad Mitchell

M ike, Chad and Joe basked in applause following their rendition of *The Draft Dodger Rag.* The Phil Ochs composition always generated laughter as it touched on almost every circumstance—except maybe bone spurs—that could excuse a young man from service in Vietnam. The laughter rang strongest when Chad changed a line from *"I gotta' water my rubber tree plan*t" to *"I gotta' water my cannabis plant,"* and when Joe dropped to a low bass register for the final chorus line *". . . and I always carry a purse."*

Topical music—songs written to satirize or mourn political and cultural events of a given point in history—don't always hold up well when performed for audiences twenty, thirty and forty years later. People must be reminded who Barry Goldwater or John Birch, or Richard Nixon were, and outside the context of their time, these songs lose some of their sting.

The four-song suite The Trio performed—beginning with *The Draft Dodger Rag*—had never—during the fifty-five years The Chad Mitchell Trio would sing them—been performed out of context.

War, it seems, is always a current event.

"You know I am an Episcopal priest," Joe told his audience, "and every Sunday during our eucharist we have a place where we remember those who have been sick or those who have died. I'm sure all denominations and all faiths have a similar way of doing things. Each Sunday I make sure I say, let us remember the 3,694 American men and women who have died in this war in Iraq and Afghanistan that is going on. And I also pray for the hundreds of thousands of Iraqi men, women and children who have died in that war so far."

Joe went into his solo performance of *Business Goes on as Usual*, written about the Vietnam War, but its meaning is timeless:

"*. . . Business goes on as usual,*
Except that my brother is dead."

Without pause following Joe's solo presentation, Bob Hefferan strummed the opening chords to *Johnnie*, The Trio's most powerful anti-war statement.

———∿———

WASHINGTON, D.C.
January 1986

Doris Justis couldn't quite believe she would pull this off. She had accomplished what every expert regarded as impossible. Through guile, threats and luck, she'd protected her secret for weeks, contorting herself to plug every leak. She'd rescued her enterprise each time it teetered at the edge of a cliff.

Now, on Saturday morning, January 25, 1986, standing in backstage catacombs of George Washington University's Lisner Auditorium, she needed only to protect the secret for a few more hours.

Then Bill Danoff tapped her shoulder and said, "Doris, did I just see Chad Mitchell?"

Doris gasped, looked quickly left and right to determine if any of the other artists milling about the area had been within hearing distance. She glared at Danoff, grabbed his arm, dragged him into the nearest dressing room, and breathed fire. "Bill," she commanded, "this is a huge secret. You will not tell a single soul! Do you understand me? Not a soul!"

Danoff, who collaborated with John Denver on *Take Me Home Country Roads* and several other Denver hits, had just joined a select group—Doris, her husband Powell, her singing partner Sean McGhee, and a couple of stagehands—who knew what was in store on the Lisner Auditorium stage later that afternoon.

∿

Doris had been a Trio fan since seventh grade. She was twelve years old in 1962, attending a Silver Springs, Maryland junior high school, when her best friend Gail asked if she'd heard of The Chad Mitchell Trio. Doris was hooked. She bought records. Her parents bought her a guitar. She joined a singing group. Twice she saw The Trio live when they performed in the Washington, D.C. area. Folk music became a focal point of her life.

Anyone interested in the folk scene around Washington D.C. in the 1960's knew of Dick Cerri, a disc jockey for WAVA FM radio where he created a Saturday and Sunday night show called *Music Americana,* devoted completely to folk music.

The show aired past her bedtime, but Doris secreted a transistor radio under her pillow so she could listen. Each show included a folk quiz contest. Cerri would pose a question, listeners would mail in their answers. A winner would be drawn from all the correct answers.

Doris's prize the first time she won was Tom Paxton's debut album.

Doris began to scour newspapers and magazines for folk music-related items. She won frequently enough that, "I became a kind of correspondent for the show." College interrupted her access to Cerri's show, but when she returned to D.C. at a time folk music was on the wane, she happily discovered that Cerri was still on the air. The prize for his folk quiz that week was tickets to a Kingston Trio concert. Doris mailed in her answer.

Cerri called to tell Doris she'd won, and they talked for two hours. At the end of the conversation, he said, "I wish I had someone as knowledgeable as you working for me."

"I said, 'When do I start?'" Doris worked for Cerri, producing radio shows and concerts, until his death in 2013.

When rock and roll displaced folk music by the end of the sixties, Cerri was among the few who held on. Through the 1990's he sponsored monthly Washington, D.C. concerts that bore the name of his long-past radio show, *Music Americana.*

By 1985, he'd become known as Mr. Folk Music.

He and Tom Paxton founded the World Folk Music Association in 1982 "to help folk artists and their fans keep the light of folk music burning brightly."

Cerri and Doris were thrilled when the public embraced folk group reunions in the late seventies and early eighties. Their monthly concerts featuring both new and reunited groups in the D.C. area continued, still under the name *Music Americana.*

Of all the groups, Cerri made clear time and again, The Chad Mitchell Trio had been his favorite. And every time a discussion arose about folk group reunions, Cerri and everyone else agreed the one group that would never perform again was The Trio. First Chad's departure, then Joe's dismissal had created too much animosity. The schism was too wide.

As 1986 approached, Cerri told Doris, "This will be my twenty-fifth year in radio. I wish we had some way to celebrate that milestone."

"Okay, how about a concert," Doris said.

"That's a great idea, Doris," Cerri said. "I want you to produce it."

Doris had never taken on such a project on her own. First, she needed a venue. Lisner Auditorium was available, but Doris's first reaction was, "It's too big." With 1,750 seats, she worried she couldn't fill it. Next, she needed acts. When she and Dick talked about the project on his radio show, word spread and, "Before I knew it, I had fifteen acts. Dick said I had to start saying 'no' to people because the concert would run too long."

Bolstered by the response, Doris thought, we need a surprise for Dick. A big name we'll keep secret.

No bigger name existed than Peter, Paul and Mary. She called Mary Travers.

"Oh, Doris, we'd love to," Mary said. "But we're already booked for that date. We can't do it."

Her thoughts drifted to The Trio. Maybe she could get at least one of the guys to attend. The last she'd heard, Mike lived in Spokane. She'd heard that Joe had become an Episcopal priest. She knew of Chad's legal troubles and had no idea where he might be.

A friend worked in the office of the Episcopal Diocese of Washington, D.C. She showed Doris a directory of all Episcopal priests in the country. It included ten Joe or Joseph Fraziers. When she called the listing for Menlo Park, California, she recognized Joe's voice on his answering machine. She left a message. Two hours later, Joe returned her call. "I'll be there," he promised.

Joe didn't know how to contact either Mike or Chad.

A few days later, Bob Flick of The Brothers Four, called Doris to apologize. They would be touring in Japan on the date of the concert. One of the folk music tidbits she still gathered for the radio show clicked in her head.

"Didn't I read that you live in Washington State?" she asked Flick.

"Yes."

"Does Mike Kobluk still live there?"

"Yeah, do you want his phone number?"

Mike answered at his office. Of course, he remembered Doris and Dick Cerri. He'd be glad to join Joe in attending the concert as a surprise for Dick.

Then Doris cautiously asked the next question, uncertain what Mike's reaction would be.

"You don't happen to know where Chad is, do you?" she said.

Mike didn't hesitate. "I last heard he was in New Orleans, doing something with a steamboat company."

She asked if Mike would be comfortable including Chad.

"If you can find him, and he says okay, I'm in." He paused for a moment, then added, "Do you want us to sing?"

"I almost died," Doris said.

How many steamboat companies could there be? She set about finding Chad.

Chad's answering machine at The Delta Queen Steamboat Company said, "You've reached William Chadbourne Mitchell. I'm on vacation for two weeks. Please leave a message."

Doris remembered The Trio had been affiliated with something called Triangle Productions in Chicago. She found a phone number and left another message. A secretary returned her call, saying Triangle was in the process of shutting down. Frank Fried and his wife were living in California. Chad Mitchell was visiting them. She gave Doris the number.

Initially suspicious that Doris's call was some sort of scam or joke, Chad had to be convinced the whole thing was on the level. "If Mike said he will," Chad said, "then I guess I will, too."

———— ❧ ————

"Dick, I've added another act."

Cerri scowled. "Doris, we've talked about this. You have twenty acts already. This thing is going to go on and on. Who is it this time?"

"I can't tell you," she said. "It's a surprise. And we're giving them thirty minutes."

Dick Cerri was used to getting his way. A man who normally controlled every aspect of his radio show and concerts, he'd turned this project over to Doris because it wouldn't look right for Dick to be arranging an anniversary celebration for himself. Now, he was regretting that decision. Doris didn't appear capable of making tough decisions regarding who to leave out.

Time to draw the line. "No one is doing thirty minutes."

The tone of his voice made his anger clear. Several other people in the room quietly slipped out, leaving Dick and Doris alone.

"Yes, they are," Doris said.

"No, they're not. Look, Doris, I don't mean to spoil your surprise. But I already know it's Peter, Paul and Mary. They don't need thirty minutes. They'll understand."

"Thirty minutes," Doris said, and walked out.

The contrast of personalities between Doris and Cerri could not have been greater, Chad noted. "Doris is truly the sweetest, most soft-spoken person you could know. Her standing up to Cerri this way showed just how determined she was."

Three more potential disasters nearly wrecked her plan.

Two weeks before the concert, Chad called.

"Doris, I'm so sorry," he said. "The company changed my schedule. I have to perform on the Delta Queen that weekend, and I can't get out of it. Do you want me to call Mike and Joe?"

Heartbroken, she said, "No, I'll do it."

She couldn't, however, bring herself to make the call. What could she say?

Two days later, Chad called back, "Guess what?" he asked Doris with a note of glee in his voice.

"What?"

"The Delta Queen ran aground!"

The second near calamity occurred the day before the concert. Doris had granted Joe permission to tell his sister so she and her family could attend. Unaware of the secret, Joe's sister called Dick to thank him for getting The Trio back together.

"Thankfully, Dick was out when her call landed on his answering machine," Doris said. "Dick's assistant let me know what had happened and erased the message."

The third close call came Wednesday before the concert when Dick and Doris taped an interview with Mary Travers and Peter Yarrow for a future radio show. When the interview ended, Dick said, "I don't want to upset Doris, but I know who the surprise act is for the concert this weekend."

"My heart stopped," Doris said. "I thought maybe he really had found out. And Mary didn't know who the surprise act was, but she picked up on our earlier conversation and played along perfectly."

"Oh, Dick," she said. "Please don't tell people. Let's keep it a surprise."

The argument about giving this surprise act thirty minutes continued until the night before the show. "Doris," Dick said, "It cannot be this way. You can't give anyone thirty minutes."

"He was so angry with me," Doris said, "I thought he'd never speak to me again."

Doris refused to back down.

———～———

Chad, Mike and Joe arrived two days before the concert. Doris picked them up at the airport and drove them an hour and a half from Washington to her beach house on Chesapeake Bay. Paul Prestopino drove down from his home in Roosevelt, New Jersey with a car full of instruments. Doris's singing partner, Sean McGhee, delivered Jacob Ander.

Doris stocked the house with food and wood for the fireplace. Joe and Chad slept in the two bedrooms. Mike drew the short straw and slept on a couch. Paul and Jacob slept on a chilly sunporch. Doris also left a stack of Chad Mitchell Trio albums by the stereo to refresh their memories of complex harmony arrangements no one had written down.

"That evening," Doris said, "everyone was sitting in the living room and it was awkward at first. Nobody knew what to do."

The last time Chad had spoken to Mike was the night in Chicago, 1965, when they'd shared a hug and handshake.

"Finally," Doris said, "I just looked at Mike and asked, 'Do you suppose you remember *Four Strong Winds*?' Well, out came the instruments, and it was as if they had never been apart. It was magical, and they knew it.

"Afterward, Chad took me aside and said, 'I didn't believe we could do this. I didn't think your audience would be all that thrilled. But now, I think maybe we can.'"

On Friday evening, The Trio and their musicians were sequestered in a motel.

Because the Saturday evening concert had sold out, Dick insisted on a matinee performance as well. That presented further complications. Sound checks for all acts were scheduled for Saturday morning. Which meant The Trio's secret sound check had to be even earlier. At that point, the soundman and the theater's stage director became privy to the secret. The Trio, along with Paul and Jacob, were hidden in a dressing room for the rest of the morning.

Doris watched Dick as the concert progressed. When time came for the final act, she saw him settle into his front and center seat in patient expectation of a half-hour with Peter, Paul and Mary.

The curtain opened to an empty stage, with a second curtain shielding The Trio and their musicians from view.

Doris took the stage and announced, "Okay, Dick, it's your turn to participate in the folk quiz."

He looked a little perturbed, and a thought occurred to her. *"Oh, no. What if he has a heart attack? He just might."*

She asked a couple of questions so broadly vague that Dick couldn't answer. Finally, she said, "I think Dick needs another clue."

Joe's voice filled the hall:

"Elizabeth Borden took an axe . . ."

A moment of stunned silence intervened before the hall erupted.

"Dick was speechless," Doris said. "I never saw him like that before or after. He was so thrilled."

The second curtain parted, and The Chad Mitchell Trio was back.

In addition to *Lizzie Borden*, they sang Paxton's *I Can't Help but Wonder Where I'm Bound, Ballad of the Greenland Whalers, A Dying Business, Johnnie,* and as a test of both their harmonic and linguistic chops, the frantic Russian language *Maladyozhenaya*.

After arriving in Washington, The Trio had only two days to rehearse," the Washington Post's music critic wrote. *"But at the concert their voices were as strong, their harmonies as tight and their stage presence as compelling as during their commercial heyday twenty to twenty-five years ago.*

"As a result of the tremendous audience response, and what Kobluk called the group's own 'indescribable' joy at singing together again after twenty years apart, the three said in interviews that they may think about doing a limited tour . . ."

They went their separate ways without any commitments regarding the future.

Mike returned to Spokane and the task of booking acts for local stages. Joe returned to his church. Chad returned to his New Orleans office.

"So, how'd it go?" Frank asked him.

Removed from the emotion and immediacy of the event, Chad admitted he'd enjoyed himself. But with passing time, reality of day-to-day life set in, and The Mitchell Trio was again consigned to his past.

Someone, though, had videotaped the concert.

Chad received a copy by mail.

Frank watched and said, "You know, Chad, I think it's time you guys did some reunion concerts. People still love The Trio. And you're still good."

---

*"Some things that once seemed so important
just don't matter as much after fifty years."*

—Mike Kobluk

SEPTEMBER 1986

Chad read the Chicago Tribune music critic's advance on The Trio's upcoming concert date at Chicago's Park West and cringed.

The story referred to him as "front man Chad Mitchell." He'd thought the reporter would offer quotes from Mike and Joe as well. The concert was promoted under the name Mitchell Trio, but the article's reference was to "the original Chad Mitchell Trio."

Their Washington, D.C. gig had been a pure pleasure. Nobody said anything about the past. Old arguments were left unspoken. Both Chad's and Joe's transgressions went unmentioned. Nobody danced awkwardly around taboo subjects. Mike's warmth and enthusiasm shouted an unstated forgiveness.

Once again, all that mattered was the music.

Inadvertently, though, this music critic had stomped on hot buttons at the core of the "original Chad Mitchell Trio's" demise.

While Mike, Chad and Joe had returned to their daily lives without expectations of anything further, concert promoters had other ideas. They chose Joe, who made clear his unqualified enthusiasm for picking up the gauntlet again, as their point of entry. Joe found an ally in Frank Fried who, long removed from any financial relationship to The Trio, simply wanted to see them perform.

Joe called both Mike and Chad about the opportunity to hold an official reunion concert in Chicago. "All the promoters say reunion concerts for sixties groups are hot," Joe told them.

Once again, Chad and Mike tossed out the "I will if he will" solution, and musicians Prestopino and Ander joined them for a week of rehearsals.

Chad's initial concern about the Tribune story seemed unfounded. Neither Mike nor Joe offered comments. The creative joy of rehearsal took over.

This time, they rehearsed on a steamboat. Mike and Joe flew to Memphis and met Chad on the Mississippi Queen. The Trio practiced for three days, performing for passengers as the boat made its way to St. Louis where they disembarked and flew to Chicago.

Despite employing all his persistence and charm in his romantic pursuit of Chris, oddly, Chad never sang to her. She knew that at one point in his life he had been a singer of some sort, but that bit of his past was not a factor in her decision to marry him.

"As I got to know Chad," Chris said, "I heard some things here and there. I might have been vaguely aware of The Chad Mitchell Trio. I knew who Peter, Paul and Mary were. But I didn't know much beyond that about folk music and didn't care.

"The first time I heard The Trio sing was that night at Park West."

Park West is a historic and intimate venue located on West Armitage Avenue in Chicago. Configured for concerts, its maximum seating capacity is listed at seven hundred.

Chris arrived early, found her way to the back of the theater and struck up a conversation with the sound man. He looked like someone you'd expect to be mixing sound for rock and heavy metal groups. Chris described him as "hard-boiled."

"How old are these guys, anyway?" he asked Chris, adding that he'd never done sound for a folk music show. He didn't expect much and said so.

Chris shrugged. "It's my first time, too," she said.

Doors opened. People rushed to their seats. Until there were no more seats. Still they came, standing in back and along outer aisles. Chris expected a raid by the Fire Marshall at any moment.

Lights went down. The musicians entered in darkness. Mike, Joe and Chad stepped into a mid-stage spotlight. And the place went crazy! Everyone seated leapt to their feet. They waved Chad Mitchell Trio albums over their heads. The ovation went on and on.

"We'd never seen anything like it," Chad said. "In all our years of performing nobody screamed when we walked on stage. And we hadn't sung a note."

They bowed in thanks. They raised their hands as a request to proceed. The ovation continued.

Chris and the sound guy exchanged amazed expressions.

Finally, the audience relented.

"Their performance," Chris said, "was electrifying. They were that good. Just electrifying."

She glanced to find the sound man completely into it, his subtle adjustments adding to the vocal and instrumental excellence.

When the show ended, the sound man turned to Chris, laughing at himself and his amazement. "That's the best performance I've ever witnessed here," he said.

"I understood at that moment," Chris said, "I would never in my life experience being that good at something. It didn't change my view of the person Chad is, but it made me realize I was living with someone who had achieved a degree of excellence that had to be incredibly satisfying."

Listening to her description, Chad laughed and, speaking to perfectionism that is a part of his psychological struggle, said, "But not to me, not until much later." Then he softened his critique. "That's not completely true. I knew we were good."

Chicago Tribune music critic Lynn Van Matre also knew they were good.

> ". . . after being persuaded to harmonize briefly once again at a folk music benefit earlier this year, (The Trio) decided to do a couple of full-fledged shows and see how things went. And that's how it happened that the urban folk boom of the early 1960's magically flowered once again over the weekend at Park West.
>
> "And magical was the word for The Chad Mitchell Trio's reunion shows. Mitchell, Frazier and Kobluk sound great separately, as they proved in solo segments; together their voices meld smoothly and appealingly. Front man Mitchell is still the low-keyed, joking showman of the group, but Frazier and Kobluk got their share of laughs . . .
>
> "This kind of reunion is always risky; far too often, things just don't work the second time around. The Chad Mitchell Trio is one of the charming exceptions. Here's hoping this 'reunion' isn't their last."

Van Matre's review once again referred to Chad incorrectly as the group's "founder."

Chad and Mike both finally understood, though, they could shout to the heavens that Mike was every bit as much responsible for the group's inception and direction as Chad. They could protest that each member of The Trio played equal roles. Chad could point out he would rather the media seek out Mike or Joe.

Interviewers, promoters and fans, though, would always embrace a familiar, simpler, though incorrect, version of the past.

They each by now had gained enough real-world experience to put celebrity into proper context.

When questioned about future performance dates, Chad said, "Well, I don't know. We all have other commitments, especially Mike, who has three kids in college."

They didn't kid themselves that a Mitchell Trio renaissance waited in the wings. But future performances would come. They would settle back into roles they played twenty, thirty, then forty years earlier. Chad would remain the principal spokesman during concerts, because he was good at it. They would each sing solos during concerts, not because Mike and Joe wanted to dispel the notion they were backup singers, but because they were wonderful solo vocalists, and the concerts were better for it. Chad could avoid the post-concert hoopla, because it still made him uncomfortable. Mike could welcome that task, because he is a gregarious, charming man, at his best in a social setting.

───※───

The next "I-will-if-he-will" came through Chad's relationship with a Mark Twain impersonator.

Hal Holbrook's phenomenally successful one-man play, *Mark Twain Tonight*, reached Broadway in 1966. By 1986, that success had spawned dozens of Twain impersonators, and according to Chad, Roger Durrett was among the best.

As entertainment director of a steamboat company operating on the Mississippi, Chad had frequent need of Mark Twain. During one Mississippi Queen cruise, in fact, Chad found himself in the company of two Twain impersonators. He had hired Roger to perform on the Mississippi Queen's main stage. A group tour had been booked for that cruise, and they hired their own Twain to perform in the boat's small theater.

"We had both these actors, in full costume wandering around," Chad said. He took his assistant aside and advised, "We'd better keep these two guys apart."

"What, do you think they'll get in a fight or something?"

Chad shrugged. "Haven't you heard that saying? Never the Twain shall meet?"

Roger's older brother, Doug, managed Roger's entertainment career. They'd produced a Mark Twain performance for Public Broadcasting System channel WTVI in Charlotte, North Carolina, and two half hour-shows on WNED in Buffalo, New York.

Roger crossed paths with The Trio on the Mississippi Queen as they were rehearsing for the 1986 Park West concert. He called Doug and said,

"You've gotta' hear these guys. They are really good."

PBS had already recorded some folk reunion shows for its fundraising drives, so Roger and Doug set about trying to sell both The Trio and PBS on a Chad Mitchell Trio reunion event. They put together a joint venture with WTVI in Charlotte.

Doug chose Spirit Square as their venue. The former church had been converted into a 750-seat performing arts center. The director of the theater—a man in his 20's—had earlier booked a Kingston Trio concert but hadn't heard of The Chad Mitchell Trio. He expressed his doubts that Doug could attract an audience large enough to ensure financial success.

"I handed him a tape of The Trio's Park West performance," Doug said. "When we met later, he dropped the tape on my table and said, 'Wow, these guys blow the doors off The Kingston Trio.'"

As preparation for the show continued, the Durretts had another idea. What if they could get John Denver to participate? Doug approached Milt Okun. Milt listened to the pitch and relayed the request to John. "I think Milt urged John to do it, because it would be good for The Trio," Doug said.

By 1987, John was on the downhill side of his popularity. His last chart presence came in 1981 with the country hit *Some Days Are Diamonds*. Just as it had bypassed The Trio in the late sixties, popular culture had left John behind as well. In a music industry swamped by Grunge, Heavy Metal and Hip-Hop, young consumers had come to regard John as saccharine sweet.

The PBS audience demographic, though, fit John Denver just fine.

The Trio performed two concerts, one on Thursday, Nov. 11, and one on Saturday, Nov. 13. Doug's and Roger's film crews shot both performances, but John was only available for the Thursday show.

As they rehearsed earlier in the week, John told Doug, "I have an idea."

John's concerts had become forums for his crusade against the Cold War proliferation of nuclear weapons, and all his shows concluded with a video presentation called *What Are We Making Weapons For?*

John toured the Soviet Union in 1985 where he met Alexander Gradsky, a leading Russian singer-songwriter. The following year at Melodiya Studios in Moscow, they recorded *What are we Making Weapons For?* offering both U.S. and Soviet perspectives.

John produced a short film for *Weapons*, the first time an American and Soviet artist had performed together in a music video. The recording included the Red Army Chorus.

John said he regarded *Weapons* as the best thing he'd produced in his career. Its release cost him his recording contract with RCA which had recently been acquired by General Electric—a company holding extensive military contracts.

Doug and Roger were glad to include *Weapons* as the concert's closing act. Showing the video on a giant screen, however, increased the technical complexity of their production. At that time, video projectors could only project one color. Three projectors—one for blue, one for green and one for red—had to be used and carefully synced.

The Durretts wanted the production to be more than just a concert. They wanted to capture the performers' personal emotions as they gathered for their first television appearance in twenty-one years. So, a separate film crew recorded interviews with Mike, Chad, Joe, Milt Okun, Frank Fried and Tom Paxton, who served as the concert's opening act.

"If I were doing it over again," Okun told his interviewer, "I'd do several things differently. When we were first meeting and talking about our very first record with Colpix, the group wanted to call themselves The Chad Mitchell Trio, because Chad has this exquisite tenor voice that was really the main asset of The Trio at first. I knew this was a mistake, and I may have said it. But if I had really insisted on a name that would not be subject to The Trio remaining the same—always having Chad in it—if it had been a general name, then when Chad left the group, it would not have caused the revolution that resulted in its demise.

"That was my mistake. I should have known better."

Milt said he wished he and The Trio's manager would have concentrated on aligning The Trio with a record company that would "take the best features of the artists . . . and cherish it rather than trying to destroy it. The fact is, The Chad Mitchell Trio was a golden name on college campuses of America. People loved them. Their record company was trying to fight the image of social consciousness and satire. Again, that was a weakness on management and a weakness on the part of their producer. Me. If I would have fought to get into a situation where The Trio had a company that would develop their best features, The Trio would have had much more influence than they did. They would have had the success they really deserved."

Milt added a little wistfully, "Of all the work I've done in recording, from Harry Belafonte right through the folk groups—Peter, Paul and Mary, The Brothers Four, John Denver, Placido Domingo—no one ever gave me as much satisfaction and pleasure as The Chad Mitchell Trio."

The film crew also recorded behind the scenes events, like John's arrival. He greeted Mike and Joe with warm hugs. He and Chad exchanged a rather formal handshake.

"I think Chad might have been a little anxious at that point," Doug said.

By the time they'd completed their Thursday performance, Chad and John were more comfortable with each other as The Trio's inner circle retired to a back-stage room and shared company until 4:00 a.m. The group included Joe, Mike and Clare, Chad, John, the Durretts and a few others.

In the early hours of the morning, John and Chad sat next to each other as John pontificated on his new interest in EST, a program aimed at "self-transformation, personal responsibility, accountability and possibility."

"It teaches getting in touch with your inner child," John said.

Chad regarded John with a bemused expression. "Yeah?" he said. "What if your inner child is an asshole?"

The Trio performed to full houses both nights.

John recorded an introduction for the taped program.

"In a few hours this hall will be full, sold out three months ago. We're in Spirit Square Performance Place in Charlotte, North Carolina. And that's a good name for it, because the spirit of folk music will be very much alive here tonight.

"I'm John Denver, and welcome to *Mighty Day*. Tonight, the original Chad Mitchell Trio will reunite on stage for television for the first time in twenty-one years. It's folk music history in the making, and I'm delighted to be a part of it."

The Trio chose a representative cross section of their music, including some songs they had dropped from their live concerts as Chad's tenure came to an end.

They opened with *Ballad of the Greenland Whalers*, Chad's adaptation that appeared on their *Blowin' In the Wind* album. Next came *The Whistling Gypsy*, a Milt Okun adaptation, in which Milt required Chad to whistle through the chorus. Whistling on pitch in live performance is no easy task. Chad demonstrated he could still do it.

They followed with one of their funniest but lesser-known songs, *Hang on the Bell, Nellie*, written by Tommie Connor, Clive Erard and Ross Parker in 1949. *Nellie* was overshadowed by *Lizzie Borden* on the *Mighty Day on Campus* album. But their live performance of *Nellie*, which ends with Chad's innocent double entendre on "swinging" is priceless.

For their solo performances, Mike's voice proved perfectly suited to the haunting *Adios, Mi Corazon*, based on a 1907 poem written by Charles 'Badger' Clark. Chad chose Yip Harburg's *Brother Can You Spare a Dime*. Joe performed *Nicaragua*, by Canadian songwriter Bruce Cobern, a song protesting modern U.S. imperialism in South America.

The concert included three more of Chad's adaptations of traditional songs: *Waves on the Sea*, *Bonnie Streets of Fyve-io* and *Tell Old Bill*.

They didn't shrink from the vocal challenges of *Which Hat Shall I Wear?* and *Maladyozhenaya*. Their most blatantly partisan political song—*Barry's Boys*—became Ronnie's Boys on the PBS stage. And finally, The Mitchell Trio portion of the concert ended "where we started," according to Chad, with *Lizzie Borden*.

Chad left the stage after introducing John Denver. Mike, Joe and John sang John's *For Bobbi*, from The Mitchell Trio's *Violets of Dawn* album.

Chad rejoined them for the concert finale, *Last Night I Had the Strangest Dream*. And one more time, Mike and Chad packed their bags, returning to separate lives, uncertain whether they'd perform together again.

Chad indulged in one more flirtation with a solo album, which flew well below the radar of Trio fans. Peter Giustra, who owned a construction company, was a Trio enthusiast who wanted to become a record producer.

He called Chad at the Delta Queen offices in 1991, introduced himself, and said, "It's been too long since you've had an album."

Giustra booked studio time in Toronto, hired musicians and flew Chad in for the recording sessions. *Virgo Moon*, recorded on the Silver City Records label, appeared later that year.

"The material is pretty varied," Chad said, "but there is one song in particular that I think the trio would have been interested in recording."

My Name Joe, by David Massengill, "is a really well-written song about an illegal working in an L.A. kitchen. Someone alerts immigration authorities to Joe's presence and an officer rounds up all the kitchen help, asking, 'so who's Joe?' They all respond, 'my name Joe' while Joe slips out the back door."

To Chad's surprise the CD's first cut—*Outbound Plane,* by Nancy Griffith and Tom Russell—began to get air play on FM stations. Suzy Bogguss, though, chose 1991 to release her version of Ian Tyson's masterpiece, *Someday Soon* on her album *Aces.* Judy Collins had a huge hit with the song in 1969, and the Bogguss interpretation did almost as well more than twenty years later. On that same album, the Bogguss rendition of *Outbound Plane* reached number nine on the chart of Hot Country Singles and immediately squelched interest in Chad's rendition.

In 2017, Chad teamed with an instrumental ensemble called the Hot Club of Spokane to record *3 Songs for a World-weary World*: *Nobody Knows You When You're Down and Out,* adapted by Chad; John Prine's *Everybody Needs Somebody*; and the traditional *Hold On (Keep Your Hands on the Plow).*

— CHAPTER TWENTY-SEVEN —

On their first wedding anniversary, Chris and Chad's daughter Anne-Claire was born. Taking up fatherhood at the age of fifty-one presented a whole new set of challenges. Chad and Chris had settled into their lives in New Orleans. Chad continued to work for Delta Queen and might have been content to stay except they didn't feel the city was a place to raise a daughter.

"The public-school system in New Orleans was bad, crime was on the rise and I'd worn out my welcome with Delta Queen," Chad said, "so we determined we would move somewhere by the time Anne-Claire started school."

Neither wanted the East Coast or Southwest. They considered returning to Oregon. Chad's mother needed assistance due to failing health, though, and that swung the decision in favor of Spokane.

Chris and Anne-Claire moved into Chad's mother's basement in 1991, and they began the difficult search for a house during a Spokane real estate boom. Chad stayed behind to wrap things up in Louisiana.

Chris knew precisely what she wanted—a brick rancher with gas heat. Every time something fitting that bill came on the market, her realtor called. She'd drop everything and rush to the property. Time after time, she met her agent on a front lawn where someone else had just made an offer. When she finally got there first, she didn't hesitate. She called Chad. "We're buying this one."

Chad arrived in time for closing.

———*e*———

SPOKANE 1992

Once again, Chad found himself wondering what he might do to make himself useful.

His time with Delta Queen had provided a thorough education regarding the cruise industry. Not many cruise lines operate out of Spokane, though.

Chad created his own job. Always a careful observer, he watched with interest the inspection and appraisal process required to complete the purchase of their Spokane home.

"I thought to myself, 'Well, I can do that.' So, I took some appraisal classes and started selling real estate. The market was hotter than could be, and everyone needed a realtor. I did that for several years and worked for a couple of different brokerages."

He specialized in putting together deals for low-income buyers.

———*e*———

Over the next two decades Mike and Chad found themselves dusting off their vocal cords to perform three or four times a year, often for benefit concerts, some related to Joe's religious or political causes, or for gatherings of sixties folk icons like *Folksongs U.S.A.*, a benefit for the 92nd Street Y in Manhattan on May 13, 1993. There, Chad and Mike witnessed one of the most emotional moments of folk music history.

The Trio joined Pete Seeger, Art Garfunkel, Eric Weissberg, Tom Paxton, Odetta, Theodore Bikel, Oscar Brand, Josh White Jr., Paul Robeson Jr. and Burl Ives on the concert bill.

New York Times reviewer Stephen Holden reported that the show featured "two notable reunions:"

". . . the first New York performance in more than three decades by The Chad Mitchell Trio," and the first time Seeger and Ives had performed together in four decades."

Holden said of The Trio, "Until it broke up in 1965, The Trio . . . was the most musically polished and politically pointed among the many '60's folk groups . . ."

The most poignant and memorable moment of the concert, though, occurred with the pairing of Pete Seeger and Burl Ives."

During Joseph McCarthy's 1950's witch hunt for communists in every cupboard, Ives was one of a few among the folk community who willingly cooperated with the House Unamerican Activities Committee. While the others—Seeger chief among them—refused the committee's entreaties, Ives did not. He told the committee that he'd unwittingly accompanied Seeger to a gathering that turned out to be a meeting of a cell of the American Communist Party. Ives became an anathema among those who were put on blacklists and disappeared from the folk music scene, but his acting career thrived.

By 1993, Seeger had been rehabilitated in the minds of network television executives and restored in popular opinion as patriarch of folk music's legacy of political activism and social conscience.

Seeger tried to beg off from the 92nd Street Y concert. He wasn't interested in sharing a stage with Ives and was having difficulty with his voice. He told the concert promoters he couldn't sing.

The Y's board members reminded him that proceeds of the event were to support the Y. They also reminded him the 92nd Street Young Men's and Young Women's Hebrew Association had provided Seeger and others a place to perform during the blacklist years when no one else would. They told him he would open the show and Ives would close it. Seeger and Ives wouldn't be on stage at the same time.

The afternoon before the concert, The Trio conducted their sound check, then retired to a row of seats near the stage to watch. While Seeger appeared robust, indeed, he struggled to sing. During his portion of the evening performance, he played his banjo and spoke most of the lyrics to his songs.

By contrast Ives, confined to an electric wheelchair, appeared frail and disengaged. He was tended by several associates, but the show's script called for him to steer himself onto the stage and hit a mark. Chad and Chris watched this afternoon rehearsal as Ives drove himself from the wings. He sat heavy in his chair, chin drooping onto his chest, eyes almost shut.

He struggled to find the mark, jockeying back and forth. They feared he might drive right off the stage into the front row.

After finally finding his mark, Ives remained, chin on chest, eyes closed. He might have been asleep. With the first notes played by the musicians behind him, though, Ives lifted his head to the theatre and adjusted himself upright in the chair. His eyes brightened with an inner light.

"And," Chad said, "he sang like an angel."

The audience that night was as stunned by Ives' performance as Chad and Chris had been. They were more surprised when Seeger strolled on stage, carrying his banjo and a folding chair. He set it down next to Ives. They conversed briefly. Then Seeger played the opening chords to *Blue Tail Fly*, one of Ives' trademark songs.

Together they sang, and Chris said, "The audience was just overwhelmed. Everybody wept."

When they finished, Seeger leaned across and kissed Ives on the forehead.

"I was just so emotionally moved by Pete's capacity for caring and forgiveness," Chad said.

Ives died almost exactly two years later at the age of eighty-five. Seeger passed away in 2014 at the age of ninety-four.

———— ❧ ————

Some of Mike's and Chad's performances were not of their choosing. On one of several Spokane Concert stops by Peter, Paul and Mary, Chad and Mike found themselves sitting in separate sections of the Opera House audience.

Mike had chatted with Peter earlier that afternoon and mentioned that Chad would attend the concert as well.

At the show's end, Peter stepped to his microphone and said, "Our friends Chad Mitchell and Mike Kobluk are here tonight. I'd like them to stand." The audience's enthusiasm prompted Peter to add, "Chad, Mike, come on up here and help us with this last song."

The applause increased.

Chad and Mike exchanged a glance from across the auditorium. Mike offered a reluctant shrug, and they made their way to the stage.

"We're going to sing that great Woody Guthrie anthem *This Land is Your Land*!" Peter announced.

Peter had urged Chad to a position next to him. "I'll get everyone started with the first verse, and Chad will lead us in the second verse!"

"And I thought, 'You, asshole,'" Chad recalls. "Nobody knows the lyrics to the second verse. I certainly didn't. So, I sort of whispered to Peter, 'I only know the first verse.' And Peter says, 'That's okay. I'll shoot you the words.'"

Peter did the Pete Seeger thing where, in the brief rest between lines, he speaks the coming line. None of which could Chad hear. "So, I'm going 'Gish fond du gottteee...' not that loud, but pretending I'm really singing this thing... I could have shot him. I just could have shot him."

Mike says he escaped Peter's attention because, "I hid behind Chad."

— CHAPTER TWENTY-EIGHT —

September 1997

I have to say it now, it's been a good life all in all . . .

Poems, Prayers and Promises
—John Denver

"Mike, I know I said I'd be there, and I hate to miss it, but this television thing I'm doing in Alaska is running over schedule. I'll be there next year. I promise."

Mike put down the phone and called to Clare, "John won't be able to make it." Mike did his best to hide his disappointment. "He said next year for sure."

Mike and Clare often had friends visit at their weekend place on Lake Christina just across the Canadian border north of Spokane. Chad and Chris had visited on several occasions. The weekend Mike planned for mid-September was something special, though.

They had invited everyone who'd been involved with The Trio for a reunion in the fall of 1997. John was among the first to say he'd be there. Chad and Chris attended. The Kobluk's daughter Lydia and their twin sons, Gerald and Justin, attended along with their families. The Rev. Joe Frazier attended. Bob Hefferan flew up from Phoenix. Guitarist Jacob Ander was there, along with Paul Prestopino.

Although by now they'd met several times, Mike looked forward to Chad and John having a chance to get to know each other.

Mike had organized a Mitchell Trio Olympics and divided the guests into four teams. He identified each team by color and provided team t-shirts. The Green Team wore yellow shirts, the Red Team blue shirts and so on.

Joe led a worship service Sunday morning.

Mike and Clare had done their best to keep John's participation a secret from the outside world but failed. Each day boatloads of fans hovered offshore hoping to get a glimpse of John Denver.

Each evening everyone sang, accompanied by three of the best musicians who'd ever taken a folk music stage. Those amazing harmonies, joined by voices of relatives and friends, drifted through the Canadian night for all to hear.

Mike recalled those evenings around a campfire at John's residence, Starwood, in Aspen, during the week they rehearsed for the 1979 benefit concert.

This, Mike knew, is what John would have enjoyed most.

OCTOBER 12, 1997

With a television droning in the background Sunday evening, Mike thought about his Monday appointment schedule and the upcoming Best of Broadway Series set to open the following weekend.

He didn't pinpoint the message at first, but some bit of something turned him toward the TV screen where he saw a picture of John. He read a headline scrolling below John's portrait as a network announcer solemnly pronounced, "... the singer and songwriter, who recorded such mega-hits as *Rocky Mountain High, Country Roads* and *Annie's Song,* died when the experimental aircraft he was flying plunged into the Pacific Ocean off the California coast at Monterey ..."

Clare, who'd heard the news snippet in the adjoining room, looked at Mike in disbelief.

"Did they say ..."

"I only caught the last little bit," Mike said.

"But that can't be right, can it?"

"I'll call Annie," Mike said.

John Denver met Annie Martell following a Mitchell Trio concert at Gustavus Adolphus College in St. Peter, Minnesota the spring of 1966. Despite John's hectic travel schedule with The Trio, they managed to carry on a long-distance romance, and John asked her to marry him.

During 1966 and 1967, The Trio appeared on the nationally syndicated Mike Douglas Show several times. Their appearance on June 6, 1967 occurred a week before John's wedding.

Only a month earlier, David Boise had replaced Joe as The Trio's third member.

John introduced their first song by explaining, "People like us who make our living doing one-night concerts on college campuses have to go on the road for sometimes more than a month at a time, and sometimes you have to leave someone you care about very much. For that reason, I wrote a song a few months ago. It's our current single on the Reprise label called *Leavin' on a Jet Plane*, and it will be out this week."

Following *Jet Plane*, Douglas surprised John by bringing Annie onstage. While John and Annie danced, Mike and David sang in Russian a Ukrainian love song entitled *My Guitar*, which they would reprise at John's wedding a week later.

Although they'd been acquainted more than a year, John and Annie had spent only a couple of months together. They would admit later they really didn't know each other.

Mike and Clare were in the process of moving to New York so Mike could become more involved with his American Theater Productions company. John and Annie moved into Mike's Chicago apartment.

Annie soon tired of the life John sang about in *Leavin' on a Jet Plane*. The Trio's frantic schedule left her alone for weeks at a time. Annie's reluctance to tour with The Trio left John open to dalliances on the road. When The Trio finally ended and John's fame blasted him to another level, the situation degenerated further. He released his first solo album, including *Jet Plane* in 1969. The album received little notice. But the same year, Peter, Paul and Mary recorded *Jet Plane,* and it became a mega-hit.

Along with Bill Danoff and Taffy Nivert, with whom John would collaborate on several hits, John wrote *Take Me Home Country Roads*. Released as a single in April of 1971, it peaked at number two on Billboard's US Hot 100 Singles that August.

Within months John had become an international superstar. He'd maintained his association with Milt Okun, boosting Milt's Cherry Lane Music Publishing Company to the top of the industry as well.

John and Annie adopted two children, Zachary and Anna Kate, as their relationship became more volatile. He admitted in his autobiography, *Take Me Home*, published in 1994, that he was unfaithful to Annie and his philandering escalated as his fame grew.

The couple experienced several separations during the seventies. *Annie's Song* was written to try and mend one of these rifts. Other songs inspired by their troubled relationship included *Goodbye Again*, released in 1972, and *I'm Sorry*, his final number-one top hit released in 1975.

Even at this peak of his success, the dismissal of John's body of work as superficial had begun. John was named Entertainer of the Year for 1975 by the Country Music Association. He also won CMA's album of the year award. It fell to Charlie Rich, the previous year's CMA Entertainer of the Year, to introduce 1975's winner. He opened the envelope, said the winner is "my friend, John Denver," then took a cigarette lighter from his pocket and burned the announcement.

Rich's son later said his father, whose judgment was clouded by alcohol and pain medication, meant the gesture as a joke. Others suggested Rich didn't consider John a worthy country singer.

By decade's end, John's star had begun to decline as tastes in popular music continued their evolution. Along with the decline came alcohol dependency.

John and Annie divorced in 1983.

John met actress Cassandra Delaney in 1986. Twenty years his junior, they married in October 1988. Cassandra gave birth to Jesse Belle in May of 1989. The couple separated in 1991, subsequently divorcing in 1993.

In 1995, John was arrested in Colorado for driving while intoxicated.

———∿———

John was not a casual pilot.

His father, Dutch Deutschendorf, a career Air Force pilot and Learjet instructor, taught John to fly. At the time of his death John had flown for twenty years and had logged 2,600 hours in command of various aircraft. He was rated to fly jets, and while he hired pilots to ferry him and his entourage around the world on concert tours, he frequently piloted the plane himself.

Mike remembers that for their 1983 concert, two of John's planes were used to transport the performers and their wives, along with sound equipment, from Aspen to Denver. John flew one of the planes.

Despite his 1968 dismissal from The Trio, Joe Frazier remained close to John for the rest of John's life. Joe told stories of flying with John during his visits to Aspen. He recalled a "scary moment" in a biplane that seemed to "scrape the mountain peaks and nuzzle the valley floors around Aspen."

A few weeks before his death John purchased a Long E-Z, a fast, highly maneuverable craft constructed from a kit by aircraft maker Adrian Davis Jr. Davis made a basic modification to the plane, which had fuel tanks in each wing. The E-Z drew fuel from first one tank and then the other. The original construction located the lever switching fuel feed from tank to tank below the pilot's seat. In this plane, though, Davis relocated the lever to a spot behind the pilot's left shoulder so the fuel line wouldn't be routed through the cockpit.

Two other pilots flew the plane after John's purchase. Both said when they twisted their bodies to the left trying to reach the lever, they inadvertently placed pressure on the right rudder, putting the highly maneuverable E-Z into a dive.

On the day of the crash, John and a maintenance tech discussed the lever's accessibility. They clamped a pair of vice grips to the lever to extend its reach, but that didn't work. They determined the only way a pilot could reach the handle would be to remove his shoulder harness.

On the afternoon of Oct. 12, John climbed into the Long E-Z, shot several touch-and-go landings, then headed out over the Pacific.

Official accident findings were issued fourteen months later:

The National Transportation Safety Board has determined today that popular entertainer John Denver fatally crashed his experimental aircraft into Monterey Bay, because his attention during the flight was diverted in an attempt to switch fuel tanks. The fuel selector valve on the amateur-built Adrian Davis Long-EZ airplane Denver was flying was behind the pilot's left shoulder, forcing him to turn in his seat to locate the handle. This action, the Board concluded, likely caused him to inadvertently apply the right rudder, resulting in loss of aircraft control.

On October 12, 1997 Mr. Denver was performing touch and go operations in his recently purchased aircraft at the Monterey Peninsula Airport located in Pacific Grove, California. The pilot touched down three times before turning west and heading out into Monterey Bay. Moments later witnesses reported hearing a reduction in engine noise. The pilot made no distress calls and the aircraft was destroyed when it impacted in the bay. The pilot and the majority of the aircraft were recovered.

Contributing to the crash was the pilot's inadequate preflight planning, specifically his failure to refuel the plane. The Board further determined that the builder's decision to locate the unmarked fuel selector handle in a difficult to access location, combined with unmarked fuel gauges, was a causal factor in the accident. Additionally, the Board found that the pilot failed to train himself adequately for the transition to this type of aircraft and was inexperienced flying the Long E-Z.

The board also confirmed that John lacked an aviation medical certificate—a requirement for a valid pilot's license—at the time of the crash. He'd been disqualified for the certificate in March 1997 after officials learned he had "violated previous FAA orders to abstain from drinking" following his 1995 drunk driving arrest.

The autopsy showed no signs of alcohol or drugs in John's body.

Some reports suggested John was despondent at the time of his death. Close acquaintances said the opposite. They said John was feeling good about himself the day he died. He played a round of golf at Spyglass earlier that day and played well. They said that, philosophically, John was unafraid of death and that he died without regrets. They said he was a good man.

———∿———

Thousands attended the memorial service held for John in Aurora, Colorado five days later. Annie organized the service and asked Mike if he would be among those to speak.

Mike and Bob Hefferan sat together, waiting for the service to get underway as mourners filed in. They began to share memories. Mike reminded Bob that when they first met John, he was so naïve he didn't even know how to pronounce the word *politics*. They talked about John's golf game, and touring experiences they shared.

As their discussion continued, somber expressions turned to smiles, smiles turned to laughter.

A man sitting three rows below in the tiered cathedral confronted them.

"Don't you two realize this is a memorial?" he demanded. "How can you sit here laughing? We're here to remember and honor Mr. Denver."

Mike replied quietly, "We thought that's what we were doing."

———∿———

A few months after joining The Trio in 1965, John wanted to thank people who had helped him reach what he considered a pivotal point in his young career. Though he had little money, he rented studio time and hired Paul Prestopino and Bob Hefferan to accompany him on his first recording project.

They produced a thirteen-song LP, which John dedicated to Milt Okun. He had two hundred and fifty copies pressed and presented them as Christmas presents to people most important to him.

Mike Kobluk cherishes his copy.

The record includes four Beatles tunes, *Here, There and Everywhere,*

Yesterday, And I Love Her and *In My Life*. Other songs include *Ann* by Billy Ed Wheeler; *When I Was a Cowboy* by B.S. Hefferan; *Blues My Naughty*, by Carey Morgan; *What's That I Hear Now* by Phil Ochs; *When Will I Be Loved* by Phil Everly; and *Darcy Farrow* by Steve Gillette.

The untitled album also includes the first-ever recording of a song he'd written, which he titled *Babe I Hate to Go*.

As the album's final cut, John sang *Farewell Party* written by Bob Gibson and Bob Connally.

As Mike stepped to the microphone for his turn to speak at the memorial service, he looked first to Milt Okun. Annie had asked Milt to speak, but he'd declined saying he'd be unable to overcome his emotions.

Mike reigned in his own emotions as he began:

"I first met John in 1965. John was recommended to replace Chad in The Mitchell Trio by Mike Kirkland of The Brothers Four. We invited John to come to New York City to audition, to sing with me and Joe Frazier, and to give us a chance to get to know him. We loved what we heard and what we saw: his vitality, his freshness, his musicality, his naivete, his unabashed exuberance.

"We asked him what his long-term goals were and without a moment's hesitation, he blurted that he wanted to become as well known and as popular as Frank Sinatra, and that he wanted to earn enough money to buy his own jet, so his father, Colonel Dutch, could become his pilot. We all know he accomplished all this and more.

"After hours, during impromptu informal singing sessions, John inevitably would offer a song written by Bob Gibson. He recorded it on his private Christmas present album. It seems terrifically appropriate to quote it here:"

"Don't want no tears shed for me when I'm gone,
Don't want nobody to sing no melancholy song.
Don't want your parting words to become my eulogy.
Just have a ragtime band to play when you say goodbye to me.
Keep the whiskey flowin' boys and raise your glasses high,
I'm pleased to see you here to say farewell and not goodbye.
Keep that whiskey flowin' boys and raise your glasses high,
And damn the man that dares to let my farewell party die."

"So, at this point, we'd like to think about some of the great times we had with John Denver.

"John wrote his first three songs as a member of The Mitchell Trio. *For Bobbi, Like to Deal with the Ladies* and *Leavin' on a Jet Plane*, each of which we recorded. We recorded three albums in those wonderful years.

"We performed at Carnegie Hall to a sold-out audience only three months after John joined The Trio. We toured and performed in Europe. We toured scores of colleges and universities across the U.S., and we sang in numerous nightclubs and folk clubs. We got to attend John and Annie's wedding, and to sing during the ceremony and after. I'm proud to say it was a great three years that created fabulous, everlasting memories.

"So, keep that whiskey flowin' boys and raise your glasses high.

"And damn the man that dares to let his farewell party die."

CHAPTER TWENTY-NINE

The Trio might never have returned to its roots for the 2007 Spokane concert if not for the owner of a major Miami real estate agency who, like so many of their avid fans, fell in love with The Chad Mitchell Trio when he was a teenager.

Alan Jacobson was a sophomore at Coral Gables High School when he found himself captivated by the folk music craze. He liked the Kingston Trio, Peter Paul and Mary and other groups, but when he heard the *Mighty Day on Campus* album, he was swept to another level.

"The Trio intrigued me because of the blend of their voices," Alan said. "They were the best of all the groups. I thought they were terrific. I bought every one of their albums and followed them through my high school and college years at the University of Miami."

He was shocked when he bought *That's the Way It's Gonna Be* in 1965 and saw someone different than Chad on the cover. Then, as folk music lost its way amid the stampede to rock and roll, The Trio faded into his life's background.

From time to time, he'd come across one of the old albums, and wonder what happened to them.

"Then in 1987 I read they were doing a reunion concert with John Denver," Alan said, "and I knew that wherever this concert was, I had to go." He wasn't aware of The Trio's initial reunion arranged by Doris Justis in Washington, D.C. or the Park West concerts in Chicago the previous year.

The newspaper article said the concert was being arranged by a man named Doug Durrett. He tracked down Durrett and asked for front row center seats "regardless of the cost."

The newspaper article also said Chad Mitchell worked as entertainment director for The Delta Queen Steamboat Company in New Orleans.

"I called The Delta Queen offices and asked for Chad. They said he was out, so I left a message."

A day later, an eighteen-year-old receptionist at Alan's real estate company came running into his office and said, "I can't believe it. Chad Mitchell is on the phone. How do you know Chad Mitchell?"

Surprised, Alan reversed the question. "Well, how does someone your age know who Chad Mitchell is?"

"My mother is a huge fan," the receptionist told him. "I grew up listening to their records."

Alan answered the call, identified himself and said, "I have to tell you, I love you guys and I'm coming to see the Charlotte concert. While I'm there, I'd like to take you to lunch. If the other guys want to come, I'd love to have them also."

Chad went to dinner with Alan and his partner Jan Hart prior to the concert. Mike and Joe joined them for a meal following the show. Alan asked if he could arrange additional concerts.

Alan wasn't a novice when it came to booking shows. He'd thrown lavish Miami parties for family and clients featuring significant entertainers. He booked operatic tenor Jan Peerce for his parents' fiftieth anniversary party. He'd booked comedian Henny Youngman for another of his bashes.

Chad and Mike pointed out they both had day jobs, and that there wasn't much money to be made in booking reunion concerts into small venues. Alan told them he wanted to provide his services "just for fun."

For the next twenty-five years, Alan became the de facto manager and promoter for The Chad Mitchell Trio. He wanted to do more to preserve The Trio's legacy, though, than just promote concerts.

"They were so good," he said, "I wanted to provide something that people could always remember them by, something for their kids to see."

The result is *The Chad Mitchell Trio Then and Now* three-DVD package that includes video of The Trio's '60s television performances, the 1987 concert including John Denver and the 2007 Spokane Opera House Concert. The set also includes interviews with each trio member, Milt Okun, Frank Fried, Tom Paxton and Paul Prestopino.

Alan preferred not to reveal how much the project cost. Mike estimates well in excess of $100,000. The video of the 2007 concert includes scenes shot both in Spokane and an earlier concert held that year in Bayfield, Wisconsin.

"We wanted to be sure we had backup material in case something didn't turn out exactly right at one concert," Alan said.

He hired a company to do lighting and video.

The most significant expense, though, came in assembling film clips from the '60's television shows. While Mike has collected copies of those clips for his personal collection, Alan had to negotiate payment for rights to use them in concert and on the DVD sets.

"The cost of buying the rights to use small little segments of two or three songs from the Ed Sullivan estate was astronomical," he said. "I also wanted Ed's introduction of The Trio and the credits that rolled at the end of the show. That cost even more."

"It was worth it, though," Alan said. "A labor of love. Tremendous fun."

"He did an absolutely first-class job of it," Mike said."

Alan recouped a fraction of his costs through sales of the *Then and Now* DVD set. He also financed the recording of The Trio's 2014 farewell concert in Bethesda, Maryland and produced that DVD.

When Alan and Jan downsized in 2016, he donated his remaining stock of DVD's and other Chad Mitchell Trio merchandise to the World Folk Music Association. The WFMA now handles sales of those materials through their website.

As years wore on, Mike and Chad became guardians of The Trio's excellence. Age, they knew, would eventually rob them of their gifts. Joe's enthusiasm for performance blinded him to deterioration of his vocal quality.

Paul Prestopino laughed when he told a story of rehearsals for the 2007 Spokane concert.

"Mike took me aside," he said, "and asked me if I could raise the key a half step on a couple of songs."

"I'm having trouble getting down to some of those low notes," Mike confessed.

Not an hour earlier, Chad had approached Paul, asking that the key be lowered a half step, explaining, "Some of those high notes are more difficult than they used to be."

Money was hardly a motivation for their post-1987 career. "We covered expenses, maybe put a little money in our pockets," Mike recalls. "But it was fun. We almost sold out the Opera House for the 2007 concert. So, we did get to take something home after we paid the musicians and other things."

For the most part, though, they'd come full circle—playing for fun and beer money, just as they'd done fifty years earlier at Gonzaga.

By the time Mike, Joe and Chad performed the 2007 Spokane concert, seven men had shared singers' roles in the Mitchell Trio. Not long after, fate and circumstance would conspire to add an eighth name to that list.

In 1962, at the age of fourteen, an Allentown, Pennsylvania kid named Ron Greenstein purchased the *Mighty Day on Campus* album. Parked at the intersection of the Big Band Era, the folk wave and emerging rock & roll, the young musician couldn't decide on which genre to focus his interest. Until he heard The Chad Mitchell Trio.

"When I heard that tight harmony," he said, "I knew which direction I wanted to go."

Like thousands of other teens, the young bass player formed a folk band and set about memorizing all the chords and harmonic nuances of The Trio's material.

He saw them perform live at the Philadelphia Folk Festival late in 1965. Typical of a rabid fan, he followed others to the concert after-party at The Trio's hotel. He found Mike and Joe in the hotel lobby, standing off to the side of a throng of women mobbed around The Trio's newest member, John Denver.

As Mike and Joe watched this spectacle with amusement, Ron introduced himself to Joe and asked, "What happened to Chad?"

Focused on the gang of women accosting John, Joe glanced to Ron and said, "Aw, he quit."

As the popularity of folk music faded, Ron's devotion did not waver, so when a folk nostalgia wave occurred with The Trio's re-emergence in the eighties, Greenstein was thrilled. He continued to form folk groups and perform around his hometown.

More so than guitarists and pianists and trumpet players, bassists are either blessed or cursed with interchangeability. The Trio was originally backed by a single instrument. Jim McGuinn played banjo or guitar. They expanded to a pair of string players when McGuinn was replaced by Paul Prestopino and Jacob Ander. The only time they used a bass player was in their television appearances when the show's producer paid the extra musician. They simply couldn't afford to travel with a bassist.

Sometime around 2000, Ron's group opened for a Tom Paxton concert. A friend knew Tom. Ron asked the friend to inquire whether Tom might want a bass player. From then on, whenever Tom performed nearby, he hired Ron to accompany him.

In 2009, The Trio was scheduled to play a concert in Sellersville, Pennsylvania. When he heard of the booking, Ron knew what he had to do.

"I had one shot at my life-long dream," Ron said. "I knew I had to give them a call."

He obtained the phone number of Alan Jacobson, who by this time had taken over management of The Trio's bookings.

"Mr. Jacobson, my name is Ron Greenstein. I live near Sellersville, and I'm excited about The Trio's upcoming concert. I'm a bass player. I know The Trio doesn't travel with a bassist, and I'd love to offer my services."

Ron heard a chuckle and Alan said, "Well, you know you're about the three hundredth guy who's told me that."

He continued with what Ron is sure was a prepared speech. "Chad, Mike and Joe are nice guys. If you come to one of the rehearsals, they'll see what you can do, but you must understand if they don't think it will work, it's nothing against you."

Alan gave Ron Chad's and Mike's phone numbers. Chad wasn't home. Mike first emphasized they really couldn't afford a bass player. Ron said he didn't want or need to be paid. Mike agreed to Ron's presence at a rehearsal but added Alan's admonishment. "You have to understand," Mike said, "that we appreciate your offer and your dedication as a fan, but if we don't think it will work, we'll have to say so."

When offers of this nature came along, Chad and Mike understood that the fan making the offer had no genuine expectation of performing with The Trio. He or she simply would be thrilled to gain access to a rehearsal, play a song or two, shake hands and be on their way.

Bass players were simpler to deal with than most because their instrument was too bulky to carry around. After they'd listened to a few numbers being rehearsed, they'd offer to go to the car and get their bass. Mike or Chad could thank them for coming and apologize that their schedule wouldn't allow them to wait.

Ron, though, brought his bass to the hotel room, unpacked it and sat in a corner to listen. Mike, Chad and Joe worked to recall the harmonies to *I Can't Help but Wonder Where I'm Bound*. Though they'd sung these songs hundreds of times over the years, as they were now going months between performances, precise recollection of the parts required the searching of memories.

As the song progressed, Ron picked up his base and started playing, fitting seamlessly with the other musicians. Mike and Chad glanced at each other exchanging an unspoken *who is this guy?* Ron didn't miss a beat or a note on anything they rehearsed.

Joe stumbled on a line of harmony.

Chad waved to cut off the musicians. "Joe . . . I think it should be . . ." and he sang the line.

"Wait, I thought we . . ." Mike said, singing a different variation.

Ron cleared his voice. "Actually, here's the way you sang it on the album."

Recognition sparked as Ron sung the line.

Again, Mike and Chad exchanged a glance.

"I . . . I memorized all your stuff when I was in high school," Ron said with a shrug.

"Okay," Chad said, "I guess now we're six members."

"You can't imagine what that was like," Ron said. "My ultimate fantasy. Something I thought was completely out of reach. I was a member of The Chad Mitchell Trio."

For the final decade of The Trio's formal activities, Ron played bass. With one exception.

They'd scheduled a second Pennsylvania concert, this one in Lancaster, where they performed on a bill with The Brothers Four, The New Christy Minstrels and Livingston Taylor. Ron had a conflicting commitment and wasn't available. The day of the show, Joe became ill and lost his voice.

"That's the only time The Trio sang as a duet," Mike said.

"Like a trooper, Joe was up there with us," Chad recalled, "but his vocal quality just wasn't there."

———

Later in 2009, two of Mike's former Spokane colleagues—Jack Lucas of West Coast Entertainment in Spokane and Kevin Twohig, CEO of the Spokane Public Facilities District—produced a three-concert Chad Mitchell Trio fiftieth anniversary tour, including concerts in Spokane, Seattle and Salem, Oregon.

Four years later, Jerry Lonn, another of Mike's connections through his work in Spokane, backed Trio concerts in Surprise, Arizona, and a couple of days later in Cerritos, California. Ron accompanied them as bassist on those performances.

Joe by now was dealing with congestive heart failure and was too weak to perform. So, Mike and Chad called on Ron to fill in on vocals. In Cerritos, Joe watched from a wheelchair in the front row of a packed house. Joe joined Mike, Chad and Ron signing autographs following the concert.

The last time Joe appeared with The Trio in concert was in 2011 at a World Folk Music Association event. Mike had become more and more concerned about hanging on too long.

"Mike had access to some recordings of these various performances," Chad said, "and I hadn't heard them. When I finally did, I thought, 'Oh God.' We weren't good. Joe's voice just wasn't blending."

Despite an enthusiastic audience response, "Mike and I came off the stage shaking our heads," Chad recalled. "We knew we hadn't performed up to The Trio's reputation. But Joe raised his fists and shouted, "We've still got it, guys! We've still got it."

"Mike thought we should have stopped earlier than we did," Chad said.

"I think we were still singing pretty good when we did our fiftieth anniversary concerts in Spokane, Seattle and Salem," Mike said. "But after that, I felt that, as a trio, we simply didn't have it anymore."

In all their history, The Trio never had to rely on a recording studio to sound good. Many of history's most successful vocal artists sound distinctly less polished on stage than on their studio-produced recordings.

Early in their career, Milt Okun would cringe to hear Peter, Paul and Mary in concert. During those early years, Mary in particular needed studio tricks to bring her onto the right pitch. During their American tour, no one could even hear the Beatles over the screaming crowd. Jimmy Buffet—among the most charismatic performers anywhere—in terms of musical quality is only a shadow of his studio self in live performance. Yet Parrot Heads walk away from a Buffet concert overwhelmed by the experience.

The adrenaline and excitement surrounding the spectacle mask the flaws.

"During a live performance (the flaws) go right by the audience for the most part," Chad said. "Our audiences were still happy because we are fairly visual. I guess I kept thinking Joe would get better. But Mike didn't. And Mike was right."

As opportunities to perform presented themselves, Chad appreciated the irony of role reversal. Where Mike was single-mindedly committed fifty years ago to keep The Trio going when Chad revealed his plan to quit, Chad now had to cajole Mike to continue during the latter years of The Trio's second life.

Chad's anger leading up to their 1965 breakup was partly rooted in Mike's insistence that they work such a constant and hectic schedule. As The Trio's reincarnation moved into the 1990's, Mike sometimes felt that a half dozen dates a year were too much.

"Alan ran the website at that point," Chad said, "and people would call him with offers, so he'd call me and ask me to talk with Mike. Mike was reluctant. And it wasn't just that he didn't think The Trio was up to performing the way we should."

For several years Mike suffered from severe back pain that made plane flights an ordeal. Many of their performance opportunities required travel to the East Coast.

"Joe wanted to perform no matter what," Chad said. "But in dealing with Mike, I was always careful to say 'if you don't want to do it, I can live with that. It's okay.' Mike and I had restored a relationship, and I didn't want to do anything to upset that."

Mike almost always eventually agreed, though, Chad said, "Because he didn't want to be the guy who kept The Trio from performing."

The Traveling Troubadour Company arranged for Chad Mitchell Trio cruises between 2007 and 2015.

"We did six altogether," Mike said, "including the Caribbean, Canada, the Mediterranean, Ireland and Alaska."

Again, compensation was negligible. The Trio and their wives got to cruise for free. "But we had to spend so much time rehearsing," Chad said, "we didn't have time to get out and see the sights."

Given their proximity, Mike and Chad could work on their parts together. Joe, though, often came unprepared, so Mike and Chad had to rehearse intently with Joe during the cruise.

Joe had signed on for The Trio's trip to Ireland in March of 2012. He realized he was too ill to make the trip.

Ron's phone rang a few days before they were scheduled to leave.

"Ron? This is Joe Frazier. I won't be able to go to Ireland. I want you to sing my parts."

Ron fumbled his way through a response. "I . . . I . . . listen Joe, you guys know I'm a good bass player," he said, "but I'm no singer. Not in your league, anyway."

"You can do it," Joe said. "You know all the parts. You'll be fine."

Ron called Chad. "I'm not a singer," he protested again. "Not of the caliber you guys are."

"Well," Chad said, "we're going to Ireland and somebody has to do it.

You're the only guy I know who knows all these parts."

An amateur baseball player might think he could step onto a field with major leaguers and hold his own. But that's a delusion. The scale of difference in ability is not a matter of degrees. The difference might be better described in light years.

The same can be said of professional musicians. Mike Kobluk and Chad Mitchell are extraordinarily talented vocalists. They sing with precision and a strength that would overpower an amateur voice if they didn't rein themselves in.

"You have to imagine," Ron explained, "I'd been singing with local groups, and I know how to harmonize. But when you're standing up there with those two guys, they are such powerhouse singers. And here's Chad, right there in my left ear blasting with this gorgeous voice, and I'm just trying to concentrate on the part."

Ron listened to tapes of the performance and said, "It was awful."

Ron continued to fill in for Joe during The Trio's few remaining concerts and, according to both Mike and Chad, he improved with time. But neither were satisfied with the result.

"Both Mike and Chad are perfectionists," Alan explained. "Mike was not satisfied because Ron wasn't Joe. And Mike and Chad wanted perfection."

"We found ourselves changing the way we sang in order to blend with Ron," Chad said, "and we simply weren't as good as we wanted to be."

Mike has softened his view of their early years in several ways. He remains, like Chad, an adamant perfectionist when it comes to The Trio's performance. In the sixties, none of The Trio members nor their musicians would even consider lack of preparation. Milt Okun was absolutely sure a piece had been perfected before The Trio took it on stage.

In later years, though, Joe's lack of preparation frustrated Mike.

Jerry Lonn, the promoter who put together the 2013 Surprise and Cerritos concerts, aware of Mike's reluctance, called Chad and asked if he would appear as a solo act in a folk music review.

"I called Mike and asked how he would feel if I did that show," Chad said, "and he was very honest. He said, 'I gotta tell you, that brings up some bad feelings.' The show didn't end up happening, but knowing Mike's feelings, I would not have done it."

Mike also appreciates their truce.

"After so many years," he said, "you forget an awful lot of stuff that may or may not have once been important. So, you concentrate on the stuff you know *is* important, and that's relearning notes and words and trying to recreate something we'd done really well all those years ago. That became more significant than any wounded relationship."

One song Joe couldn't seem to get right in the later years is *The Story of Alice*. In concert, The Trio's audience loved *Alice*, by Jerry Bock and Larry Holofcener. The song relates an ill-fated love between Alice and Algernon, two physically flawed people who found each other.

They performed Alice in three pieces, early in a concert, mid-concert, and near the end, a wonderful device to surprise audiences and emphasize the song's humor.

They'd planned to do *Alice* for one of the cruises, but Mike—as was the right of any Trio member—vetoed it because time after time in rehearsal, Joe failed to get it right. Finally, Mike swore in frustration he'd never perform *Alice* again.

Living only a couple of blocks apart, Chad and Mike attend the same neighborhood Christmas parties where friends ask them to sing one of their religious-themed numbers like *The Virgin Mary*. They usually accommodate the request. One year they sang and afterward, sitting together at a table, each ventured the opinion they'd done pretty well.

"Who knows," Chad said, "maybe we could even try *Alice* again."

They both laughed at the memory, then sat, lost in thought.

Finally, Chad said, "I'm sorry about the way I behaved at the end. I'm still not sure what drove my anger."

Mike nodded and said, "Well, I'm sure I did things that only complicated the situation."

Pleas kept coming, though, and in order to respond to their fans, they did a series of "song circles" in New Orleans and Las Vegas. In that forum, The Trio didn't sing as a group. Everyone in the circle was invited to offer songs, so many fans realized their fantasy of singing with Chad Mitchell and Mike Kobluk. The events didn't require extensive rehearsal.

Chad and Anne-Claire sang together again as Chad Mitchell Trio fans gathered for the New Orleans Song Circle on November 29, 2016. The occasion coincided with Chad and Chris's thirtieth wedding anniversary, and Anne-Claire's twenty-ninth birthday.

She and Chad prepared several numbers for the evening, including John Prine's *Everybody Needs Somebody,* Hal Atkinson's *Do You Mind Lord,* and Shelly Markham's *Blow Away*.

"She stole the whole show," Chad said.

Mike smiled through her performance, then told Chad and Chris, "Boy, she can really sing."

— CHAPTER THIRTY —

OCTOBER 2007
SPOKANE OPERA HOUSE

C had allowed applause for *Johnnie* to dissolve into silence before continuing.

"About this time in most programs," he said, "artists tend to string together a variety of their biggest songs, and in that tradition, we would like to perform a medley of our hit."

Mike sang lead for *The Marvelous Toy,* the song that, if not for the assassination of a president, might have been the hit that always seemed to just elude The Trio.

They closed their magical return performance to Spokane with the frantic Russian language *Maladyozhenaya,* then bowed, and sprinted off the stage. Tom Paxton returned with them for an encore to sing his masterpiece, *Can't Help but Wonder Where I'm Bound.*

And finally, Ed McCurdy's *Last Night I Had the Strangest Dream.*

OCTOBER 2007

SPOKANE SPOKESMAN-REVIEW

By Jim Kershner

When The Chad Mitchell Trio strolled onstage for their first show in Spokane since 1964, I was prepared for the worst.

What I heard instead was the best. I would go so far as to call it a triumph, and if that sounds over-the-top, I'm confident that most of the people in the nearly full (Opera House) would agree.

Before I explain why, I should clarify why I was apprehensive. Before The Chad Mitchell Trio even took the stage, a '60s film clip from an appearance on "The Ed Sullivan Show" played above the stage.

This clip (and two others later) established convincingly that this Gonzaga University-spawned group possessed world-class vocal talent and stage presence, equal to the Kingston Trio, or Peter, Paul & Mary.

Yet showing those clips was risky. Anybody who has watched a PBS pop-rock-folk reunion special knows that the contrast between then and now can be downright depressing. Those old acts almost never sound as good as they once did, especially vocally.

The Chad Mitchell Trio turned out to be a shining exception to that rule. Nearly five decades after they began, their voices on Saturday sounded exceptionally clear and powerful, with perfectly rehearsed three-part harmonies blending gorgeously.

I'm tempted to say they sounded better than the old days, but that would be going too far. They had some serious lung power in those days, as proved by a "Dinah Shore" clip. Suffice to say that their current sound is absolutely pleasing to the ear, and they haven't lost a step when it comes to stage presence, emotional intensity and comic timing.

Sorry if I gush, but I was won over completely from the very first song, a raucous and well-timed version of "I Was Born About 10,000 Years Ago," when Mitchell scurried frantically behind Mike Kobluk and Joe Frazier in a mostly vain attempt to get a verse in edgewise. How many putative band leaders would open a show with a joke, essentially on themselves?

Yet it was this spirit of irreverence and fun that made the '60s folk movement such a great chapter in pop, and it was especially the spirit that animated The Chad Mitchell Trio.

And still does.

Mitchell introduced one song with this pithy, out-of-nowhere phrase: "Speaking of dirty Scottish folk songs . . ."

He also thanked the organizers of the concert for their persistence "in convincing the people at the home to let us out."

Not all was fun and games. Their version of "Four Strong Winds" was exceptionally beautiful, squeezing all of the pensive longing out of this Ian Tyson classic. Their version of Woody Guthrie's "Reuben James" showed off their prodigious individual talents to breathtaking effect, with Frazier generally handling the lower registers, Kobluk the middle and Mitchell still perfectly capable of hitting the thrilling highs.

And they haven't lost their taste for cutting political satire either. They unveiled a new version of "The John Birch Society," with new words written by Rep. Dave Obey, a Democratic congressman from Wisconsin titled, "The George Bush Society." It was a scathing indictment of the current administration . . .

However, their mixing of the triumphal "When Johnny Comes Marching Home" with the heartbreaking Irish tune "Johnnie We Hardly Knew Ye," on which it's based, was an even more devastating, and more subtle, anti-war song . . .

By the way, the last time The Chad Mitchell Trio performed in Spokane, the reviewer for The Spokesman-Review criticized them for being too political. Almost 44 years later, this reviewer is happy to say: That guy was dead wrong."

2014

Probably no entity other than The World Music Folk Association and their old friend Tom Paxton could have convinced Mike and Chad to take the stage in concert again. The WFMA had hosted a fiftieth anniversary concert for The Trio on March 31, 2011, at the Cedar Lane Unitarian Universalist Church in Bethesda, probably the last time Joe performed with full voice. But in 2014, the WFMA was determined to honor The Chad Mitchell Trio one last time.

Joe had been ill for much of 2013 when planning for the final concert began. Mike and Chad realized he would not be able to perform, so again they called on Ron Greenstein to join them.

Joe did not survive to see the November concert. He continued to be plagued by heart issues after having a pacemaker implanted in July of 2012. He died at the age of seventy-seven on March 28, 2014. He was laid to rest at St. Columba's Episcopal Church in Big Bear Lake, California. He was survived by his life partner, John Tveit, who died in 2019.

The Kobluks and Mitchells traveled together to Joe's funeral.

Following the service, they drove to Beverly Hills to visit Milt Okun, who was also in ill health. Milt sat in a chair propped on pillows for their visit. He could walk only with assistance.

When he'd finished speaking with Milt, Mike withdrew, leaving Chad and Milt alone.

"I wish," Chad said in an emotion-filled moment, "that we'd been able to continue our work together."

Milt gripped his hand. "So do I, Chad. So do I."

Frank Fried passed away in January 2015. Milt died Nov. 15, 2016. Alan Jacobson's partner, Jan Hart, died in September, 2019.

Tom Paxton's wife Midge passed away after a long illness in 2014. They had been married fifty-one years. During his subsequent concerts, Tom mentioned occasionally that some of his songs were more difficult to sing now.

In 2019, however, Clare Kobluk received a phone call from her sister Peggy, who mentioned she'd recently been seeing Tom.

"Wow," Clare said. "Are you two an item?"

Mike subsequently asked Tom, "Well, *are* you and Peggy an *item*?"

Tom's response: "We're not an item. We're a book."

The WFMA concert took place November 15, 2014 at the Bethesda Blues and Jazz Supper Club before a full house of fans from all over the world.

The Gaslight Singers opened, followed by Doris Justis and her partner Sean McGhee performing as Side-By-Side. They'd shared the stage with The Trio ten times since Doris engineered the initial reunion in 1986. Tom Paxton followed with an eleven-song set, then offered a tribute to The Trio.

"I've enjoyed their friendship, and I've admired their career," Tom told the audience. "They have put together fifty years of integrity. They sang the songs they needed to sing. I salute them, and adios."

Following intermission, WFMA president Chuck Morse made the introduction saying, "I have never been disappointed in a Chad Mitchell Trio concert. We're in for a great treat tonight."

Doris Justis read greetings from The Brothers Four, the Highwaymen, Peter Yarrow, and Rick Dougherty, a veteran of both the Limeliters and the Kingston Trio.

The Trio opened with *Mighty Day, My Name is Morgan* and *Vaichazkem*, sung in Hebrew.

Then Mike introduced the musicians, guitarist Bob Hefferan and Greenstein on bass. His most emotional introduction was for Paul Prestopino—guitar, mandolin, banjo and harmonica—who, since joining the group in 1962, "has played in every one of The Mitchell Trio's concerts, including with both Chad and John Denver, since then."

The Trio concluded with *The Unfortunate Man, Tell Old Bill, James James Morrison Morrison,* and then, the song that set The Chad Mitchell

Trio inextricably on its path: *Lizzie Borden.*

Joe had always recited the poem that prefaced *Lizzie:*

"Elizabeth Borden took an ax..."

Now the task fell to Ron, who told the audience, "I've been waiting fifty years to do this."

Their encore was The Marvelous Toy.

Throughout their history, The Trio set itself apart from others by performing with a dramatic and comedic flair. They ended in just that fashion, guided by Mike Kobluk's unique sense of humor.

They didn't finish the song. They sang, *"And whirr when it stood still. I never knew just what it was. . ."* then trotted off the stage.

The audience laughed. Then cheered. Then waited.

Finally, The Trio returned. Chad said, "Well, all right."

They sang.

*". . . We never knew just what it was
And we guess we never will."*

— Acknowledgements —

T his is by far the most complicated acknowledgements statement I've undertaken. No project like this, though, could be written in isolation. First, I want to thank Mike and Clare Kobluk and Chad and Christine Mitchell for their willingness to engage in this task. Recollection of details sometimes can't span fifty years. Mike's efforts to assemble memorabilia of The Trio's rich history were vital to this effort, as were the "crapbooks" his mother carefully assembled. Chad's willingness to bare his soul in order to tell the full story was both brave and invaluable.

Thanks to Tom Paxton, not only for his incredible body of work, but for his contributions to this book. Where would we be without "The Marvelous Toy?"

Thanks for Doug and Roger Durrett who are responsible for the 1987 reunion concert featuring the original Chad Mitchell Trio and John Denver. Upon learning Chris Mitchell would not be able to attend the concert because of pregnancy, Doug and Roger went out of their way to make video recordings and other records of many off-stage events so Chris could have a record. Chad and Chris generously allowed me access to the full copies of these materials.

Huge thanks, also, to Alan Jacobson who is responsible for the three-DVD set "Then and Now" which includes video of The Trio's earliest television performances, the full DVD of The Trio and John Denver concert in 1987, and the incredible production of the 2007 Chad Mitchell Trio Concert in Spokane. Alan went to great expense to make sure these productions were of the highest quality. Most of the detailed quotations in this book from Milt Okun, Frank Fried and Joe Frazier were only available through the outtakes of interviews from both Jacobson's and Durretts' projects.

Thanks to Chuck Morse and the World Folk Music Association for their dedication and invaluable help in keeping both The Trio's and folk music's legacy alive. Thanks to Doris Justis for the retelling of her determined efforts to resurrect The Trio in 1986. Of all the anecdotes collected here, that one is my favorite. Thanks to my former *Spokane Spokesman-Review* colleague Jim Kirshner for being a character in my book. And thanks to Ernie Sheldon for *The Ballad of Murder Incorporated.*

Other valuable background sources for this project include The Chad Mitchell Trio website; the Peter, Paul and Mary website; *The Weavers 1949-1953 by Dave Samuelson;* John Denver's biography *Take Me Home*; Milt Okun's biography *Along the Cherry Lane;* an on-line memoir written by Frank Fried entitled *From Lennin to Lennon;* and *The Heritage Music Review* blog by Doug Bright.

Thanks to my editor Laura Taylor and my formatter, Debra Kennedy who helped beyond the call of service for this project. Thanks to Jessica and Holly at Acorn Publishing.

Finally, thanks to Nancy, who continues to make our wonderful adventure possible.

Poems "Red, White and Blue Cross," "Shall I Write a Letter to My Congressman," and "An Atom a Day Keeps the Doctor Away." from Rhymes for the Irreverent, 2006 edition,
by E.Y. Harburg
Copyright 1965 The Yip Harburg Foundation and the Freedom from Religion Foundation.
Used by permission of the Estate of E.Y Harburg and Glocca Morra Music LLC.

Unfortunate Man
adapted by Jimmy Driftwood
Used by permission of Walden Music Company Inc.

Ship of State
by William Mitchell
Used by permission of Anne-Claire Music.

The Marvelous Toy
Words and Music by Tom Paxton
Copyright (c) 1961 BMG Ruby Songs and Reservoir Media Management, Inc.
Copyright Renewed
All Rights for BMG Ruby Songs Administered by BMG Rights Management (US) LLC
All Rights for Reservoir Media Music Administered by Reservoir Media Management, Inc.
All Rights Reserved Used by Permission
Reprinted by Permission of Hal Leonard LLC

I Can't Help But Wonder (Where I'm Bound)
Words and Music by Tom Paxton
Copyright (c) 1963, 1964 BMG Ruby Songs and Reservoir Media Music
Copyright Renewed
All Rights for BMG Ruby Songs Administered by BMG Rights Management (US) LLC
All Rights Reserved Used by Permission
Reprinted by Permission of Hal Leonard LLC

The '68 Nixon (This Year's Model)
Words and Music by June Reizner
Copyright (c) 1968 BMG Ruby Songs and Reservoir Media Management, Inc.
Copyright Renewed
All Rights for BMG Ruby Songs Administered by BMG Rights Management (US) LLC
All Rights Reserved Used by Permission
Reprinted by Permission of Hal Leonard LLC

What This Country Really Needs Is...
Words and Music by June Reizner
Copyright (c) 1967 BMG Ruby Songs and Reservoir Media Management, Inc.
Copyright Renewed
All Rights for BMG Ruby Songs Administered by BMG Rights Management (US) LLC
All Rights Reserved Used by Permission
Reprinted by Permission of Hal Leonard LLC

LIZZIE BORDEN
Words and Music by MICHAEL BROWN
Copyright © 1952 CHAPPELL & CO., INC. (ASCAP)
All Rights Reserved
Used By Permission of ALFRED MUSIC

THE JOHN BIRCH SOCIETY
Words and Music by MICHAEL BROWN
Used By Permission of Brownstown Music Inc.

THE BALLAD OF MURDER INCORPORATED
Words and Music by RICHARD POWELL and ERNIE SHELDON
Copyright © 1963 UNICHAPPELL MUSIC INC. (BMI) and CHAPPELL & CO. INC. (ASCAP)
All Rights on Behalf of UNICHAPPELL MUSIC INC.
Administered by WARNER-TAMERLANE PUBLISHING CORP.
All Rights Reserved
Used By Permission of ALFRED MUSIC

FAREWELL PARTY
Words by ROBERT B. CONNELLY, Music by ROBERT GIBSON
Copyright © 1966 WC MUSIC CORP. (ASCAP) and ROBERT JOSIAH MUSIC INC (BMI)
All Rights Reserved
Used By Permission of ALFRED MUSIC

Review, "Trio Extremely Talented but Somewhat Depressing"
by Ed Costello.
Used by permission of Spokane Spokesman-Review

Review, "I was prepared for the worst . . . what I heard instead was the best"
by Jim Kershner
Used by permission of Spokane Spokesman-Review

Excerpt from "The Pop Life"
by John Rockwell
From The New York Times.
Copyright 1975 The New York Times Company.
All rights reserved. Used under license.

Made in the USA
Middletown, DE
06 September 2021

47710468R00187